TELEVISION POLICY

Television Policy
The MacTaggart Lectures

BOB FRANKLIN

EDINBURGH UNIVERSITY PRESS

© Copyright in this edition Edinburgh University Press, 2005
© Copyright in the individual contributions is retained by the lecturers

Edinburgh University Press Ltd
22 George Square, Edinburgh

Typeset in 11/13 Apollo by
Servis Filmsetting Ltd, Manchester, and
printed and bound in Great Britain by
MPG Books Ltd, Bodmin

A CIP record for this book is available from the British Library
ISBN 0 7486 1717 5 (hardback)
ISBN 0 7486 1718 3 (paperback)

The right of the contributors to be identified as authors of this
work has been asserted in accordance with the Copyright,
Designs and Patents Act 1988.

Contents

Acknowledgements

All books, but especially edited collections, are collaborative projects which bring together the skills and talents of writers, editors, publishers and a host of others involved in their production. This is my opportunity to offer thanks to colleagues who have contributed to this book but whose names do not appear on the contents page. Janet Allaker, Fran Barlow, Sarah Barnett, Sarah Edwards, John Eldridge, Lord 'Gus' Macdonald, Julian Petley and Brian Winston each deserve thanks for their help and support with this project. I am also deeply indebted to the MacTaggart lecturers across almost thirty years, who have given permission for their work to be edited and reproduced in this collection.

Foreword

Just as T.S. Eliot's J. Alfred Prufrock laments 'I have measured out my life with coffee spoons', British broadcasters could equally have measured out their lives with MacTaggart Lectures. From the early explorations of naturalism by John McGrath and Marcel Ophuls to John Humphrys' accusation that some programming has become 'meretricious, seedy and cynical', the MacTaggart Lectures have offered us a route map across the shifting sands of British broadcasting, a compelling insight into the preoccupations, passions and ambitions of television's leaders. Bob Franklin is to be congratulated for compiling this unique collection of the MacTaggart lectures which offer readers invaluable insights into the development of television policy across three decades.

At the end of August every year, hundreds and now thousands of television workers, from young students trying to break into the industry to media moguls, gather in Edinburgh to hear the MacTaggart. The atmosphere resembles the beginning of the school term where the pupils come to hear what one of the senior teachers has to say or perhaps to a hushed cathedral waiting for a major sermon from a senior archbishop. Indeed, for many years the lecture was actually held in a church so British television's great and good solemnly squeezed into rows of rock-hard pews to hear the McTaggart Lecture delivered as if from heaven. The current venue, the McEwan Hall at Edinburgh University, with its grand D-shaped hall and elegant semi-circular galleries, has the grandeur and scale of a cathedral even if it isn't one and was in fact built by a brewing philanthropist.

Whatever the venue, this is the biggest event in the British television calendar. The most imaginative of these lectures are thermometers of the temperature changes in broadcasting, critical guidance as to where we are all headed and how hot or cold television will be. When Rupert Murdoch tore into television's leadership in 1989 the contrast with the perspective of, say, Denis Forman just a few years before was startling. You knew you were witness to a historic moment, a fundamental shift in the power base of British television. When Murdoch said, 'much of what passes for quality on British television is no more than a reflection of the values of the narrow elite which controls it and which has always thought that its tastes are synonymous with quality – a view incidentally, that is natural to all governing classes', the audience understood, or at least should have understood, that the days of a cosy, insular duopoly were over forever.

As Chair of the Television Festival Committee, I introduced five MacTaggart lecturers. In the green room beforehand some were relaxed, some were surrounded by a daisy chain of advisers and one wanted a glass of Scotch to steady the nerves. Looking back, half-remembered soundbites still stand out, echoing down the years. Janet Street-Porter (1995) derided the M People, 'middle-class, middle-brow and male, Masonic in their tendencies and, not to put a point on it, fairly mediocre'. Perhaps mindful of being an M person himself, Peter Bazalgette (1998) talked about the 'sleek barons of British broadcasting'. Michael Grade (1992) championed the BBC because it kept the rest of television honest and now, of course, as the BBC Chairman he has the chance to keep it that way.

The lectures seem to divide almost into two. A large number of them highlight the dangers to creativity of ratings tyranny or management over control. In 1984 Denis Forman said, 'for us the people who create television programmes are the most important people in the world and it is our task to create the right conditions for them'. Seventeen years later David Liddiment claimed that the soul of British television was in danger and that 'we're losing sight of the innate value of programmes'. On the other hand there have been a string of speakers whose MacTaggart Lecture centred on the structure and shape of the broadcasting industry. From Peter Jay's 1981 talk on 'The Future of Electronic Publishing' through David Elstein's treatise on 'Market Forces and Social Values' (1991) to Tony Ball's (2003) view that the market could more than adequately provide the needs of viewers, MacTaggarts have been as obsessed with the economics of the industry as with the creative process.

In almost all the lectures that unique British institution, the BBC, sits centre stage. Whether it's Michael Grade, John Birt, Richard Eyre, Greg Dyke or Tony Ball, it is the BBC that the lectures always come back to: its power, its independence, its creativity, its role in a digital world and its relationship with the British state.

From the many fine lectures, for me one stands out, Dennis Potter's 1993 oration, 'Occupying Powers'. This was partly the theatre of the occasion, one of television's true geniuses, fist-clenched, embittered and passionate, spitting out his words. It was also the angry eloquence of his language, a skill no other MacTaggart lecturer could hope to match, however talented. Potter talked about the careless treatment by the BBC of his first television play in order to 'offer up one small strip of sticking plaster for the suppurating wounds of the poor wretch who is the present Director General'. That was the end of Potter's compassion. He said of John Birt, the Director General, and Marmaduke Hussey, Chairman of Governors, 'you cannot make a pair of croak-voiced Daleks appear benevolent even if you dress one of them in an Armani suit and call the other Marmaduke'. He went on, 'put Rupert Murdoch on trial and televise every single second of it'. But he returns to Murdoch's damage to the BBC. 'The insecurities and contradictions of the BBC's only half-digested and half shamefaced definitions lay like rubble spread in inviting heaps in front of the supercharged, savage-toothed JCB of his [Murdoch's] unslaked appetite.'

Yet, it is not just the muscular poetry of his language nor the brutality of his full-frontal assaults on the biggest names of the industry that mark this out as special. The whole lecture is knitted together by his absolute passion for television. 'I first saw television when I was in my late teens. It made my heart pound,' he said dramatically emphasising the word 'pound'. 'Here was a medium of great power, of potentially wondrous delights that could slice through all the tedious hierarchies of the printed world and help to emancipate ourselves from many of the stifling tyrannies of class and status and gutter-press ignorance. We are privileged if we can work in this, the most entrancing of all the many palaces of variety.' Listening to Dennis Potter and to many of the other MacTaggart lecturers it is hard to disagree. At its best, television can indeed be entrancing and a privilege to be part of.

John Willis
Director of Factual and Learning, BBC

Introduction

Bob Franklin

The origins and development of the James MacTaggart Memorial Lecture and the Edinburgh International Television Festival (EITF) are typically, and in some ways appropriately, regarded as inextricably connected, but the MacTaggart Lecture can claim rights of *prima geniture*. The first lecture, delivered in Edinburgh by radical playwright and director John McGrath on 25 August 1976, formed part of a retrospective celebrating the work of the recently deceased, Scottish television producer and director, James MacTaggart. The retrospective had been organised by the BBC in association with Granada Television and the highly successful and prestigious Edinburgh International Film Festival, which had begun some thirty years earlier. It was in the following year, that an Advisory Committee,[1] chaired by Gus Macdonald[2] with William Brown (then Managing Director of Scottish Television) and Alastair Hetherington (Controller, BBC Scotland) as joint Presidents, organised the first Edinburgh International Television Festival at which distinguished documentary maker Marcel Ophuls discussed 'Naturalism and Television' as his theme for the second MacTaggart Lecture. But the mutual success and continued close association of these two events has blurred recognition of their staggered birth.

Across the subsequent three decades, MacTaggart lecturers have been drawn from the ranks of the most celebrated and distinguished programme-makers (Verity Lambert and Norman Lear), producers (Janet Street-Porter, Christine Ockrent, Marks and Gran), playwrights (John McGrath, Troy Kennedy Martin, Dennis Potter), journalists (John Humphrys, Peter Jay) and authors (John Mortimer), as well as senior media executives from both the public (Michael Grade, Greg Dyke and Mark Thompson) and private/independent (David Liddiment, Richard Eyre, Jeremy Isaacs, Denis Forman and David Elstein) sectors of broadcasting, alongside significant owners of media corporations such as Rupert Murdoch and Ted Turner[3].

The MacTaggart Lectures provide insights into the policy and programming ambitions of key individuals in the world of television, but they offer more than a miscellany of personal statements, with little to unite them but a common platform. Across almost thirty years, the MacTaggart Lectures have created a unique and authoritative forum for the significant debates which have helped to shape the major developments in television policy and programming since 1976: they articulate and record a response to the challenges posed by such developments.

The impact of the lectures within the industry is considerable, because of the opportunity they provide to set an agenda, to place an issue centre stage for industry and public discussion: an opportunity seized by BSkyB Executive Tony Ball in 2003 when he used the MacTaggart to 'kick-start' a discussion about BBC programming, funding and audiences in the run-up to Charter renewal. For the MacTaggart audience of television programme-makers and broadcasters there is an undoubted irony in having to acknowledge that the occasion provides 'proof that the public lecture, a form of communication that reached its apogee in the 19th century, can still make an impact today . . . And this for a straightforward 50-minute talk with no graphics or video clips' (McCormick 2000: 10).

The MacTaggart Lectures, along with the Television Festival, have developed against a backcloth of extraordinary and rapid change in British television, triggered by government policy and technological developments in cable, satellite and digital delivery systems. In 1974, when James MacTaggart died, the three terrestrial channels (BBC1, BBC2 and ITV) still employed 'tower on a hilltop technology' to transmit television pictures for a few hours each day to an audience which still largely viewed in 'black and white'. It was the age of the 'comfortable duopoly', although it was drawing to a close. The BBC and ITV divided the national audience between them, a consensual commitment to public-service broadcasting prevailed and the licence fee provided the only income to fund BBC services. Commercial television was regulated by the IBA[4] political broadcasting was still in its infancy,[5] the recently appointed Annan Committee held the future of broadcasting[6] in its hands and *Porridge, Monty Python, Upstairs, Downstairs* and *South Riding* provided the popular programming of the day.

By contrast, the BBC's current, expanded portfolio of national tele-vision channels (see Dyke's 2000 lecture), complemented by Channel 3, Channel 4, Channel 5 and approximately 260 digital, cable and satellite channels, including a number of 24-hour news services, are funded by a mixed economy of licence fee, advertising, subscription, pay to view and increasingly sponsorship. The funding of television has shifted radically. For the first time in 2004, revenues from subscription (£3.3 billion) outstripped advertising (£3.24 billion), while the BBC allocated £2.3 billion of licence fee revenues to television services (Ofcom 2004). These burgeoning channels now deliver approximately 40,000 hours of programming each week (DTI and DCMS 2000: para 1.1.2): in colour, round the clock and targeted at 'fragmented' audiences. Some offer opportunities for interactivity. In the new millennium, broadcasters' and politicians' commitments to public-service broadcasting are less apparent, following a series of Broadcasting (1990 and 1996) and Communication Acts (2003) that have deregulated the ownership of the broadcasting market, regulated content with an increasingly 'lighter touch', increased competition between broadcasters and enthroned the viewer as sovereign in the television market place.

This brief introduction to the MacTaggart Lectures is in three parts. The first explores the history of the MacTaggart Lectures and the Edinburgh International Television Festival, most recently redesig-nated the MediaGuardian Edinburgh International Television Festival in recognition of the Festival's major sponsor. The second part consid-ers the changing political and policy context against which the lectures have been delivered. The final part analyses and explores the key themes of the lectures.

The MacTaggart Lectures and the Edinburgh International Television Festival

The MacTaggart Lectures: 'A Commentary on the Art of Television'

The playwright and producer John McGrath (billed as 'Director of the 7:84 Group') delivered the first James MacTaggart Memorial Lecture on the theme of 'TV Drama: The Case against Naturalism', at 7.30 p.m. on Wednesday, 25 August 1976, at the Royal College of Physicians, in Queen Street, Edinburgh. The lecture concluded the first day of a two-day retrospective celebrating the contribution of the distinguished director James MacTaggart to television drama (McIntyre 1977). The event had been organised by John Gray from the BBC and was described in the programme as 'A contribution to the 30th Edinburgh International Film Festival' (BBC 1976). In a brief Foreword, Anne MacTaggart spoke of her late husband's strong commitment to the belief 'that television was an art form in its own right, not the lesser hybrid of an arbitrary union of theatre and film'; he would have been 'immensely satisfied to know that tacit acknowledgement of this belief was being made by the inclusion in the Edinburgh International Festival of a retrospective programme of his work as an individual television Director' (BBC 1976).

The retrospective featured public showings of MacTaggart's most acclaimed work, including *Candide*, *The Orkney Trilogy*, *Good Morning Yesterday*, *The Duchess of Malfi*, *All The Way Up* and a television film version of *Robinson Crusoe*, which MacTaggart had written and directed on location in Tobago shortly before his death (*The Times* 1974: 18). The retrospective concluded with an 'Open Forum' but there is little doubt that the highlight of the event was John McGrath's formidable lecture. McGrath began anecdotally, recounting recollections of working with James MacTaggart at the BBC on innovatory series such as *Z Cars* in the early 1960s, but concluded with what Troy Kennedy Martin described in his later MacTaggart Lecture (1986) as a 'swingeing attack on naturalism'.

McGrath's finely crafted combination of conceptual analysis and polemic delivered a highly contentious and subsequently contested lecture. The television image, he argued, is unsuited to naturalist drama since it lacks sensuality. A cinema screen can 'flood the senses' but a 'television shot is at best nice': it is like trying to 'listen to a symphony over the telephone'. The television image, moreover, lacks empathy with viewers merely 'looking at the screen, not being drawn into it'. McGrath offers two laments.

First, the mood music at the BBC in the 1960s, in news, current affairs, documentary and satire, no less than drama, was tolerant, encouraging of innovation, accepting of critical voices. McGrath suggests that the BBC was a 'benign anarchy in which almost anything could happen'. But by 1976, this had been replaced by 'centralised control' and 'elaborate systems of command, supervision, check and review'. McGrath argued that the inevitable consequence was that subsequently 'naturalism has flourished as the dominant mode of television drama'.

Second, McGrath regrets that while James MacTaggart, Sidney Newman, Ken Loach, Tony Garnett and others at BBC Television in the 1960s were eager to discuss 'all the paraphernalia of naturalism' and other questions concerning the development of television drama, these issues were 'no longer discussed, because no one seems to be asking what this medium [i.e. television] can do'. McGrath concludes his lecture with a clarion call to the 200 people attending this first MacTaggart Lecture:

> There are many people here who are working in television. They should ask themselves why so much critical intelligence is raising the level of debate about film, and so little exists about television. Why there is not one decent forum, publication, programme or magazine, of television criticism. Why television drama is still thinking the way it did twenty years ago . . . Why the power to initiate has gone from the creators and is now the prerogative of the institution. Why plays are getting fewer, and later at night, and series getting more violent and sensationalist. Why television has failed to produce its own Dickens or even an approximation to one.

McGrath believes the answers lie 'partly in the hands of television executives' but the greatest responsibility must be borne by 'the writers and directors, who need to acquire the habit of theoretical discussion'. Given this analysis, McGrath proposed a forum for discussion and reflection about television, its relationship to film and theatre and the possible future of this relatively young medium: there was still a need to pose the question 'What can this medium do?' The MacTaggart Lectures and the Edinburgh International Television Festival fit the bill neatly.

Less than a month after McGrath's inaugural MacTaggart, Sidney Newman, who was Head of Drama at the BBC in 1963 and appointed MacTaggart as producer of a new series called *Play For Today*, delivered what might be termed the second, albeit unacknowledged, MacTaggart Lecture on 20 September. Entitled 'Liquorice, Lollypops for the Masses or Some Ruminations on Drama as Communication', the lecture was dedicated to the 'memory of James MacTaggart', discussed MacTaggart's contribution to television drama and represented 'the fulfilment of a dream' (Association of Directors and Producers (ADP) 1976). The Newman lecture was announced as 'the first of many', although there is no record of any subsequent lectures in the series.

Marcel Ophuls delivered the second 'official' MacTaggart Lecture at the 1977 EITVF and underlined the continuity with McGrath's lecture by revisiting and contesting the theme of naturalism and television; Troy Kennedy Martin addressed similar concerns in his 1986 MacTaggart. Subsequently, lectures have explored topics such as censorship and truth

(Mortimer, 1980 lecture), the relationship between government and broadcasters (Dyke, 1994, and Humphrys, 2004 lectures), the impact of media ownership on broadcasters' freedom (Whitehead, 1987, and Forman, 1984 lectures), the future of public-service broadcasting (Eyre, 1999, Murdoch, 1989, Ball, 2003 lectures), the impact of markets on pro-gramme quality (Elstein, 1991, Lambert, 1990 lectures), debates about whether and how television should be regulated (Ockrent, 1988, Jay, 1981 lectures), the differences involved in making film for television or cinema (Schlesinger, 1985, Kennedy, Martin, 1986, McGrath, 1976 lec-tures), whether taboo subjects should be addressed in sitcoms (Lear, 1978 lecture), the imbalances of power between 'talent' or 'creatives' and broadcasters (Street-Porter, 1995, Marks and Gran, 1997, Bazalgette, 1998 lectures), the inadequacies of BBC management (Grade, 1992, and Potter, 1993 lectures), the declining quality of television programming (Liddiment, 2001, Thompson, 2002, and Humphrys, 2004 lectures) and whether television is truly 'male, middle class, middle aged and mediocre' (Street-Porter, 1995 lecture). Always topical, typically contro-versial and invariably delivered by a senior professional within televi-sion, John Mortimer (1980) claimed the 'MacTaggart lectures have discussed what may now without pretension, be called the Art of Television' (unedited lecture).

But why was MacTaggart's name chosen to be associated with this prestigious series of lectures? Did it reflect little more than the coinci-dent timing of the establishment of the EITF and the retrospective of MacTaggart's work outlined above?

James MacTaggart: 'On a Mission from God'

Verity Lambert (1990 lecture) addressed the issue directly: 'What was so special about him that this lecture should be given in his name?' She recalls 'working with James as a writer and director'.

> He was a friend and colleague when we worked at the BBC in the sixties. He was producing the *Wednesday Play* and I was producing, among other things, *Dr Who*. Looking back what I remember most about him was his courage, enthusiasm, and his passion – his courage to innovate and entertain – to give the viewer an opportunity to per-ceive and experience television drama in different ways. Whether it was the drama-documentary realism of *Cathy Come Home*, or in the non-naturalistic *Candide*, in which he used innovative technology, he never patronised his audience. He knew that television was there

to entertain, to reflect the society in which we live, to increase awareness and understanding of ourselves and of others, and to communicate with people. And because of his commitment and passion, more
often than not, he did. It was because he stood for those kind of
values of television that the founders of this lecture decided to give
his name to it in perpetuity. (unedited lecture).

Gus Macdonald, one of 'the founders' of the MacTaggart Lecture, confirmed this view. 'MacTaggart was very distinguished,' Macdonald
suggested, 'a very independently spirited and creative person who
challenged a lot of the conventions. And because what we were trying
to achieve in the Television Festival was a closer debate between film
and television, MacTaggart seemed to be a bridge between the two. He
was also a Scot. MacTaggart was the Scot who had done the best work
since Sandy McKendrick' (Macdonald, 2003). Troy Kennedy Martin in
his 1986 lecture recalled MacTaggart's passion and commitment to
innovation within the fledgling medium of television. In 1962, he and
'Jimmy MacTaggart . . . set forth . . . on a similar quest. We were going
to destroy naturalism,' he claimed, 'if possible, before Christmas. We
were, like the Blues Brothers "on a mission from God"' (Kennedy
Martin, 1986 lecture).

Across his career as an actor, playwright producer and director
James MacTaggart undoubtedly won the respect of his peers. Phillip
Whitehead declared that he did not know him but 'admired his work,
as did we all' (Whitehead, 1987 lecture). A number of lecturers mention
MacTaggart's contribution to television in their opening remarks with
an effusive admiration that suggests more than mere good manners.
Michael Grade described him as 'a brilliant iconoclastic figure' (1992
lecture), for Street-Porter, he was 'one of TV's greatest innovators'
whose 'vision not only created some of the most memorable TV for
viewers, it inspired television's talent to reach further than they had
done before, to follow his example' (Street-Porter, unedited lecture).
For John Mortimer (1980), MacTaggart 'gave enduring life to TV drama
by his direction and production of plays as diverse as *Up the Junction*,
the *Duchess of Malfi*, or works by Dennis Potter, John McGrath and
Voltaire' (unedited lecture).

James MacTaggart was born in 1928 and educated at Glasgow High
School and Glasgow University. During his national service in the
Army, he volunteered to become a parachutist in the 15th Scottish
Battalion. He worked as a freelance radio actor ('of high skill') with the
BBC in Scotland before joining the staff as a General Programme

Producer in radio in the 1950s (*The Times* 1974: 18). He was the driving force, along with the writer Eddie Boyd, of the radio magazine *Scope*. He produced several major radio dramas for Scotland and the radio network. In 1956 he moved to BBC television as a Drama Production Assistant for a salary of about £15 a week. Shaun Sutton, Head of BBC Drama in 1976, recalls finding a note from Appointments dated January 1956 expressing doubts about the suitability of MacTaggart as a BBC employee. A second 'sinister, unsigned, undated note' said meaningfully, 'it would probably be another week before we knew about J. MacTaggart'. Sutton adds 'it wasn't long before we all knew about him' (BBC 1976).

MacTaggart moved to London as producer/director in 1962. Sidney Newman, who was Head of Drama at the BBC in 1958, appointed MacTaggart as the producer of a new series of plays, to be called *The Wednesday Play*. MacTaggart was responsible for such notable productions as *Up the Junction*, *Stand Up For Nigel Barton* and *Vote, Vote, Vote For Nigel Barton*. His productions included single plays and groups of plays under the series titles of *Storyboard*, *Teletale* and *First Night*. MacTaggart eventually became a freelance writer/director for the BBC and wrote for such programmes as *Adam Adamant Lives*, *Detective*, *The View From Daniel Pike*, *Menace* and *Scotch on the Rocks*.

Appraisals of his work were always glowing and typically emphasised his technical mastery of the television medium as well as his artistic gifts. MacTaggart, for example, experimented with the then highly novel 'video' recording technology, using early chromakey and basic electronic effects to bring non-naturalist styles to classic as well as new plays (Housham 2000: 15). The biographical preface to Newman's 1976 commemorative lecture for the Association of Directors and Producers claims that 'as a director [MacTaggart] achieved the elusive alchemy of combining the elements of the creative artist and the master craftsman. His gift for storytelling, whatever the content, was rarely challenged. In his last years, he again excited colleagues and audiences with his adaptations and direction of *Alice* and *Candide*, using colour separation techniques with an audacity that stemmed from his unrivalled authority and rare ability' (ADP 1976). Shaun Sutton endorses this view of MacTaggart as the all-rounder, possessed of great talent and industry, who enjoyed a rapport with all his colleagues involved in the creative process which he brought alive: he was the consummate professional.

> [MacTaggart] glowed with skill and enthusiasm. He was sharp and witty. He was theatrical in that his huge sympathy with actors

smacked of greasepaint and footlights. Yet with a film camera in his hands he could rival the best of the feature filmmakers. Almost as an accidental, he wrote scripts of the highest quality. Jimmy was good at it all. The record of his work is full of successes . . . It's easy to say that a man was a giant in his world – the phrase has become tarnished with misappliance. But that's what he was – a giant, a television all rounder, a rare occurrence. (BBC 1976)

Towards the end of his life, MacTaggart received the Society of Film and Television Arts (SFATA now BAFTA) and the Desmond Davis Award for outstanding contribution to television drama. This gifted producer/director, who made films for television, exemplified one of the key purposes of the emerging Edinburgh International Television Festival: to bring together the two cultures of television and film. MacTaggart's work exemplified the soundbite attributed to Peter Fiddick that the British film industry is not dead – it's alive and well and its called television (Macdonald 1977).

The Edinburgh International Television Festival: The 'wee gabfest' becomes 'Channel 4 in Waiting'

Accounts of the origins of the first EITF in 1977[7] offered by its originators are, to say the least, prosaic. Jane Mills, who served as Festival organiser from 1977 to 1979, describes a 'dreary, drizzly day in Soho' in March 1977, and a meeting with '*World in Action*'s lean, lefty-looking, droopy-moustachioed executive producer, Gus Macdonald' over copious drinks at the Tatty Bogle – 'a dark, disreputable drinking club just north of Golden Square'. Two hours later she had 'agreed to spend what he [Macdonald] had promised would be no more than a day a week organising a "wee gabfest" for a "wee handful" of programme makers' (Mills 2000: 5). Mills acknowledges that she had previously organised nothing more adventurous than a dinner party, but two days later she flew to Edinburgh and for the next five months she worked 'non-stop as the "wee gabfest" grew into a week long fully fledged festival attended by almost 300 delegates': and all this for less than £5 a day (Mills 2000: 5).

Macdonald, who was deputy Chair of the Edinburgh International Film Festival, had already secured funding for the event from within the television industry (Fiddick 1977b). This phase of the event had been organised over food rather than drinks, but organisational matters continued to be informal. Macdonald explains that

I went round to Jeremy Isaacs at Thames and Alasdair Milne at Scottish BBC, Denis Forman and David Plowright, who were my bosses at Granada, and I also approached Alastair Hetherington, who was running BBC Scotland at the time, as well as seeing Phil Brannon, Paul Fox and Cyril Bennett at LWT. I got most of them together at Bianchi's, an Italian restaurant down in Soho, which is where John Logie Baird might or might not have invented television, and they agreed to back it on the one condition that they wouldn't have to attend because they knew it would be really radical and they would probably come in for assault. I said that was fine because what we really needed was a creative festival that would encourage and embolden programme-makers. So I got their support and money for it. (Macdonald 2003)

Macdonald identifies a number of ambitions for the new television festival. First, television needed an autonomous festival to showcase the best in television programming and to discuss controversial issues exploring the emerging medium; 'Britain had the best television in the world, but no television festival, what better venue than Edinburgh?' (Macdonald 1977). Macdonald had grown increasingly troubled by the Edinburgh Film Festival's 'adulation of foreign film-makers' which coexisted with 'almost a dismissive attitude' to the people that he saw as 'brilliant film-makers who were working in British television' (Macdonald 2003).

Second, this separation between film and television cultures was 'unnatural'. The EITF might 'bring the two cultures closer together' especially since technological changes were making 'filming more ambitious and affordable' (Macdonald 2003). Macdonald's *World in Action* team – 'just one current affairs series in one ITV company – had shot half a million feet of film in the last year' (Macdonald 1977). One benchmark of the Festival's success was the establishment of the National Film and Television School, 'which started as a film school' (Macdonald 2003).

Third, the festival provided 'the only forum for programme makers to come together to discuss their work' (Allen 1977); this was a Festival 'for the programme makers and not the administrators' (Mills cited in the *Sunday Telegraph*, 3 July 1977). But what began as a forum for programme-makers developed into a much broader based event. Macdonald claims the 'the hope was that the Festival would allow the voice of programme-makers to be heard . . . and that people would be allowed to speak freely because their bosses wouldn't be there. But the problem arose that after a while people said this raises huge questions but there is no one here to answer them. So we ended up demanding that executives come and answer for their policies; why they were so cautious or why their comedies were so poor, or their current affairs so craven' (Macdonald 2003).

The 1977 Festival programme offered the 175 full and 300 temporary delegates (*The Scotsman*, 3 September 1977) a radical agenda of paper presentations, panel discussions and film screenings 'designed to assist the development and promotion of a critical perspective on the small screen' (*Festival Times*, 2 August 1977) and to show that television drama is as 'worthy of serious intellectual thought and criticism as theatre and film' (*Sunday Telegraph*, 3 July 1977). The Festival also included showings of a number of films which had previously been banned, including Peter Watkins' *War Game* and Dennis Potter's *Brimstone and Treacle*, which the then Director General Alasdair Milne had decided the BBC should not screen only days before its scheduled slot; these films were highly significant for the press interest and festival publicity which they generated (see, for example, Fiddick 1977a, 1977; Purser, *Sunday Telegraph*, 4 September 1977; Church in *The Times*, 2 September 1977; Davidson in *The Scotsman*, 2 September 1977). Despite the success of the 1977 Festival, the fragility of organisational arrangements was illustrated by the uncertainty about whether there would be a similar event the following year. Before the closing lunch 'unfolded into full alcoholic bloom', Gus Macdonald and Jane Mills announced, 'we shall all get together in a fortnight's time and talk about it' (*The Scotsman*, 3 September 1977).

Macdonald's expectation of a 'really radical' event was certainly fulfilled in the first ten years of the Festival. In 1977, for example, Jeremy Isaacs, then Director of Programmes for Thames Television, invited delegates to pass a motion calling on the BBC to televise Potter's *Brimstone and Treacle* and invited the audience to telephone the BBC *en masse* to insist on the play's transmission (*The Scotsman*, 1 September 1977). In the following year, Michael Grade, Head of Programmes at LWT, was heavily criticised for the insensitive use of stereotypes in the company's comedy programmes (Williams and Griffin-Beale 1978: 12), while in 1980, the Festival screened *Death of a Princess*, which had been criticised by the Thatcher government for its radical portrayal of Islamic culture. In 1982, there were 'angry scenes' as broadcasters challenged military censors about the restrictions on coverage of the Falklands war. Two years later, miners' leader Arthur Scargill was applauded loudly as he denounced television coverage of the coal dispute, while the

Festival's tenth Anniversary in 1985, attended by 695 delegates, witnessed a major row about *Real Lives*, a documentary about Northern Ireland which Home Secretary Leon Brittain had persuaded the BBC Governors to postpone and re-edit: Prime Minister Thatcher wanted to ban the programme without having seen it on the contentious ground that it offered terrorists 'the oxygen of publicity' (Clarke 2000: 6; Franklin 2004: 76).

The mood of the Festival programme was rather cerebral, as well as radical, with papers for panels on topics such as censorship and drama, soap operas and women and realism and non-naturalism, presented by Raymond Williams, Melvyn Bragg, Richard Dyer, Anthony Smith, Dennis Potter and John McGrath. Perhaps unsurprisingly, given the contributions by such intellectual heavyweights, the *Sunday Telegraph* declared the event less a festival 'than a conference' (4 September 1977). But tensions between programme-makers and academics were apparent. John Birt, for example, began his 1996 MacTaggart Lecture by recalling the mood music of the early festivals. 'Our early cosiness – exploring our own obsessions,' Birt (1996) claimed, 'was first invaded by the semiologists – missionaries emerging from the new world of "Media Studies". They baffled us by proclaiming in one early session about soap operas that: "characteristically it may be precisely when capital becomes the dynamic principle of cultural production that the ideological functions secured by the production escape social control and become less problematic"' (unedited lecture). Macdonald deployed a less adversarial invective to identify a similar schism but derived a distinctive conclusion. 'We had this great influx of Marxist and radical academics, which got quite embittered as their critique tried to demolish everything that we as practitioners were doing, including in my own case any concept of objectivity' (Macdonald 2003). But from the earliest days, Macdonald acknowledged the value of what he termed 'the sharp and disconcerting critique of outside observers'. The television industry's 'own insularity, complacency and philistinism, which comes with age,' he suggests, 'pose greater threats to the health of the medium than any number of semiologists or opaque Althusserians who drift in from the cold to warm themselves at the camp fire' (Macdonald 1978). Eventually the 'leftist academics began to fade away and in their place you got an influx of PR people, agents and others who were looking for talent and deals' (Macdonald 2003).

This shifting festival demography has prompted the criticism that the Festival has metamorphosed from a 'Marxist forum' to a 'corporate jolly'; from 'radical chic' to 'corporate sharks' (Housham 2000: 15–17).

In the early days, some observers identified festival participants as 'products of the late 1960s/early 1970s radical campus culture', along with young programme-makers from the 'glamorous drama and current affairs departments' who believed their work was 'part of the "ongoing struggle for truth"' (Housham 2000: 15). But since the mid- to late 1980s, the Festival has 'grown and prospered as a more formal, conservative business convention' with consultancies, new media and marketing and finance business all wanting 'some of Edinburgh's now respectable glitz to rub off on their activities' (Housham 2000: 17).

Two reasons help to explain the shift. The first is political. The successive Conservative governments of the 1980s embarked on a programme of reform for the television industries which was part of the broader Thatcherite project. The hallmarks of this project were an emphasis on individualism and competition rather than collective action, the alleged supremacy of markets above public service, the efficiencies to be gained from 'privatising' public-sector assets and the need to tackle restrictive practices resulting from trade-union activity. Against the backcloth of this new policy mood, the BBC and ITV felt vulnerable and grew increasingly wary of 'a big event that (albeit unwittingly) was handing ammunition to their vulture like critics in Fleet Street' (Housham 2000: 16). The BBC and ITV cut both their funding for the Festival and their sponsorship of programme-makers to attend the event.

Second, changes in the television industry, especially the emergence of independent production, were significant. Macdonald (2003) recalls chairing a session and commenting jokingly that he was

> Old enough to remember when socialists used to come to the Edinburgh Festival but they were now called independent producers . . . I wrote a headline for a laugh to wind them up saying they were the 'Trojan Ponies[8] of Thatcherism'. During the 1980s the business became more commercialised and the Festival was working very hard to establish a greater sense of independence for programme-makers. The natural extension of that was independent production because at the start you were claustrophobically trapped between the BBC and ITV. So we saw the future of television as opening up to independent production and I think the best description of Edinburgh in that period was that it was Channel 4 in waiting. It was Channel 4 in assembly. We encouraged that process along but we did so for creative reasons, although we were aware of the commercial implications. Survival became a big issue for independents and

Edinburgh was their opportunity to meet commissioning editors and others. So it developed into much more of a networking gathering where people could meet, greet, make contacts and pitch ideas.

Housham identifies 1985 as the watershed year in the transition. One festival session featured a critical discussion of the BBC's decision to buy the US mini-series the *Thorn Birds* at a time when Granada was broadcasting *Jewel in the Crown*, allegedly signalling the BBC's diminishing commitment to public-service broadcasting. Roger Bolton, a mid-ranking BBC executive 'with a brilliant record in current affairs behind him and a track record as a potential director general', made an intervention from the floor in support of this conjecture. He was subsequently carpeted by then Director General Alasdair Milne and told that 'he should have known better'. Bolton's 'brightest career prospects at the BBC bit the dust at that festival, and everyone took note' (Housham 2000: 16). The illusion that EITF was an enlightened forum where individuals could support any view and 'express their feelings freely without fear of retribution was finally smashed in 1985' (Housham 2000: 16).

This transition from a forum for radical discussion to a festival where networking and commercial concerns became prominent is reflected in the distinctive programme sessions available in 1977 compared to 2004 (see Appendix A for the 1977 programme). The intellectually heavyweight panels on 'Realism and Non-naturalism' and 'Censorship and Television Drama', which featured in the earlier Festival, with papers by Raymond Williams, Richard Dyer and Anthony Smith, have been replaced in 2004 by more popular sessions including Chequebook vs Notebook Journalism with Max Clifford (PR Consultant), Rebecca Loos (David Beckham's former PA), Peter Horrocks (Head of Current Affairs at the BBC) Steve Anderson (Controller of Current Affairs at ITV), David Yelland (former *Sun* Editor) and Monica Lewinsky. In 2004 there was also a session on *The Court on Camera* with Lord Falconer and O. J. Simpson's sister-in-law, Denise Brown.

One constant feature of the Festival, amid the changing elements of who attends and what subjects are discussed, is provided by the bar of the George Hotel, which is the 'festival nerve centre', which rarely closes before 3 a.m. and provides the 'perfect networking opportunity' where 'commissioning editors stripped of their voicemail, controllers unprotected by their phalanx of assistants, and presenters naked without their agents' listen to pitches from young talent and independent producers. John Willis claims that in 'three days, a heavy drinking independent can meet more key television people in the George Bar than in the rest of the year put together' (Willis 2000: 8).

Another constant is the open democratic access to debate which the Festival provides. In his introduction to the 1978 Festival, Gus Macdonald claimed that one of the great strengths of the new Festival was that the key issues of British Broadcasting could be publicly confronted. 'All guns are checked in at the door in Edinburgh – we don't encourage delegates or factions. Everyone who chooses to come does so as an individual and we welcome them, in the words of John Grierson, to the simple braveries of the public forum' (Macdonald 1978). In 2003 Macdonald argued that whatever else might have changed, these same rules applied: 'There's still a television festival and it's a very lively event where all the industry can get together . . . everybody is equal, any researcher can just walk in and pick a fight with the Director General, if he's old enough to come there – and that still works.'

The MacTaggart Lectures: The Political and Policy Context

There is a broad scholarly consensus that the history and development of British television can be divided into five distinctive, if at times overlapping, periods, with each period or phase characterised by a distinctive policy mood and broadcasting developments (see, for example, Blumler 1996 and Smith 1974). This fivefold periodisation of television history, but particularly the final two periods, provides a very useful backdrop against which to contextualise and interpret the MacTaggart Lectures.

The first period, which Blumler terms 'monopoly', begins with the BBC's early television broadcasts in 1936 and concludes with the Television Act 1954, which ushered in commercial broadcasting in the subsequent year. In this early phase television was judged to be little more than 'radio with pictures' and consequently there seemed a compelling logic to the suggestion that television, like radio, should be organised as a public service, funded by licence fee, regulated by the BBC Governors, with programmes informed by Reithian ambitions to 'educate, inform and entertain' (Briggs 1979: 4; Franklin 1997: 160).

The second phase of 'creative competition' extends from 1955 to the publication of the Pilkington Report and the creation of BBC2 in 1962. The period was characterised by the debate concerning the impact of commercial television on programming and the suggestion that standards were falling on ITV, while the BBC was achieving a new rapport with audiences. Pilkington criticised ITV for the triviality and narrow range of some programmes as well as the increasing portrayals of violence in programmes (Pilkington 1961: para 572). But ITV targeted previously neglected 'mass tastes', delivered regional programming and offered a new informality in programming – especially in news programmes – which radically reduced audiences for BBC programming and obliged the Corporation to justify licence fee funding given its diminishing audience share. The BBC responded with increased provision of sports, the development of television drama such as *Play For Today* and the innovatory news and current affairs programmes *Tonight* and *Panorama*.

The third period of 'stable competition' between 1963 and 1970 witnessed a new mood of confidence among broadcasters, expressed in the suggestion that BBC Director General Hugh Greene had 'dressed Auntie in a mini skirt' along with a flurry of new, highly critical programmes, which for the first time challenged powerful interests in society: especially politicians and governments. The satirical review *That Was The Week That Was* exemplified this new mood, along with dramas emphasising social realism and criticism such as *Cathy Come Home*, *Up the Junction* and *Z Cars*.

It is the fourth and fifth periods in television's development across the twentieth century, however, which are most significant in providing the broader setting for the MacTaggart Lectures, as well as being helpful in explaining the timing and emergence of particular themes within the lectures reflecting lecturers' reactions to salient issues of policy and politics being played out in the broadcasting industry and the wider society.

Broadcasting under Cultural Attack or 'Death on the Rack for Death on the Rock*'*

The period which Blumler describes as 'broadcasting under cultural attack' extends from 1970 to 1983 and is characterised by a 'public backlash' to broadcasters' confidence which distinguished the previous phase of 'stable competition'. Across the period, there was 'a growing belief that television had grown over-dominant, that it was beginning to "trivialise" politics and to be careless in its effects on public morals, on the level of violence and on respect for authority' (Smith 1974: 17). The policy preoccupation across the period articulated by public and press was the demand for greater regulation and public accountability for television.

The backlash against broadcasters was multi-pronged. The public, for example, increasingly voiced concerns about explicit portrayals of sexual and violent behaviour on the small screen, while Mary Whitehouse's Viewers and Listeners' Association enjoyed expansive press coverage and burgeoning membership. Academic critiques of broadcasters' treasured professional and public-service commitments to objectivity and impartiality were touted loudly in the Glasgow Media Group's series of books denouncing *Bad News*, while at the Centre for Contemporary Cultural Studies at the University of Birmingham, Stuart Hall and his colleagues were analysing the moral panic about 'black muggers' stemming from ideological messages which broadcasters encoded into television news reports; what Rod Allen called the 'seismologists' had arrived (Allen 1977). Another seemingly paradoxical critique emerged from within broadcasting itself, reflecting some programme-makers' unhappiness with the broadcasting duopoly of the BBC and ITV, which limited employment opportunities, stultified creative work, protected duopoly interests and sanctified the status quo of broadcasting organisation. The most significant policy outcome in this respect was the establishment of Channel 4 in 1982 with its remit to broadcast innovative programmes to minority audiences and provide opportunities for independent production (Blumler 1996).

But the significant backlash came from politicians in all parties and of all political hues. Blumler cites politicians' widespread criticism of the flippant tone of *Yesterday's Men*, a documentary about Harold Wilson and the Labour Party, as illustrative of this trend. However, it was the election of the Thatcher government in 1979, followed by a number of very public spats, which deteriorated relations between politicians and broadcasters to the nadir of the late 1980s.

The list of critical engagements between politicians and broadcasters grew year by year. In 1982 broadcasters objected to the government's very forceful management of 'war news' via the number 10 press office and the Ministry of Defence (Harris 1983), which worked so effectively that Glasgow Media Group's analysis of BBC programmes declared them to be little more than rehashed government handouts with some background from ministerial briefings (*The Guardian*, 8 October 1985, p. 1). In 1985 the government objected to an edition of the BBC's *Panorama* which showed armed members of the IRA policing a road block at Carrickmore (Bolton 1990: 64–83), while later the same year the Home Secretary intervened to secure the postponement and re-editing of the BBC's *Real Lives* programme to deny terrorists the 'oxygen of publicity'. In 1986 Norman Tebbit, then Chairman of the Conservative Party, used the party's conference platform to berate the BBC for its coverage of the American bombing of Libya, denouncing it as a 'mixture of news, views, speculation, error and uncritical carriage of Libyan propaganda' (Milne 1988: 190). In 1987 Special Branch raided the offices of BBC Scotland, removed journalist Duncan Campbell's note and address books and impounded film relating to the *Secret Society* series. Alan Protheroe, then Assistant Director General of the BBC, described the 28-hour raid as 'a shabby, shameful disgraceful state sponsored incursion into a journalistic establishment' (Protheroe 1987: 4).

Finally in 1988 the government attempted to prevent Thames Television from showing the *Death on the Rock* programme, which challenged the government's account of the shooting of three members of the IRA in Gibraltar. The independent Windlesham–Rampton Report concluded that the programmes did not breach impartiality and did not 'bribe, bully or misrepresent those who took part' (Windlesham and Rampton 1989: 142). The government 'utterly rejected' the report, which served merely to strengthen Mrs Thatcher's 'determination to shake up the ITV companies and the BBC' (*The Independent*, 27 January 1989, p. 1). As David Elstein commented in his 1991 MacTaggart Lecture, the Broadcasting Act 1990 was a piece of 'political revenge' designed to inflict on ITV licence holders 'death on the rack to make up for *Death on the Rock*'.

Governments' increased intervention in broadcasting was evident in other ways: the appointment of Marmaduke Hussey as Chair of the Board of Governors in 1988 to 'bring the BBC to heel' (Milne 1988: 188); the stacking of the BBC Board with Conservatives across the early/mid-1980s; the sacking of Director General Alasdair Milne in 1988, the redrafting of the Official Secrets Act in 1989 in ways which many observers believed resulted in a more restrictive Act than its predecessor (Ponting 1988: 15); and the introduction of censorship in the reporting of Northern Ireland affairs on 19 October 1988 (Franklin 2004: 30–3).

The period which Blumler designated 'broadcasting under cultural attack' was undoubtedly an extremely difficult time for television, in which programme-makers, producers and broadcast journalists experienced a backlash from the public, press and politicians and these challenges to television broadcasting were reflected in MacTaggart Lecture discussions across the period.

Deregulation and Markets

The fifth and final period of 'deregulation and markets', which extends from 1984 to the present, is distinguished by the prominence of the market as the organising principle of broadcasting and the elevation of the viewer to a consumer sovereign whose market choices guarantee popular rather than quality programmes. The period is also characterised by the increasing deregulation of both ownership and programme contents resulting in greater concentration, conglomerate and cross-media ownership of television and other media, along with new regulatory bodies which operate with an ever lighter touch. In this climate of policy change, broadcasters' commitments to public-service broadcasting seem less certain than previously, prompting concern and discussion about programme quality and the alleged 'dumbing down' of television schedules in order to 'chase' ratings and audiences.

Since the mid-1980s, television in both the public and commercial sectors has been subject to unprecedented change in its organisational, financial and regulatory aspects. At certain key points, technological developments in cable, satellite and digital delivery systems have quickened the pace of change, as well as raising significant policy problems reflecting increasing media convergence. A flurry of Green and White Papers, Broadcasting Acts and policy documents articulating broadcasters' responses to government policy initiatives (for example, *Extending Choice: The BBC's Role in the New Broadcasting Age* (1992)), articulate these developments.

The 'curtain raiser for this tide of radically revisionist commercialism' (Blumler 1996: 242) was the Peacock Committee, which concluded that funding the BBC by advertising was incompatible with the Corporation's public service commitment's to quality programming, but acknowledged an expansive future role for market forces in shaping the television industry. Peacock recommended an index-linked licence fee as the funding mechanism in the short term to be replaced by subscription, in a staged process of change, leading eventually to a 'full market system characterised by multiple channels, diverse delivery systems and a diversity of payment options' (Peacock 1986: 133–4). Peacock's legacy has subsequently been unravelled and implemented with the publication of a number of policy documents and statutes ranging from the 1988 White Paper *Broadcasting in the 1990s: Competition, Choice and Quality* to the recent *Communications Act* (2003), which have transformed many aspects of the broadcasting landscape.

The commercial sector of television, for example, constitutes a more competitive environment since the Broadcasting Act 1990 required would-be Channel 3 licence holders to bid for franchises in a 'blind' auction, revised funding arrangements for Channel 4 initiating a battle with Channel 3 for advertising revenues, legislated for the launch of

Channel 5 in March 1997 and facilitated the expansion of satellite and cable services funded by subscription or advertising. More recently the explosion of digital television services offers further competition to channels operating in the commercial sector.

Regulation has also changed radically, with the IBA superseded by the ITC in 1991, which, along with the Cable Authority, Radio Authority and all other regulatory bodies (excepting the BBC Board of Governors) has been incorporated into Ofcom under the provisions of the Communications Act 2003. The Act also revised regulatory arrangements governing media ownership by abolishing the restriction on non-EU companies owning ITV and the prohibition limiting any ITV company to a maximum 15 per cent share of audience, thereby clearing the way for a single owner of Channel 3: Carlton and Granada pre-empted the Act by three months announcing their proposed merger in October 2003. Other regulation changes have relaxed restrictions on Channel 5 allowing ownership by any UK or overseas company, including newspaper groups with 20 per cent or more of the UK market, subject to plurality test (a key amendment to the Act proposed by Lord Putnam), which will require the new ownership arrangements to sustain the quality and range of programme provision.

Press and government speculation about possible broadcasting policy change has also fuelled discussion within the industry across the period of 'deregulation and markets'. Michael Grade's angry speech to the Edinburgh International Television Festival on 26 August 1996, following press reports in June that the Conservative government was considering a plan to privatise Channel 4, illustrates this point. Grade argued fiercely and persuasively that privatisation was incompatible with Channel 4's remit. Four years later, similar speculation that Chancellor Gordon Brown favoured privatising the Channel prompted Grade's successor, Michael Jackson, to use the annual Fleming Lecture at the Royal Television Society as a platform from which to announce his implacable opposition to any such plan (Franklin 2001: 65–6). By contrast, however, Chief Executive Mark Thompson, just prior to becoming Director General of the BBC in June 2004, presented the Board of Channel 4 with controversial plans to merge with Channel 5 in order to cut costs, increase efficiencies and allow more creative risk-taking in programme-making without undermining the Channel's core remit of delivering high-quality programming targeted at minority audiences (Wells and Milmo 2004: 2).

Change has also been evident in the public sector, but, curiously, given the antipathy of successive Conservative governments to the BBC across the 1980s, the extent of change is perhaps less notable than in the commercial sector. The predictable policy preoccupation has been the suitability and legitimacy of the licence fee as a funding mechanism for the BBC in circumstances of declining audience share in a multi-channel television environment. The Department of National Heritage, the precursor of the Department of Media, Culture and Sport, discussed the pros and cons of the licence fee, direct taxation, advertising, sub-scription and a mixed financing system for the BBC, in *The Future of the BBC*, before concluding in favour of the licence fee on the rather ten-dentious ground that 'No one has devised an obviously better system' (Department of National Heritage 1992: 31).

In the mid-1990s, the BBC responded to various financial proposals, including the abolition of the licence fee as a regressive tax (Boulton 1991) and the suggestion that the BBC might be privatised (Hargreaves 1993), by proposing cost cuts via initiatives such as Producer Choice, which attempted to make efficiency savings by creating an internal market for production resources within the BBC, as well as requests for an increase in the licence fee to fund new services (Birt, 1996 lecture). The 1999 Davis Report on funding the BBC recommended a digital licence 'top-up' fee to facilitate the roll-out of digital services, but Chris Smith, then Secretary of State for Culture, Media and Sport, eventually rejected the idea. In July 2004, the report *What You Said About the BBC*, commissioned by the Department of Culture, Media and Sport, confirmed the public's view that the licence fee remains 'the least worst option' for funding the BBC, although only one-third of the 5,500 respondents believe the BBC should be funded solely by the licence fee. The report also noted that the 'unanimity about the sense of decline in quality of BBC Television output is startling' (*The Guardian*, 21 July 2004, p. 2).

Regulation of the BBC remains the remit of the Board of Governors, but the initial report of the review of public-service broadcasting, chaired by Ed Richards, for Ofcom in April 2004, suggested that the BBC Governors 'should take a lead' in preventing the corporation from indulging in copycat programming, aggressive scheduling or buying too many programmes from abroad; it also suggested that that every service on the BBC should demonstrate a public-service value and the licence fee might be shared with other broadcasters to help them meet public-service commitments. Peter Bazalgette, Chairman of Endemol, claimed, 'Ofcom has parked its tanks right in the middle of the BBC lawn' (*The Guardian*, 22 April 2004, p. 3). Michael Grade appeared to be listening to Ofcom announcing in the BBC Annual Report in July

2004 that the Governors would be commissioning an independent review of the quality and range of programming on BBC1. Grade challenged the regulatory effectiveness of the BBC Governors in his 1992 MacTaggart, but, on his return to the BBC in May 2004, he announced his determination to counter the post-Hutton criticism that the BBC's managers had captured the Governors and held them in thrall. Grade envisages Governors acting more independently, supported by a 'Governance Unit' intended to prevent attempts by managers 'to bamboozle' them (*The Guardian*, 30 June 2004, p. 8). The Governors will also commission independent reviews of various aspects of the Corporation's activities.

In June 2004, *Building Public Value* set out the BBC's case for Charter renewal. Once again it seemed clear that the BBC had heard Ofcom's message concerning public-value outcomes from BBC services. The document insisted that the licence fee remains the only funding option compatible with the essential character of the BBC, but suggested that the responsibility for setting the value of the licence fee should be transferred to an independent body in much the same way the government transferred responsibility for setting interest rates to the Bank of England in 1997 (BBC 2004). Accountability for the use of public funding, moreover, should be guaranteed via a new public-value test. In future every BBC channel and service will be granted a 'service licence' by the Board of Governors, which will set its remit, targets and budget (an idea mooted by Tony Ball in his 2003 MacTaggart Lecture). Every service will be subject to a public-service test in which 10,000 people will be asked their views of BBC services (Wells 2004: 8).

In summary, the period of 'deregulation and markets', which began in 1984, has witnessed an unprecedented shift in broadcasting policy and provides a backcloth of policy change against which to set the MacTaggart Lectures. Many of the themes raised in the lectures – the changing relationship between politicians and broadcasters, censorship and a culture of dependency, the nature of quality programming, the prospects for quality programming in an increasingly market-driven system, the growth and role of independent production and creative talent, the future of the BBC and Channel 4 and the prospects for public-service broadcasting – reflect the changes in the television industry, driven by broadcasting policy, technological changes and the choices of viewers in the expansive, multi-channel television environment. The lectures also articulate a response to the challenges posed by such change.

The MacTaggart Lectures: Changing Concerns and
Continuities

A persistent if only half-joking theme which traditionally finds a place
in the opening paragraphs of many MacTaggart Lectures is the idea that
the lecture forms part of a job application. The tradition has its roots in
Jeremy Isaacs' 1979 lecture 'Signposting Television in the 1980s: The
Fourth Television Channel', which was widely interpreted as a bid to
run Channel 4 (see Dyke, 1994, Bazalgette, 1998 lectures); Isaacs was
successful. In 1992 Michael Grade used the MacTaggart platform to
'pitch for' the job of Director General of the BBC, but didn't get it
(Bazalgette, 1998 lecture). By 1994, Greg Dyke felt obliged to declare
himself 'the first genuinely unemployed MacTaggart lecturer' but
denied that he was 'here tonight . . . to pitch for my next job in television' (Dyke, 1994 lecture). Such denials have become commonplace.
Three years later, Marks and Gran (1997) announced themselves as 'the
first lecturers since Rupert Murdoch who aren't looking for a new job
or trying to hang on to their current one' (unedited lecture), while
Phillip Whitehead (1987) announced unequivocally, 'this lecture is not
a job application or a valedictory' (unedited lecture, see also Elstein,
1991 lecture). In 1999, Richard Eyre acknowledged this tradition of the
'MacTaggart as job application' but expressed his reluctance 'to pioneer
its use as a resignation letter' (Eyre, 1999 lecture). According to Peter
Bazalgette, it was Janet Street-Porter who pioneered such innovation in
1995, when she alleged that British television was being badly managed
by middle-class, middle-aged, middle-brow, male executives, one of
whom promptly sacked her from the now defunct cable station *Live TV*
(Bazalgette, 1998 lecture). But predictably perhaps, it was Dennis Potter
who brought this tradition to its apotheosis in 1993 when he concluded
his highly critical but eloquent lecture with the following declaration:

> I hope it is clear by now that I happen to care very much about the
> medium that has both allowed and shaped the bulk of my life's work,
> and even my life's meaning. However, I do have the odd hour or two
> in each day in which to pretend to be a Saint George rather than a
> Saint Sebastian. I therefore hereby formally apply, in front of wit-
> nesses of substance, here at the Edinburgh International Television
> Festival, for the post of Chairman of the Governors of the British
> Broadcasting Corporation.

Another favoured theme, according to John Birt (1996), is 'BBC
bashing'. Indeed, Birt suggests that it is 'one of the Festival's favourite

blood sports, along with pig-sticking the Director General of the day' (unedited lecture). Phillip Whitehead's claim that 'the BBC draws the lightning' proved farsighted, presaging Michael Grade's and Dennis Potter's devastating critique of senior managers at the BBC. In the 1992 lecture, Grade accused BBC executives of adopting 'a sort of pseudo Leninist style of management which relies on the exercise of central control' resulting in 'an enervating caution which starts at the top and quickly becomes the culture of the whole organisation'. Addressing the MacTaggart audience, Grade asked 'Can anyone in the hall see the BBC in its current mood even making, let alone transmitting, *Death on the Rock*?' (Grade, 1992 lecture). Worse opprobrium followed in the following year when Dennis Potter's 'personal statement' or 'cry, as much from the bile duct as the heart' referred to John Birt as 'the poor wretch who is the present Director General' and famously characterised the Director General and Chairman of the BBC Board of Governors as 'a pair of croak voiced Daleks' who could not be made to appear 'benevolent even if you dress one of them in an Armani suit and call the other Marmaduke' (Potter, 1993 lecture).

A related theme was inaugurated by John McGrath in the first MacTaggart Lecture, which offered a critique of realism in television drama and, ahead of Grade's 1992 lecture, lamented the corrosive effect of 'centralised control' and 'elaborate systems of command, supervision check and review' on the creative mood of the BBC. 'The bully boys,' McGrath claimed, 'have moved in to stay' (McGrath, 1976 lecture). The list of 'bully boys' identified has varied across the years, reflecting the character and perspective of those who have been 'bullied', but a number of lecturers have returned to McGrath's focus on power and pluralism within the television industry.

One obvious persona for the bully boys are the politicians who censor programmes such as *Real Lives* and *Death on the Rock*, or who censor less directly by nurturing a climate of dependency which obliges broadcasters 'to spend their time currying favour with government' which is unhealthy for broadcasting and democracy (Dyke, 1994, Elstein, 1991, Whitehead, 1987, Mortimer, 1980 lectures). In the USA, the bully boys assume the guise of the conservative politicians in various lobbying organisations which are determined to reinstate 'old taboos' and inhibit television discussions of 'homosexuality, abortion . . . drug abuse and the menopause' (Lear, 1978 lecture).

Alternatively, the bully boys might be the broadcasters at the BBC, ITV or even Channel 4 who stifle the creative energies of 'talent' and independent producers, denying them ownership and distribution rights over programmes (Lambert, 1990, Marks and Gran, 1997, Street-Porter, 1995, Bazalgette, 1998 lectures). Working for the BBC or ITV involves being 'under-respected, under-consulted, under-rewarded': the BBC and ITV 'betray the behind-the-camera talent'. Channel 4 is a 'creatively liberating partner' but the Channel drives 'some of the hardest and cruellest bargains financially' (Marks and Gran, 1997 lecture).

The senior managers and Governors of the BBC constitute a third set of bully boys characterised by their Leninist managerialism uttered in the Dalek-voiced croaks, mentioned above (Grade, 1992, and Potter, 1993 lectures). In another formulation they are 'male, middle class, middle aged, middle brow and mediocre' but their stultifying effects on creative work is essentially the same (Street-Porter, 1995 lecture).

Media moguls like Rupert Murdoch, owner of BSkyB ('Rupert in the sky with gems of yesteryear' – Forman, 1984 lecture), perhaps exemplify the archetypal bully boy who defines public service in ways which promote his corporate interests, attempts to monopolise the media market, prioritises the messenger (BSkyB) above the message (quality programming) and, as Verity Lambert (1990) states, who wishes 'to see British television promoting the views to be read daily in Rupert Murdoch's most commercially successful newspaper' (unedited lecture). And all this, while entering a Faustian pact with the Conservative Prime Minister, Margaret Thatcher, which guaranteed her the support of the Murdoch press while News International's majority ownership of BSkyB was exempted from consideration by broadcasting legislation (Dyke, 1994, Whitehead, 1987 lectures).

In an interesting twist, the 'self interested, narrow, broadcasting elite' which dominates British television with its 'propagandist ideology' of public-service broadcasting may also be cast in the role of bully boy; elite members are 'akin to Plato's Guardians' (Murdoch, 1989 lecture). This particular bully boy restricts the freedom to broadcast, limits choice (certainly compared to American television) and supports unnecessarily restrictive regulatory structures; the attitudes of this elite are 'fundamentally undemocratic' and the restrictions on broadcasting which it endorses are 'incompatible with a mature democracy' (Murdoch, 1989, Ball, 2003 lectures).

Some MacTaggart lecturers have anthropomorphised market forces into the latest bully boy on the block. Market forces emphasise the priority of 'chasing ratings', which allegedly prompts a 'dumbing down' of the programme schedule (Elstein, 1991 lecture), but certainly results in a 'creative deficit' in television which makes too many programmes appear 'dull and mechanical and samey'(Thompson, 2002 lecture) and which places the 'Soul of British television at risk'. Television is about more than 'just putting bums on seats'; broadcasters have 'to take risks' (Liddiment, 2001 lecture).

The final near-perennial bully boy is regulation. Bazalgette (1998 lecture) argues for an 'end to the era of over-regulation' which insists on applying ill-informed criteria of 'quality' to programmes and fails to achieve a healthy competition which is beneficial to viewers. Eyre (1999 lecture) is glad to see the end of such regulation and eager to herald the new era of public-*interest* broadcasting. Regulators will be simply over-whelmed by the expansive amount of broadcast materials in a multi-channel environment and be replaced by 'You and me . . . and the viewers . . . there is no other grand design,' he argues, 'to relieve us individually of such burdens'.

But despite this continuing preoccupation with identifying different ills in television, there is a notable shift in the themes and concerns of the MacTaggart which can be located at the turn of the 1980 into the 1990s. Prior to that date, the broad concern of lectures was with pro-gramming, what constituted 'quality' programmes and how to make them. It involved the musings and reflections of distinguished film- and programme-makers such as John Schlesinger, Norman Lear and Troy Kennedy Martin about their own experiences and commitments to programme-making for television. Post-1990, the emphasis shifted to questions about the changing environment in which such programmes were made, whether such programming was possible, or more radically even desirable, in the emerging market-driven, expansive multi-channel television environment, and if not, what policy remedies were necessary. The questions, moreover, were typically posed by television executives rather than programme-makers; Rupert Murdoch, Greg Dyke, Richard Eyre and Tony Ball exemplified this trend.

A number of lecturers refer to this changing emphasis in their opening remarks. John Birt (1996), for example, observes that, 'in the early years of the Festival, the concerns were overwhelmingly about programme matters. We discussed naturalism or non-naturalism in drama. And the frontiers of taste, decency and free expression were fiercely debated year after year' (unedited lecture). But the 'Festival's early idealism' was slowly replaced by the arrival of 'big game' like Ted Turner and Rupert Murdoch. By 1990 the focus is on policy with lec-tures exploring market forces and social values (Elstein, 1991 lecture), the future of the BBC (Grade, 1992 lecture) or public-service broadcast-ing and the BBC (Ball, 2003 lecture). The year 1990 does not constitute a clear and unbreached divide, of course, since the development of ideas is rarely characterised by such stark watersheds; an overlapping of themes and concerns across periods is more typical of such developments. Thompson's (2002 lecture) lament for the 'creative deficit' in British television and Liddiment's (2001 lecture) expressed concern for the 'soul of television' explore clear programming concerns, while Phillip Whitehead's 1987 lecture on power and pluralism in broadcasting analyses the changing policy and political context for programme-making. But 1990 offers a sufficiently distinctive shift in emphasis from programming to policy, such that by 1997, Marks and Gran felt obliged to open their MacTaggart with the ambition to 'reclaim the MacTaggart Lecture for those of us who make programmes rather than policy' (Marks and Gran, 1997 lecture).

This 'divide' moreover approximates the broad division noted above between 'broadcasting under cultural attack' and 'deregulation and markets', without coinciding with it precisely. In the former period characterised by the public, press but mainly political backlash against broadcasters, the concern of the lectures is with the external constraints on programme-making, censorship in television drama and more widely, as well as a claim for the necessity of autonomy and freedom for successful and creative programme-making. In the latter period of rapid and extensive broadcasting change initiated by government policy, the focus of lectures shifts to explore the impact of deregulation, market forces and the emergence of a multi-channel environment on programming, the future of the BBC and the public-service tradition in broadcasting. In brief, the changing focus illustrates the extent to which the MacTaggart Lectures articulate the different ways in which the various lecturers interpreted the challenges of change for British broadcasting and how they thought those challenges should be met. They constitute a repository of responses to political and policy change concerning broadcasting across almost three decades.

The year 1989 is also significant for Rupert Murdoch delivering a 'two-finger, up yours attack' (Brooks 1989: 30) on the 'dignitaries of the British Television world' (Rees-Mogg 1989) which criticised the public-service tradition and argued for a greater 'Freedom in Broadcasting'. The significance of Murdoch's lecture resides not merely in its contents, or its ambitions to change government broadcasting policy, but in the target of his attack which an *Independent* editorial identified as 'the British broadcasting elite' (*The Independent*, 28 August 1989). This reveals a second substantive feature of this collection of MacTaggart

Lectures, which is the degree to which they illustrate the very 'British-ness' of British television and of discourses about it. The preoccupation in the lectures across the last thirty years is with the legacy of Reithian paternalism, the towering dominance of the BBC as the biggest '800 pound Gorilla' in the television 'jungle', the legitimacy of the licence fee and mechanisms for the funding of public-sector television, the impact of deregulation of ownership and programme schedules and the implications of an increasingly market-driven broadcasting industry on public-service broadcasting. Indeed the uniqueness and pervasive-ness of public-service principles in both the public and commercial sectors of British television prompted Barry Cox, Director of Corporate Affairs at LWT at the time of the Murdoch lecture, to claim that 'com-mercial television in Britain is not really commercial, it is the BBC funded by advertising' (Cox 1989: 9).

The MacTaggart Lectures cataloguing these reactions to change in British television across thirty years constitute a valuable resource for those interested in plotting broadcasting policy developments across the period. The style of the different lectures is highly variable, indi-vidualistic but always thought-provoking. When reading the essays, either individually or as a collection, it is impossible not to be impressed by their eloquent and authoritative voice. Editing the essays has certainly proved difficult. The task of reducing a highly condensed and articulate text from ten or twelve thousand words down to little more than three thousand words has triggered more than a few moments of reflection by the editor concerning the possible damage inflicted on the work of such consummately talented word-smiths expressed in these finely crafted essays. Some essays will engage more than others because of their sophistry of argument; others will amuse while others will simply impress with their sheer eloquence. Every reader will have her or his favourite. Whichever that may be, there is a general consensus, reflected not least in MacTaggart lecturers' own preferences, that the Dennis Potter lecture was a par-ticular triumph. Even the Chief Executive of Sky acknowledged Potter's 1993 performance as 'by far the most brilliantly crafted and funny MacTaggart' despite the fact that Potter opened his lecture by claiming that 'Sky's introduction of choice into television was verging on the criminal' and that Rupert Murdoch should be given 'a show trial complete with gallows' (Ball, 2003 lecture). When Sarah Barnett (2003), the Director of the MediaGuardian Edinburgh International Festival, was asked what she believed made a good MacTaggart, she claimed:

Well, it could be a number of things. A lecturer who is very senior, well regarded creatively, someone who will make a policy impact, someone who wants to discuss a burning issue. But what is good about the MacTaggart is that people rise to the challenge. People don't agree to do it unless they know they're going to have something to say. I think it then becomes a self-fulfilling prophecy. So if you agree to do it, you know you are going to have to build your corporate policy around your MacTaggart like Greg Dyke, or like David Liddiment, who went and sat in his garden for hours thinking 'What can I say? What do I want to say?' And I think it is great that people have delivered for us. So we don't always know what the burning issue is, but a lecturer is unlikely to do something unless they feel quite passionate about an issue.

She's right. Read and be moved by the passions of the MacTaggart lecturers, whose work is presented below.

References

Allen, R. (1977), 'Ophuls "Attack" on "Academic" Critics Opens Edinburgh' in *Broadcast*, 5 August.

Association of Directors and Producers (ADP) (1976), *The ADP Lecture in Memory of James MacTaggart*, 'Liquorice, Lollypops for the Masses or Some Ruminations on Drama as Communication', Sidney Newman, London: ADP.

Barnett, S. (2003), An interview with the Festival Director at the Guardian Edinburgh International Festival offices in London, 15 September.

BBC (1976), *A Retrospective Presentation of Some of the Distinguished Television Programmes Directed by James MacTaggart (1928–1975)*, Edinburgh: BBC Scotland.

BBC (2004), *Building Public Value*, London: BBC.

Blumler, J. G. (1997), 'British Television', in H. Newcomb (ed.), *The Encyclopedia of Television*, Chicago: Fitzroy Dearborn.

Bolton, R. (1990), *Death on the Rock and Other Stories*, London: W. H. Allen/Optomen Books.

Boulton, D. (1991), *The Third Age of Broadcasting*, London: Institute of Public Policy Research.

Briggs, A. (1979), *A History of Broadcasting in the United Kingdom*, vol. 4: *Sound and Vision*, Oxford: Oxford University Press.

Brooks, R. (1989), 'Murdoch's Pie in the Sky', *The Observer*, 27 August, p. 30.

Church, M. (1977), 'Television at a Turning Point', *The Times*, 2 September.

Clarke, S. (2000), 'Edinburgh at a Glance', *Broadcast*, 25 August, p. 6.

Cox, B. (1989), 'Why Murdoch's Vision Fails to Bring Quality into Focus', *The Scotsman*, 28 August, p. 9.

Davidson, J. (1977), 'Television Festival: The Unacceptable Trinity', *The Scotsman*, 2 September.

Department of National Heritage (1992), *The Future of the BBC*, Cmnd 2098, London: HMSO.

DTI and DCMS (2000), *A New Future For Communications* London: The Stationery Office.

Fiddick, P. (1977a), 'Devlish' in *The Guardian*, 2 September.

Fiddick, P. (1977b), 'Air Time at Last, for the Banned', *The Guardian*, 23 August.

Franklin, B. (1997), *Newszak and News Media*, London: Arnold.

Franklin, B. (2001), *British Television Policy: A Reader*, London: Routledge.

Franklin, B. (2004), *Packaging Politics: Political Communication in Britain's Media Democracy*, London: Arnold.

Hargreaves, I. (1993), *Sharper Visions: The BBC and the Communications Revolution*, London: Demos.

Harris, R. (1983), *Gotcha! The Media, the Government and the Falklands Crisis*, London: Faber and Faber.

Housham, D. (2000), 'Radical Cheek', *Broadcast*, 25 August, pp. 15–17.

McCormick, J. (2000), '50 Minutes To Change the World', *Broadcast*, 25 August, pp. 10–12.

Macdonald, G. (1977), 'Introduction', *Edinburgh International Television Festival, 1977* [Official Programme] London: Broadcast.

Macdonald, G. (1978), 'Introduction', *Edinburgh International Television Festival, 1978*, [Official Programme] London: Broadcast, pp. 4–5.

Macdonald, G. (2003), Interview with Lord Macdonald of Tradeston, CBE, at the House of Lords, 15 September.

McIntyre, E. (1977), 'TV Buffs to Have their own Festival', *Glasgow Herald*, 16 July.

Mills, J. (2000), 'A Star is Born', *Broadcast*, 25 August, p. 5.

Milne, A. (1988), *DG: The Memoirs of a British Broadcaster*, London: Hodder and Stoughton.

Ofcom (2004), *The Communications Market 2004*, 9 August, available at www.ofcom. org.uk/research/industry_market_research/m_i_index/cm/cmpdf/?a=87101

Peacock, Sir A. (1986), *The Report of the Committee on Financing the BBC* [the Peacock Report], Cmnd 9824, London: HMSO.

Pilkington, Sir H. (1961), *Report of the Broadcasting Committee*, Cmnd 1753, London: HMSO.

Ponting, C. (1988), 'A Fundamentally New Approach to Controlling Information', *UK Press Gazette*, 31 October, p. 15.

Protheroe, A. (1987), 'The Use and Abuse of the Official Secrets Act', *The Listener*, 12 February, pp. 4–5.

Purser, P. (1977), 'Television: Images of Fact and Fiction', *Sunday Telegraph*, 4 September.

Rees-Mogg, W. (1989), 'A Free Market Alone May Not Offer Quality Programmes', *The Independent*, 29 August.

Smith, A. (1974), *British Broadcasting*, Newton Abbot: David and Charles.

The Times (1974), 'Obituary, Mr James MacTaggart, Actor, Writer and Producer', 30 May, p. 18.

Wells, M. (2004), 'Free TV Licence from Politics', *The Guardian*, 30 June, p. 8.

Wells, M. and Milmo, D. (2004), 'Channel 4 Chief Faces Tough Questions over Merger with Five', *The Guardian*, 10 May, p. 2.

Williams, P. and Griffin-Beale, C. (1978), 'Edinburgh Television Festival: Bright Lights and Brave Words', *Broadcast*, 11 September, pp. 12–14.

Willis, J. (2000), 'Wide-Eyed and Legless', *Broadcast*, 25 August, p. 8.

Windlesham, Lord and Rampton, R. (1989), *The Windlesham/Rampton Report on Death on the Rock*, London: Faber and Faber.

Notes

1. In addition to Gus Macdonald (Chair) and William Brown and Alastair Hetherington the joint Presidents, the 1977 Advisory Committee members were Rod Allen, David

Bell, John Birt, Cecil Clarke, David Cunliffe, Chris Dunkley, Brian Gibson, Clive Goodwin, John Gray, David Hanley, Barry Hanson, Jerry Kuehl, Paul Madden, Lynda Myles, David Rose, Norman Swallow and Colin Young.

2. Gus Macdonald was Executive Producer of Granada Television's current affairs flagship *World in Action*. John Birt in his (1996) MacTaggart Lecture described Macdonald as the Festival's 'real progenitor'. Macdonald later became Chairman of Scottish Television, Minister for Trade and Industry at the Scottish Office and eventually a member of the House of Lords.

3. Ted Turner, along with Jonathan Miller, was unwilling for his MacTaggart Lecture to be reproduced in edited form in this collection. A summary of the key concerns of each lecture is presented in Appendix B.

4. The Independent Broadcasting Authority (IBA) was replaced by the Independent Television Commission (ITC) following a provision in the Broadcasting Act 1990.

5. Television coverage of general elections only began in 1959; the election of that year was dubbed the 'first television election'. There was no television coverage of Parliament. Broadcasting from the Lords began in 1985 and from the Commons in 1989.

6. The report of the Annan Committee, established to consider the possibility of launching a fourth television channel, along with the 'constitutional, organisational and financial arrangements' for such a channel, was called *The Future of Broadcasting* (Cmnd 6753).

7. 1977 marked the first Edinburgh International Television Festival specifically organised and designated as a *television* festival. In the previous year, a retrospective of the work of James MacTaggart was held under the auspices of the Edinburgh International *Film* Festival. It hosted the first MacTaggart Lecture delivered by John McGrath and the first independent television festival emerged from the event. 'The Television Festival sprang from the older Edinburgh Film Festival's loins' (Housham 2000: 15). Much contemporary press coverage of the 1977 EITVF referred to the Festival as the first television festival. See, for example, the *Glasgow Herald* (16 July 1977), *Variety* (6 April 1977), The *London Evening Standard* (14 February 1977), and the *Press and Journal* (6 May 1977).

8. A reference to signal an early reaction to independent producers that they would be used as cost cutters to lower wages across the industry.

The James MacTaggart
Lectures

The James MacTaggart Lecture 1976

TV Drama:
The Case against Naturalism

John McGrath*

John McGrath shapes his recollections of working with James MacTaggart in London in the early 1960s into what Troy Kennedy Martin (1986) described as a 'swingeing attack on naturalism'. Naturalism he argues imposes a certain 'neutrality about life on the writer, the actor and the audience': it presents a world that is 'static, implied and ambivalent'.

McGrath argued that the television image is not conducive to natural-ist drama because it lacks sensuality. While a cinema screen can 'flood the senses', a 'television shot is at best nice': it is akin to listening 'to a symphony over the telephone'. Also, it lacks empathy: viewers are 'looking *at* the screen, not being drawn into it'. Finally, television images are situated in the context of reported reality: viewers watching television drama will have witnessed, 'napalmed women in Vietnam running about on fire'.

The 'new drama' which emerged required a style of 'writing, directing, designing, sound plotting and lighting which was specifically for the lens of a television camera, not for the opera house'. James MacTaggart who produced and directed a series called *Storyboard, The Wednesday Play* and *Diary of a Young Man* was crucial to its development: his ingenuity in 'attacking the directorial problems that the narrative drama raised was truly remarkable'.

The early *Z Cars* and *Storyboards* emerged from sustained discussions about the theory and practice of television among a group of committed enthusiasts working in the medium. The timing of these discussions was not accidental. McGrath suggests the 'British ruling class were on a high'

---

* John McGrath was a socialist, playwright, director and founder of the 7:84 theatre company. He died on 22 January 2002.

and 'the liberal gesture is easy to make when you're secure and unchallenged'. But that mood has passed. Tolerance has given way to centralised control. Naturalism has flourished as the dominant mode of television drama. McGrath concludes with a challenge. People working in television should ask themselves why there is so much critical debate about film but so little about television.

□

I would like to talk tonight about what was going on in television drama in the early 1960s when Jimmy MacTaggart came to London. At that time there was a level of serious thought about the medium which seems to have become impossible today. I'd like to ask why this is so. And to raise once again some of the issues we debated then, issues of form, of naturalism, realism, narrative and alienation.

What were we talking about? There are two basic questions about television as a medium for drama. One is: 'What goes?' This is the pre-occupation of Heads of things and Executives. To us the answer was obvious: unending streams of assorted naturalism. The other question is: 'What can this medium do?' That seemed to be the interesting one. This is what some of us thought at that time about naturalism – if I may quote Troy Kennedy Martin:

> The recent naturalistic drama began in America, where TV theatre was overwhelmed by a new and dynamic naturalism which came to be identified with Chayevsky and others . . . It was a theatre of dialogue, a theatre of performance. It was a writer's theatre. But, first and foremost, which one tends to forget – it was still theatre. But because the new writers, their works and their artists won public acclaim through the television medium before going on to Broadway and Hollywood, the medium claimed that it had founded television drama.

But there was more to it than that. Naturalism contains everything within a closed system of relationships. Every statement is mediated through the situation of the character speaking. Mediated to the point of triviality. It is a way of *not* saying anything, of indicating that everything is tangential, and relative to its own milieu. In terms of presenting a picture of society, it can only reveal a small cluster of subjective consciousnesses, rarely anything more. Naturalism, of course, can and does achieve a great deal. But as a *form*, it imposes a certain neutrality about life on the writer, the actor and the audience. It says: here's the way things are for these people, isn't it sad – if a tragedy: isn't it funny – if a comedy; isn't it interesting – if by a good writer; God, it's boring – if by a bad one. It encapsulates the status quo, ossifies the dynamics of society into a moment of perception, crystallises the realities of existence into a paradigm, but excludes what it refers to. In the naturalistic play few characters are allowed to be articulate: they are more likely to emote incoherently. Every meaning is implicit and ambivalent. Naturalism forces itself to present a world that is static, implied and ambivalent. This world picture inherent in the form of the naturalistic drama, from Chayevsky to *Coronation Street* can be transcended in the theatre by great writers – like Chekhov, Gorki, D. H. Lawrence, Ibsen. But can this be achieved on television?

There are several distinguishing features of the television image. One is that it lacks sensuality *per se*. A cinema screen can flood the senses; within each frame an elaborate pattern of shape and colour can affect, overwhelm the consciousness, emotionally, sensually. A brilliant set, well lit, in the theatre can create a positive impression on the mind by way of the eye. But a television shot is at best nice. The eye is not overwhelmed. To expect more is to expect to listen satisfactorily to a symphony over the telephone.

This leads to the next feature of the television image: its objectivity. In other words its reduction of empathy in the viewer to the point where one is looking *at* the screen, not being drawn into it. The spectacle of the weeping close-up on television is rarely more than repelling. The same actor or actress in the theatre could reduce the audience to massed sympathetic lumps in throats, with much the same performance.

The third characteristic of the television image is that it is conditioned by all the other images that have preceded it. Napalmed women in Vietnam running about on fire constitute an image of reality that few can forget. To expect to shock or horrify an audience with a nasty setback to our hero demands coming to terms with real shock and horror – even though the viewer has different terms of reference for each experience and a different framework of response.

These three characteristics of the television image – its non-sensual informative nature, its lack of empathy and its situation in the context of reported reality – are, I think, unique and in their way admirable. None of them is particularly conducive to naturalist drama. What are their consequences? The first quality clearly indicates that information should flow in a linear manner, rather than dwelling on endless emoting faces. The second quality, the objectivisation of the image in television implies that involvement of the viewer comes from a build-up of information, from a form of montage, from being carried into a story that moves forward at a pace that quickens the imagination rather than dwelling on the emotions. Watch any football match. The emotion comes from the movement to the goal – and is rarely contained in the emotions of the emoting footballer. And that leads to the consequences of the third quality of the television image: its relationship to other images that pour out. When we think of drama in this context, two things are immediately noticeable. One is that drama images tend to be patently faked, slower moving and more ponderous than those of almost any other department. And secondly, they are totally lacking in variety. The resources of television for putting an image on the screen – film with voiceover, stills, animation, split-screen, reporter talking to camera, freely illustrated song – these simply do not come into the vocabulary of naturalistic drama, so they are unspoken by the drama departments by and large.

One thing emerged from consideration of these characteristics. It was clear that although naturalistic drama would, and did, 'go' on television, it was not the only thing the medium could do – in fact it was a strait-jacket from which we wanted to release the poor patient. To quote Troy Kennedy Martin for the last time:

> The new drama will be based on story rather than plot. It will relate directly, man's relation to God, to other men, to things – and to himself. Its actions will be distilled and presented in a condensed form. It will be much more personal in style. It will compress information, emphasise fluidity, free the camera from photographing faces and free the structure from the naturalist tyranny of time. But if this drama is ever to get off the ground it must create a new grammar, especially in relation to editing . . . It must develop new designs leading to maximum fluidity in the studio by doing away with the old box sets and creating acting areas specifically through the use of lighting. It must re-emphasise the importance of the nature of sound on drama (totally ignored up to now). It must develop sound to the level of the art it is on radio for the purpose of both design and dramatic action. Lighting, Sound and Editing and Design therefore become not just points that make up a whole but inextricably parts of each other. Design evolves through lighting, editing through sound, editing through design and design through editing.

This meant more than a new technique, however. The form would be part of the content: this narrative style would present a different world picture from that inherent in naturalism. It would show a world that moved, pressures on that world, and essentially a world that changed, or could change. We felt we could show more of the world we lived in, more excitingly, and in a manner uniquely suited to television and we knew that we could hold the mass audience with it.

Various groups of programmes came out of all this. The early *Z Cars* emerged from a similar but *different* line of thinking, about the meaning of a series as form. What was needed to make some of this thinking into television was a director who could see what we were getting at. When Jimmy MacTaggart arrived, he more than understood, he topped us all, with argument, with enthusiasm, above all with practical ingenuity. He produced and directed a series called *Storyboard*, six shortish plays mostly written by Troy Kennedy Martin. Then before starting *The Wednesday Play*, he produced *Diary of a Young Man*, by Troy and myself, directed by Ken Loach and Peter Duguid, all in the early sixties. Apart from his contribution to the theoretical discussions and the shaping of the scripts, it was Jimmy's ingenuity in attacking the directorial problems that the narrative drama raised which was truly remarkable.

In order to create narrative drama, we had to have thirty locations in the studio; or, as in one *Storyboard*, thirty-six in thirty minutes. More than that, we wanted to get away from the whole pseudo-theatrical approach to television. What had to be done was to create a style of writing, directing, designing, sound plotting and lighting which was specifically for the lens of a television camera, not for an opera house. Each scene or episode had to be thought of in terms of the shot: what were the minimum requirements to tell that bit of the story? And what were the best resources to do it?

If a soundtrack could establish a forest, and lighting tell you visually you were meant to be in a forest, why did you need trees? If the actors acted as if they were in a forest as well, the information had been conveyed three times over. And not one piece of stock scenery had cluttered your studio. The story was what you were involved in anyway. Jimmy MacTaggart put together a team of designers, lighting-designers, cameramen, sound men and production assistants who could create, together with himself and the writer, the bits and pieces to make the shots that would tell the story.

There were other features of this style which were to us exciting. The liberation of the medium from Chayefsky meant that a lot of other sources of entertainment, pleasure, even of art, could be put to use. Like actual verbal style, wit, articulacy, satire: by allowing a character to narrate his own story, on the soundtrack and relating it dynamically to the images, you could actually write with a bit of verve. Music: not for background emotive effect, but as a statement in itself that made its contribution to the meaning. Or animation – cartoon helping to say what happened. Or movement, stylised actor's movement, usually when the story took off, with the help of music and wanted to have a little bop to itself.

The early *Z Cars* grew out of that same kind of thinking. Troy and I were both fascinated by an American super-cop series called *Highway Patrol*. It had action, pace, narrative drive, but was cheap, nasty and American. It was the pace that grabbed us, I suppose. We began to think about the series as an indigenous television form. It seemed, and still seems to me, to relate to the endlessly unrolling linear quality of television. The news is a series, so is *The Underwater World of Jacques Cousteau*, *The Big Match*, *Steptoe and Son*, *Hancock*, *Coronation Street* – all the things that really matter to a lot of television viewers. But the drama departments were not taking them seriously. Nor the writers and directors who preferred the prestige of an *Armchair Theatre* or a BBC Sunday night play. Right then we thought, let's take the series as a form worth bothering about. Let's go for the pace, the relationship with the audience, of *Highway Patrol*, but let's go for something that will unfold in narrative form all the minor stories that make the fabric of our own society so alive. Use cops, OK, but as a device for getting into the small but important realities of the lives of the people who are going to be watching. No master criminals, super-sleuths, gentlemen experts, cunning detectives – the police are *not* our heroes; the people are the heroes.

Stylistically, I went for one rigid rule: no camera move, no cut, until the next piece of story was to be revealed. But the stories unfolded very quickly, so there were a lot of cuts, and a lot of locations. For some, we used filmed inserts and cut them in as the show went out. Most locations were in the studio. I used six cameras and we tried to light and design for the lens, using a lot of set pieces and a highly mobile camera crew. I worked with the actors on a style of acting that simply told the stories, usually several, involved in each episode. One episode called *Friday Night* actually had eight or nine stories going through it, all linked by the roving of the crew of one car on one evening. A motorbike crash, a bloke coming home drunk from his retirement party – just little stories, events of an evening. We needed a style that would make these stories move, hold the attention. We placed a conscious emphasis on narrative – society, real and recognisable, but in *motion*. No slick tie-ups. No reassuring endings where decency and family life triumphed. It seemed to work. But one feature of the series as a form that Troy and I had not reckoned with is that when successful, your series gets taken over by forces beyond your control. Suddenly, people who didn't even know what you were doing a month before were telling us how things had to be. The old-fashioned liberal respect for the artist has its limits; one of them is offending the police. Another, far worse, is being successful. We left. The series rapidly became a lot of naturalistic dramas about how difficult is the policeman's lot . . .

The style of the early *Z Cars*, as of Troy and Jimmy's *Storyboards*, and later our *Diary of a Young Man*, grew out of long discussion of the theory and practice of television. This was possible because there was a group of people energetically committed to the medium, because it was the medium the people of this country experienced. A group of people who knew the medium were part of it – and who knew they would eventually be given the chance to do what they believed in, and be respected for it? Was it an accident that this situation arose at this time? No, of course not. Similar groups were beavering away in other corners of the BBC. On *Tonight*, Jack Gould and Kevin Billington were beginning, Ned Sherrin was directing the studio, Donald Baverstock and Alasdair Milne were editing the programme. Peter Watkins was doing battle with Huw Weldon on *Monitor*, where Ken Russell was doing his best work. *That Was The Week That Was*, initiated by Sherrin, brought a great crowd of writers and performers into an atmosphere of satirical daring that was, in its form, pure television. John Boorman was making films in Bristol, Dennis Mitchell producing his hand-crafted documentaries, Phillip Donnellan working in Birmingham . . . All these people had two things in common: they were deeply concerned and articulate about form, and they had immediate, unmediated access to the resources and the audience.

There must have been, and there were, good reasons for this. Historically, the British ruling class was riding high on the Harold Macmillan wave. We'd never had it so good. And this high riding confidence was not being seriously challenged. Macmillan could afford to make liberal statements about the winds of change in Africa, and could let Peter Cook take the Mickey out of him publicly and not sue. The liberal gesture is easy to make when you're secure and unchallenged.

So the BBC, an institution ever sensitive to the mood of the ruling class, could encourage young rebels to have a go – could even allow Stuart Hood to be Controller of Programmes, Television. It could absorb, indeed it needed, a lot of controversial, energetic, imaginative young people to push it on apace or two, while the going was good. So the artist could still be an artist, even in front of 20 million people, but within limits of course. So structurally the BBC allowed a benign anarchy in which almost anything could happen.

That era has died out. Historically the economic collapse of Britain has undermined the confidence of the ruling class. Politically, they *do* feel threatened. So the BBC, sensitive as ever, has altered its structure. Anarchy is over. Centralised control, elaborate systems of command, supervision, check and review have been introduced. And on the personal level, the bully boys have moved in to stay. The drive to power is more in evidence than civilised, sharp critical intelligence.

In terms of the ideas of a few of us in television drama in the early sixties, the results of these changes have been predictable. Naturalism, of course, has flourished as the dominant mode of television drama. The excitements now are not about the *form* of the drama, but about its content; with no realisation that the naturalistic form itself *is* the content, that it distorts what the writer is trying to say, contains it within safe limits. Take *Days of Hope*. I would estimate that if *Days of Hope* had said clearly what its makers wanted to say, it would never have been made – certainly never shown. Why then was it made and shown? Simply because the naturalistic form allowed it to imply, but never to *say*, what they meant. Its meaning could become blurred, mediated. It could, indeed, be excused, passed off as something else.

Now I admire Jim Allen and Ken Loach and Tony Garnett who made *Days of Hope*. They are serious creators. But why do they take it for granted that serious meaning has to be wrapped up in order to make television drama, in cloaks of fiction, emotion, human relationships and all the paraphernalia of naturalism? Because the meaning of form is no longer discussed. Because no one seems to be asking What Can This Medium Do? But everybody accepts What Goes. Our thinking in the early sixties, the analysis and the answers we came out with, only begins to scrape the surface of the theoretical and practical problems involved. And I feel that our attack on naturalism is just as valid now as it was then.

There are many people here who are working in television. They should ask themselves why so much critical intelligence is raising the level of debate about film, and so little exists about television. Why there is not one decent forum, publication, programme or magazine, of television criticism. Why television drama is still thinking the way it did twenty years ago. Why in the absence of theoretical discussion, the *form* of drama remains unquestioned, the content impotent and style a matter of pretty pictures. Why the power to initiate has gone from the creators and is now the prerogative of the institution. Why plays are getting fewer, and later at night, and series getting more violent and sensationalist. Why television has failed to produce its own Dickens or even an approximation to one.

The answers to these questions lie partly in the hands of television executives who create structures and impose their personalities. They lie mostly in the hands of the writers and directors, who need to acquire the habit of theoretical discussion before churning out yet another ten years of naturalism.

The James MacTaggart Lecture 1977

Naturalism and Television

Marcel Ophuls*

Marcel Ophuls, the maker of television documentaries such as *The Sorrow and the Pity*, *Sense of Loss* and *Memory of Justice*, opens his lecture on a biographical note, expressing his admiration for his father, Max Ophuls, and describing how he himself became what he deprecatingly describes as 'a self indulgent specialist of four-and-a-half talking-head marathons': i.e. documentaries. Ophuls declares himself the spiritual as well as the biological offspring of his father, sharing fully 'his assessments of the shallow, anti-creative, anti-humanist and authoritarian theories which seemed to us . . . the systematic foundations of the naturalist tendency'. His critique of naturalism explores, but strongly contests, themes addressed by John McGrath a year earlier at the initial festival in 1976: 'John McGrath and I do not agree at all,' he acknowledges, 'on the nature, on the causes or the definition of the naturalist tradition.'

Ophuls begins his lecture with a recollection of a damp, November evening in London when, as a freelance seeking a job, he went to a meeting in Golden Square. As the discussion moved to the 'techniques of naturalism – its social functions and its social mission and its social purpose' Ophuls recalls the 'irresistible urge' to say that he 'much preferred the realism of Noel Coward's *This Happy Breed* . . . to the elaborately bleak naturalism of *Cathy Come Home*'.

◻

That is when the inevitable happened. I don't remember who introduced that particular element into the conversation – it might even

---

* Marcel Ophuls, like his distinguished father, Max Ophuls, was a documentary-maker.

have been me, although I doubt it – but suddenly I heard myself participating in a debate about the advisability and the possible methods of mixing fiction and non-fiction for pursuing documentary techniques in drama: for injecting new blood into TV drama by using such techniques; for vouchsafing authenticity and avoiding the stale routine of television plays. I found myself mostly listening, involved in a discussion on actors and non-actors, on professionals and non-professionals, on distancing and *cinéma vérité* techniques. In other words, a debate about all things – the function of naturalism in television.

Now, anyone who has spent any time at all shooting the bull in the offices of any TV bureaucracy knows that particular topic of conversation comes up with monotonous frequency. I am not complaining; I thought it was interesting then and I hope it will be interesting now, and I certainly found John McGrath's view on the subject presented here last year far more than interesting. But, frankly, on that particular afternoon, as the winter darkness was falling all around us, and we were sitting round in the twilight gloom, I couldn't help but find our discussion on the techniques of naturalism – its social functions and its social mission and its social purpose – just a bit too theoretical.

After a while, the conversation got around to *Cathy Come Home* and, inevitably, to how it is a shining example of how to portray social conditions and the class struggle in our society: as a pioneering effort in our common, permanent necessary attempt to describe reality in the course of our work. Now it so happens that I share my father's love of artifice, of classic theatrical traditions, of glitter, of high style, of elegance and of grace in the arts. Consequently, I am at best a very reluctant documentary film-maker, and I absolutely loathe pseudo-documentary form, no matter how noble in intention, talented in execution, successful in their results.

So, having seen and rediscovered an old classic of the English cinema, just a few nights before on BBC2, I remember suddenly feeling the irresistible urge – fully conscious of how such a seemingly frivolous statement would be received within the context of such a socially earnest and politically progressive debate – to say that I much preferred the realism of Noel Coward's *This Happy Breed* – Tory or not, West End boulevard or not – to the elaborately bleak naturalism of *Cathy Come Home*.

Now why do I mention that encounter here at this particular time? Why do I bother to expose what would appear to a great many as a very crude piece of mere flippancy? Because I feel that, to a very large extent, I must be prepared to defend such judgements right here and now, during these days in Edinburgh, whether half-jokingly or not, whether flippant or not. And it is fitting in a way that it is Gus Macdonald – one of the men with whom this conversation took place on that bleak, job-hunting afternoon – who should have invited me here to address you today. That way, at least, we get an opportunity of trying to defend my outrageous, frivolous and seemingly superficial remarks. 'Seemingly superficial' – I always thought that one of the most fitting epitaphs for my father's work would be a quotation from one of his last pictures; it's when Charles Boyer, the general, says to Madame Deut: 'Be careful, my dear, our marriage appears superficial – only superficially.'

MacTaggart, McGrath, Macdonald: these are important names in the evolution of television's constant and necessary battle to come to grips with reality, and let's not forget John Grierson while we're at it. If I am going to disagree with any one, I do so at my own risk and peril because I am perfectly aware of doing it on their home ground. And, of course, I am well aware, ignorant though I am of Scottish history, of the cultural influence of John Knox, and of this being a traditional citadel of high moral purpose, the fight for virtue and justice, for the true faith, the home ground of religious Puritanism and, perhaps, of some other kinds as well. And it seems to me that, in any serious discussion of the social function of the mass media and the role of naturalism in the evolution of TV drama, a bit more Mary Stewart frivolity and muddle-headedness and a little less Knoxian high-seriousness would tend to stimulate the creative juices in us all.

To me, strangely enough, there is a definite connection between the austere demands of the Puritan ethics and the search for naturalism in the performing arts. Puritanism, it seems to me, is always, more or less, the attempt to deny others the rewards of certain activities which you are not too sure that you can perform yourself. In sex, religion, politics, the puritan tradition is rooted in deprivation and poverty of certain kinds, and self-denial is often the rationalisation for that which is being denied to you in any case. Lack of imagination, lack of potency lack of vitality, lack of a sense of joy, of life and of love must, in any period of history, be codified in some manner, in some fashion, and the envy of others who possess gifts that we lack must be channelled. The Puritan tradition can help us to do that. It has some good sides, too, but it certainly has those; it can help us enjoy our misery while inflicting it on others.

To me, the excessive preoccupation with naturalism in our profession – the documentary ethic, the virtues of *cinéma vérité*, the rejection of artifice, the self-righteous rejection of the corruption of the star system, the distaste for emotion, for tears, for laughter, for jokes, for anecdotes, for song and dance routines – all of this seems to me to evoke the sour taste of Puritanism in my mouth. So does the urge to find new recipes for ill-defined notions of what reality is, and how it is to be transmitted, on film or electronically, to the hungry masses into a little box standing in millions of living-rooms, kitchens and even bathrooms: the ever-present, often repeated wish to get away from actors, from dialogue, from close-ups of the human face emoting – the theoretical and systematic methodical surge for authenticity, for objectivity, for truth in the raw.

I won't presume to try for an exact definition of naturalism. Suffice it to say that, to me, naturalism evokes rejection of what is the most attractive in artistic creation, the rejection of personal invention, the generosity of the fable and the storyteller, the substitution of self-righteous grubby, dreary, bloodless theorising for the sheer emotional, almost animal, joys of creative productivity, whether artistic or biological. That is what the concept of naturalism means to me, and I hope I've made it abundantly clear that I don't like it.

In the famous controversy in the history of documentary filmmaking between the Scotsman John Grierson and the romantic, whimsical, muddle-headed Irishman Robert Flaherty, my heart and my mind is very much on the side of the Irishman, naive though he may have been politically, in his approach to *Noble Savages*, for instance. Just before coming up here, my wife, my daughter and I spent forty-eight hours in London, and we saw what I thought was a splendid performance of a work of another Irishman, *Man and Superman*. And listening to that particular Irishman's glorious mixture of badinage, intellectual and ideological speech-making, paradox, love, jokes and politics, experiencing once again the profoundly original generous nature of such a mixture – the keen intelligence and the sincere generosity of it – I wondered once again what the hell the controversy about depiction of reality in our profession is all about. It made me want to shout out in sheer joy, without certainty of my own powers of invention and without envy for those whose imagination is 110–1,000 times greater than mine can ever be: 'Listen, fellows, some of us have got it and some of us ain't.'

No theory at distancing, no *cinéma vérité*, no jump-cuts, no cameras in the street, no grainy archive material, no multi-media techniques, no demiological critics, no Eisenstein in montage theory can ever replace the pure and mysterious gifts of the creative, individual, subjective, original, eccentric imagination. 'Have I not told you that the truly damned are those who are happy in hell?' says John Tanner in *Man and Superman*. No amount of Godardian jump-cuts, no documentary and pseudo-documentary techniques is ever going to match up to such a line, I am afraid, because I am glad – on the contrary, I am glad because my hopes for the future, such as they are, are not pinned to puritanical systems or ideological theory. I am placing all the trust I have left – such as it is – and betting every cent I haven't got on the individual power of the imagination.

So you see, by sticking up for Noel Coward in the face of the socially significant onslaught of pseudo-documentary techniques, I intend to enjoy, as much as I can, not only the privilege of startling the neutral and the well disposed among you, but, perhaps, even more importantly, I intend to antagonise and challenge those that I have chosen some time ago to be my adversaries. Since Ophuls junior, the stubborn, self-indulgent specialist of four-and-a-half-hour, talking-head marathons considers himself, rightly or wrongly, not only the biological but also the spiritual offspring of Ophuls senior, the equally stubborn and self-indulgent champion of apparently gratuitous and frivolous camera movements, I fully share his attitudes, his assessments of the shallow, anti-creative, anti-humanistic and authoritarian theories which seemed to us, in various forms at various moments in cultural history and according to various fashions, the systematic foundations of the naturalist tendency. And I fear and resent – as he did – the greyness, the blandness, the false sense of objectivity and the pedantic pompousness of most of its results. So I fancied myself to be able to adopt the pose of Shavian paradox; I hoped to play the mischievous role of the Ponchinell springing out of his box, by agreeing with John McGrath, relishing in advance the prospect of appearing before you as a slightly eccentric and mildly orthodox figure, an anti-naturalistic documentary film-maker, which, indeed, according to my own rights and to my own definition, I am. And then, over the weekend, I asked for a copy of Mr McGrath's speech.

Catastrophe! Instead of being allowed the perverse pleasure of upsetting other people's plans for me, I was abruptly confronted with the necessity of changing my own, for after reading the brilliant and articulate exposé of my talented predecessor I found myself disagreeing with almost everything he said. Not, of course, with the results of his keen sense of observation, not, most emphatically with the sometimes bitter fruits of his experiences with the management and the managers of television bureaucracies, and their *ever* increasing usurpation of power and their evermore heavy-handed repressiveness. No, it is with most of what seemed to me to be his theoretical assumptions that I disagree. As far as I can see, as far as I can read, John McGrath and I do not agree at all on the nature, the causes, or the definition of the naturalist tradition. To put it in a temporary nutshell, I do not see, as he does, the connection between the bleak, listless vulgarities of *Coronation Street*, the condescension of *Coronation Street*, the cynicism of *Coronation Street*, and the exhilarating, compassionate subtlety of Chekhov's theatre, the joyful vigour of D. H. Lawrence's grassroot romanticism, or the cold ruthless eye of Gorki's revolutionary faith. If there are some structuralist disciples of Lacan and Roland Barthes among us tonight, they may well judge these distinctions as futile, Epicurean, hopelessly bourgeois, and, God help us, gastronomic. I, for one, am not willing to cut off my nose to spite their pale complexions.

No, to see the connection between soap opera and Chekhov, or between *Mission Impossible* and *Citizen Kane*, I would have to admit their simpleminded if incoherently stated theories of the inadequacies of language, approve of their monotonous and repetitive use of the word, humanism, as the ultimate insult, except to reject, along with them, psychology as a tool for dramatic investigation; I would have to approve and even idolise the threadbare paraphernalia of pseudo-Brechtian subterfuge, share their congenital distaste, as Mr McGrath apparently does to some extent, for actors' and actresses' tears in close-up; I would have to abandon his idle reactionary bourgeois luxury, my love for game-playing as a legitimate form of communication, for idle anecdotes, for song and dance routines, for sex, for life, for love. I would then have to classify as naturalist for the old and obsolete school not only Chayevsky, as he does, but Orson Welles, Jean Renoir, D. W. Griffiths and Ernst Lubitch, whose *To Be or Not to Be* happens, in my opinion, to be the most accurate portrayal of national socialist society ever put on the screen. And, of course, Noel Coward, whose *In Which We Serve* I remember as the best war picture that I have ever seen.

If I may interrupt this diatribe for a second with another personal anecdote. When I was a kid in Hollywood, and my father was out of work for four years, we rented a small, rather run-down place on Whitley Heights opposite the Hollywood Bowl, and on Sunday mornings, after we had seen *In Which We Serve*, my father, who was a late riser, for many months, would get up out of his bedroom, which was on the first floor, and come to the landing, and he would impersonate the British commander taking over the destroyer – that upper-class, British commander played by Noel Coward – and he would shout down from the landing: 'This shall be a happy and an efficient ship.' And I, representing, naturally enough, the British working class in uniform, would snap to attention and reply smartly: 'Aye, aye, Sir.' So, in order not to be a bourgeois gastronome, with one or two or three stars in the *Guide Michelin,* or a blasted naturalist according to Mr McGrath's definition, it seems to me, in some mysterious way, that I would have to abandon nostalgia as well: my fondest memories which nourish my deepest convictions. This would, indeed, be like abandoning my own ship in the storm, like putting my own identity in mothballs. This request, I fear, wherever it may come from, is indeed puritanical terrorism, and has as little to do today with compassion for the oppressed, or solidarity with the working classes, as it has ever had in the past.

In my time, in my profession, I have had to face by force of circumstance quite a few tests of radical commitment. I have faced censorship and managerial usurpation in several countries, and heard the silent songs of collective conformity in several languages and to various tunes. I don't want to sound pompous or self-righteous about this. I do not see myself as a lonely champion of integrity, fighting the organised corruption of neo-capitalist brainwashing. And, so, having passed a number of these tests, I am damned if I am going to be apologetic about my love for Chekhov, or *Citizen Kane* or Ernst Lubitsch, or for my father's camera movements, or even for my own weakness for good food, good hotels, first-class accommodation and skiing in Switzerland. In other words, I'm damned if I'm going to stand idly by and let Chekhov be blamed for *Coronation Street*. On the contrary, I'm going to put my foot in it up to the elbow in the name of liberalism, bourgeois ambiguity and social democratic wishy-washyness.

While I refuse to acknowledge any resemblance between soap opera and Ibsen on the basis of the alleged inadequacies of language, any kinship between Orson Welles and Louis B. Mayer on the basis of overt or covert collusion with what the semiologists refer to as the prevailing ideology, while I fail to see the profound similarities between Ingmar Bergman and Stella Dallas on the basis of the disgusting habit they share of showing actors and actresses emoting in close-up, I do not see the fatal and thoroughly unpleasant resemblance between *Coronation Street* (and, please excuse me, I do respect the film-makers of what I'm going to name now for the second time) and *Cathy Come Home* and, yes, the resemblance with *The World at War*. On the basis of what? Above all, on the basis of condescension, on the basis of a lack of creative verve. And now I think we have come to the point where I must try to define my own undoubtedly very biased understanding of the notion of naturalism, which I dislike as much as Mr McGrath dislikes his notion of naturalism. Or, come to think of it, I think I've already done that.

I, for one, am happy and proud to acknowledge not only my own father's paternity but my debt, our common debt, to D. W. Griffiths: Griffiths, the American primitive, the Southern racist, the inventor of the tearful close-up, the unrepentant sentimentalist and the craven reactionary. The worldwide conspiracy between the Hollywood system and the TV establishment is very real. We experience it every day. We are growing up every day in the routine, managerial machinery which ensures consumer standardisation, banality, blandness, repression of individual thought, promotion of vulgarity and appeal to the lowest common denominator. Well, perhaps I am an accomplice of that by my professing to be the disciple of theatrical tradition but, if so, it will come as news to the bosses of Paramount, to the executives of CBS News and to Gunnar Rugheimer of the BBC. Admittedly, my showbusiness anecdotes make me somewhat biased and excessively verbose in my defence of the theatrical tradition but, basically (and this will come as no surprise to you), I think my position is sound and that it will endure future storms, and survive future revolutions.

The James MacTaggart Lecture 1978

Taboos in Television

Norman Lear*

Norman Lear's lecture recalls the progress of television programmes, especially situation comedies, in addressing previously taboo subjects such as homosexuality, abortions and black family life. He regrets the current backlash which seeks to reinstate these old taboos: they grow back 'like weeds in an unattended hothouse'. The pretext of those who censor is the need to protect viewers from offensive material, but the real concern is to 'block content which might be too informative and provocative'.

These taboos were overturned following confrontations between writers and producers like Lear and the Program Practices Department – which 'is the euphemism for censor': cuts in portrayals of sex and violence were typically the focus of their concerns. Lear always responded by saying that if the edit was made 'they could not expect to find us at work the next morning'. He suggests this stance was not heroic since he knew the 'network would eventually buckle', but reminds that the power of the three networks over creative workers' products is considerable: 'Remember that the American television writer has only three doors on which to knock'.

Lear suggests that taboos arise from the fears of pressure groups and the 'denigrating belief' that American television audiences are 'basically children'. But the most significant trigger of taboos is ratings and the 'fierceness of competition to be number one': this also explains the absence of ballet, art and drama in prime time. Lear claims that television reflects

* Norman Lear was formerly a highly successful pioneer producer of situation comedies broadcast on American television during the 1970s.

American society, where a similar message encourages children not to do well but to be the best.

◻

Exactly, six years ago this week – 25 August 1972 – the cover story on *Time* magazine featured a photograph of Archie Bunker, Fred Sanford and Maude, and the big banner headline above them read: 'The New TV Season: Toppling Old Taboos'. Inside, the article began with a reference to a talkshow host, Jack Paar, who in 1960 walked off his show because NBC had excised the words, or rather the initials W.C. from his previous taped show. In 1968 Petula Clark momentarily rested her white hand on the black arm of guest star Harry Belafonte – and the Chrysler Motor Company struggled for weeks to have the moment cut out of the broadcast. *Time* magazine went on to say: 'That was the way it was on network entertainment shows. Blacks were visible but untouchable, and bathrooms simply did not exist.'

That was *Time* magazine in 1972. But since then, here are some of the taboo subjects that *Maude*, *Mary Hartman, Mary Hartman*, *One Day at a Time* and other of our television shows touched upon. For the first time we saw married couples in the same bed. Our stories dealt with death, black family life, homosexuality, abortion, criticism of the economy and foreign policy, drug abuse and the menopause. Until *Maude* no heroine of a regularly scheduled series had ever been divorced; Maude was on her fifth marriage. And until *Mary Hartman* there was no discussion of child abuse, wife abuse, mass murder, transexuality, lesbianism, multiple orgasm, death by chicken soup . . . and dozens of the emotional and physical agonies that occur in the delicate threads of family relationships.

Some of you may still wonder why we sought to find *comedy* in such serious subjects. Well, speaking for myself, even as a child I saw humour in whatever the life struggle that was going on around me. Later, as a teenager, when my father grew impatient with me he would say: 'Norman, you are the *laziest* white kid I ever saw!' I used to ask him why he found it necessary to put down a whole race of people just to tell *me* that I was lazy. He insisted that's not what he was doing. There was no way I could win the argument – until I wrote it into the very first episode of *All in the Family* thirty-one years later – all the time appreciating that however unfortunate his attitude was, it was also somehow laughable.

All of the men and women – writers, directors, producers, actors – who work on our shows have learned to see life through the end of the telescope which finds the humour even in the depths of tragedy. Each of the subjects is like a jacket which we turn inside out until we find the comedy that lines it.

But now we are experiencing some backlash regarding the toppled taboos. For example, a small but very vocal minority persists in asking: 'What makes today's TV writers and producers think that they have the right to express a personal point of view in an entertainment programme on the public airwaves?' Well, there are many answers, like grown-up people do think about group issues: plus more esoteric reasons, such as artistic freedom and the First Amendment. But when I hear that question I am consumed by a question in turn: what makes anyone believe that a steady diet of comedy *without* content expresses no point of view?

Throughout the fifties and sixties American television was surfeited with a steady diet of television comedies, in which the most serious problem was the roast was ruined and the boss was coming to dinner, or mother had dented the fender and the kids had to keep father from finding out. Fifteen or twenty hours a week of that kind of programming was, in my opinion, and by omission, shouting its largest message in the world. It was saying to the country: you *have* no race problems; there *is* no economic concern in the nation; we are *not* in trouble in Vietnam and all mothers and fathers and children live in absolute harmony – the loudest noise in the house being the popping and crackling of the breakfast cereal in the morning!

I don't think that any subject we have touched – in all of our shows – has expressed as strong a point of view as the omission of all social awareness on all of the TV comedies of the fifties and sixties. But that is exactly what the very vocal minority would like: a return to the old taboos. Under the guise of fighting sex and violence on TV, the war is on against substantive content. These warmongers know that you can't deal with society's ills in entertainment without altering, informing, offending and provoking some of your audience.

How did it happen then, that these taboos were, eventually, overrun? In January 1971, we had completed the first four episodes of *All in the Family* when the first episode was about to be aired. From the day they read the script, the Program Practices Department, which is the euphemism for censor, objected to a moment in the first scene which they termed 'explicit sex'.

The show, like its antecedent, Johnny Speight's *Till Death Us Do Part*, had a young couple living with the daughter's parents. The first episode opened with this young couple at home alone on a Sunday morning. Edith Bunker had, for the first time in years, convinced her husband, Archie, to accompany her to church. Mike and Gloria, alone in the house – a situation that occurred rarely – decided to take advantage of it and repair to their bedroom upstairs. As they started up the staircase, Archie, who had been offended by his preacher's liberal sermon that Sunday, came barging back into the house much earlier than expected. Looking at his daughter and her husband on the staircase, he sized up the moment and drew a big laugh with the line: 'At eleven o'clock on a Sunday morning?'

This was the moment of 'explicit sex' that Program Practices wished out of the script. We refused to delete it and taped the show that way. Twenty-four hours before the show was to air we were still refusing – and now they were telling us that they were going to make the edit in New York. It was then that we took a position we were to take many times in the years that followed. If the network executive knew better than us how the show should be made, let him take it over all together. If the edit was made, they could not expect to find us at work the next morning. Then they bore in. They reminded me that I had a contract, that the network was well within its legal rights, that I could lose everything, not just the show, if I were to persist. My answer was always the same: 'Okay, take my house, back up the truck and take my furniture, but I know you can't touch my wife and children – and I'll find another typewriter someplace.'

By the way, there were no heroics in our position: we weren't even taking a stance. There was simply no doubt that the network would not consider taking over the production – the network would eventually buckle. And they did. The conflicts never really ended. They receded, they abated, but they recurred constantly.

I alluded earlier to a small but vocal minority who, in the guise of protecting the viewer from offensive material, was really seeking to block content which might be too informative and provocative. The way, to establish new taboos or re-establish old ones, is to establish a climate of general fear and anxiety among the networks and in the creative community – in which new approaches and innovative ideas simply will not grow. Such a climate is being created today by the attack against sex and violence in the American mass media.

I'm not about to defend excessive sex or excessive violence. I'm not inclined to approve of excesses of any kind: they are boring. But I'd like to give you a personal perspective on the question of sex and violence in American television.

Violence, now one of the *big* taboos, was rife on American television for many years. It got there because, like any other industry, television operates under the laws of supply and demand. For years the networks demanded violence – on behalf of sponsors and agencies – and writers and producers, with families to support, delivered it.

It's interesting how the 'demand' was often handled. I told you about the censor, or Department of Program Practices. The other big department at each network is called Programming. *Both* departments interface with the producers who supply the shows to the networks' demand. On the surface you would think that these departments would work closely together. Not so in practice. In practice, Programming Practices is only trying to anticipate what will or will not offend or provoke the viewer. The Programming Department's only concern, on the other hand, is winning in each time slot. Anything that they believe will attract ratings, which in turn attracts sponsors, and which in turn increase revenues, is more than all right with them.

To see how this works, let's imagine a writer submitting a script for a dramatic series. And let's assume that the script, whatever the story, leans heavily on character – on interpersonal relationships – and that these relationships and the revelation of character is the material upon which the dramatic tension builds. Program Practices, interested only in putting a lid on violence, applauds the writer's effort. But the Programming Department, with research that indicates that violence has sold in the past, is asking the writer separately but simultaneously: 'Where is the action? You've got a seven-page scene here with two people talking.'

He takes the seven-page scene out of the living-room and puts it in a car. Now he has his two characters in *action*. He adds to the action by having the driver so intent on the discussion in the car that he loses control for a moment – crosses into the other lane – causing another to veer off the road, tumble over an embankment, with three bodies spilling out of it in flames! The Programming Department has its – action. Since the networks, and the sponsors who supported them, were responsible for the violence that is now taboo, what, you may wonder, are they doing for action now? Well, that's where the new accent on sex enters: the incidence of gratuitous sex is up. But not really 'sex'. It's titillation, sexual exploitation, smarm. And now because smarm is mistaken for sex, sex has become taboo on television.

Three years ago the networks, the National Association of Broadcasters, the FCC,[1] reacting timorously to the narrow interests of pressure groups, met secretly – as the creative community eventually proved in court – and instigated what became known as Family Viewing Time. There were no guidelines. When asked what it really meant, one network executive said: 'We want a parent and his family to be able to sit and watch television – between 7 and 9 p.m. – without ever being offended.' Of course, he failed to say which parent and which child he was talking about. Obviously what might offend one family might not offend another. There was also the problem of the time zones, which went unaddressed.

Without dwelling on this futile, misguided, misbegotten, mischievous and purely cosmetic plan to ward off the protesters – and despite the fact that the Superior Court struck it down as born in conspiracy and an abridgement of the First Amendment – that climate, in which all the old taboos began growing back like weeds in an untended hothouse, is still with us. But its most chilling effect is on the creative drawing board where tomorrow's shows are contemplated. Remember that the American television writer has only three doors on which to knock. The networks represent three theatres for over 240 million people. So it is reasonable that a writer, sitting down to conceive a series, would be greatly influenced by the climate I have described.

Now I'd like to address myself to the cause of this inhibiting, chilling, creative climate. There are some of them – who see sex and violence as a plot to break down the family, belief in God, America's moral fibre, its military might and who still tell us we are Communists and we should go back to where we came from. Then there are responsible, forward-thinking groups who really attack the major problems. Why isn't there better children's television? Why are commercials, generally, so sexist and cheapening? By the way, if you care to know where the only real sex is on American television, it is in commercials: check out the scores of models running toward camera in slow motion without bras, selling automobiles, beer, shampoo and what have you.

Speaking of protest, there are also letters – angry letters sometimes – from citizens who are simply writing to express a point of view. They have been agitated by a legitimate piece of drama – and good drama will agitate now and then – and they are simply writing to express themselves. They are not writing to pressure shows off the air – not writing to censor – but writing as citizens of a free society.

The networks and the advertising agencies and the sponsors have never seemed to understand that point. Every letter of thoughtful disagreement is thrown into the same pile and is seen by them only as pressure to create or re-establish another taboo. Of course there is the true hate mail. Actually, most of them are postcards.

So letters are misunderstood out of fear, and out of that ancient, mythical belief that the average American has a thirteen-year-old mentality. People still ask me, for example, if our mail indicates that *All in the Family* has done anything to dissipate bigotry and prejudice, or if it doesn't really act to reinforce the stereotype. Actually, I don't think *any* television show can do much to unseat deeply held attitudes. On the other hand, there is every indication that *All in the Family* has *not* enforced the stereotype. We've received thousands of letters from people who believe Archie is right. But no matter how much they cheer him on, we have never received a letter where the writer isn't fully aware of the show's attitude towards Archie's intolerance. No less an expert than Richard Nixon himself summed it up once. He watched an episode in which Archie's attack on homosexuals was blunted by the discovery that one of Archie's pals, an ex-football star, was himself a homosexual. 'That was awful,' said Mr Nixon. 'It made a fool out of a good man.'

Taboos, then arise out of fear of the pressure groups, out of a basic misunderstanding of the nature of the American public, out of the denigrating belief that they are basically children, and out of one item that I have saved for last. The biggest single reason for the lack of innovation in American television, for the presence of many taboos, is the fierceness of competition to be Number One. For the first time the *New York Times* prints the top ten shows each week. The *Wall Street Journal* projects stock earning for the three networks based on the weekly ratings. Only one network can be Number One, or Number One in any given slot. What do you suppose is going on inside the mind and stomach of a TV executive as he enters his office in the morning with the *New York Times* that has told him he was Number Two or Three last week under one arm – the *Wall Street Journal,* which is predicting a fall-off in the company stock under the other arm – and crosses behind his desk to find a warm xerox of the overnight ratings for last night, again showing him out of the Number One position?

It's because of this fanatic drive for ratings and profits that we see no ballet on American television in prime time. We see no art. There is very little drama of historical significance. There is no science. And, most shockingly, there is little opportunity to groom a television Eugene O'Neill or Arthur Miller or Tennessee Williams. *Because* the networks' need for 'action' precludes a concentration on simple, powerful good talk.

In conclusion, I'd like to say that in discussing television and its taboos, I never like to divorce the TV industry from the rest of the American business scene, because it is my belief that the three television networks do at least as well in terms of their responsibility to the public interest as the world's three largest oil companies who, between them, have had to recall 18 million cars in the last two years in America alone simply because they were not sufficiently safe on the highway. Speaking of violence, isn't there a kind of violence to the public inherent in that statistic?

I talked about a television climate in which taboos are nourished and grow. There is a world climate that has resulted in the misuse of human potential for profit only, or for short-term gain. Commerce and governments alike are constantly selling the future short for a moment of success. That is the real violence of our time. American television with its taboos is a symptom.

The instruction to children in American television – and all over the world – is that life is made up of winners and losers. If you are not Number One, or in the top five, you have failed. There doesn't seem to be any reward in our society for simply succeeding at the level of doing one's best. You are happy if you are doing your thing – not necessarily achieving excellence, simply reaching for it – in a life that allows you to. I believe in that with all my heart. The joy is in the doing, the striving, the reaching towards excellence.

Note

1. The Federal Communications Commission, established by the Communications Act 1934, is an independent US government agency directly responsible to Congress for regulating interstate and international communications by radio, television, wire, satellite and cable. The FCC is directed by five Commissioners, appointed to serve for five years by the President and confirmed by the Senate.

The James MacTaggart Lecture 1979

Signposting Television in the 1980s: The Fourth Television Channel

Jeremy Isaacs*

Jeremy Isaacs' MacTaggart Lecture articulates his vision for the new fourth channel. He envisages broadcasting in the eighties as being characterised by a confrontation between 'a BBC on two channels and an ITV on two channels'; the former 'poorly off and getting poorer', the latter 'rich' and getting 'richer'.

While Pilkington's (1962) assessment of ITV was critical, Annan (1977) found much to praise. The change reflected the impact of Pilkington's remarks in shifting the Independent Television Authority (ITA) from being a 'friend' of the companies in the direction of more rigorous regulation. Isaacs argues that ITV enters the 1980s with a secure financial base and consequently the second ITV channel must be resourced to deliver quality programming without any diminution of programming on ITV 1. By contrast, BBC has witnessed a decline although it remains the 'best television service in the world'. The BBC has been underfunded since the establishment of BBC2 in 1962 and this is evident in programming: shortages of drama; an increase in American imports; and too many repeats. This decline is crucial since the BBC serves as a sheet anchor for all television programming and Isaacs' hope for the 1980s is that 'BBC television will be guaranteed the funding it will need'.

Isaacs details the broad principles informing the operation of the new fourth channel. He believes it must extend choice to viewers as well as

* Jeremy Isaacs is a producer and broadcaster who has made some of the most significant historical documentaries for television including *The World at War* (1975) and *Ireland: A Television History* (1981). He was Director of Programmes at Thames Television, the first Chief Executive of Channel Four Television and was Director General of the Royal Opera House in Covent Garden between 1988 and 1996.

the range of programmes; cater for minorities; explore the full range of political opinion; encourage independent production, and pursue broad educational purposes. The brief is for a fourth channel 'that everyone will watch some of the time and no one all of the time'. The fourth channel must, 'somehow, be different'. Returning to his theme of confrontation, Isaacs concludes with the hope that the competition between BBC and ITV will be competition 'not to grind each other down, but competition to serve all the publics we strive to reach, competition to excel'.

In Wales, if they are not written in the right language, they knock the signposts down.

In Ireland they tend to put road signs at or after the crossroads, not before. Here I am then, in language I hope we share, putting up signposts to the eighties just before we come to them. And this close, certainly, the way ahead looks very much clearer than it did a year ago.

Hansard for 15 May: The Queen's Speech to a new Parliament:

> Proposals will be brought before you for the future of broadcasting. A Bill will be introduced to extend the life of the Independent Broadcasting Authority,[1] which will be given responsibility (subject to strict safeguards) for the fourth television channel.

The words 'subject to strict safeguards' appear in parentheses, almost as if they were inserted in the Gracious Speech as an afterthought. No one has yet made clear precisely what the safeguards will be, or, indeed, what it is they are intended to protect or from whom. There is some hesitation about whether the channel should actually be called ITV 2, though in my view it should and it will be.

The basic new face of the eighties is ITV 2,[2] a fourth channel which will, and this is important, provide guaranteed access for the first time to the independent producer, but which will also, and I think much more tellingly in the long run, bring into confrontation a BBC on two channels and an ITV on two channels, one public broadcasting service which has been kept seriously short of funds, which is poorly off and getting poorer, and another public-broadcasting service which is rich, and will get richer. British broadcasting in the eighties will be characterised by this confrontation and by the alarming and widening discrepancy between the funding of the two systems.

I am asked to talk not really about the future, but about the next ten years. Satellite and the video recorder will change television utterly, we are told. But not before 1990. So I leave the nineties cheerfully to others and confine myself to the two networks that we have now, the four channels that we shall have from 1982, and to the next ten years.

I shall begin, where I began myself, with ITV.

Pilkington on ITV: 'The service falls well short of what a good public service of broadcasting should be.'

Annan on ITV: 'The achievement and success of the British system of organising commercial broadcasting ought not to go unrecorded.'

How was this change brought about? It happened because, as Annan[3] notes, Pilkington's[4] castigation, even though their recommendation to scrap the system and start again was rejected, did in effect change the face of ITV. An authority, which in early days had seen itself as friend and partner to the companies which took the early risks, now exerted itself to improve the service for which it was responsible. In 1968 one company lost its franchise, another, half of its [franchise]. The others were encouraged.

Nearly twenty-five years from its beginning, the single most important characteristic of ITV is not that it exists to make profit, but that it was set up in the image of the BBC, was given public responsibilities which do not differ markedly from the objectives set out in the BBC Charter, was placed firmly under the control of a public regulatory body with powers under statute to achieve its ends, and is peopled by programme-makers who seek to emulate the achievements of their BBC colleagues.

The second most important characteristic of ITV is that it is a monopoly. Except in London, each company enjoys a monopoly of advertising revenue in its own area. The monopoly has one great public advantage; those who possess it and profit by it can properly be asked to pay a public price for it, and this will be of crucial importance when we come to ITV 2.

The third most important characteristic of ITV is its regional base. The five major companies have supplied the bulk of the network schedule but from now on the five bigger regional companies – Anglia, HTV, Southern, STV and Tyne Tees – should play a larger part in making programmes for two channels. Too many of the voices we hear on television are too blandly similar. We need to hear the different accents of this country on our screens louder and clearer than we do.

ITV did not get an unqualifiedly good report from Annan: 'Some companies are really only doing just enough to get by either in programming, or in the treatment of their staff.' But for ITV in the eighties, there will be no alibis. ITV's high programme aspirations notable for years in documentaries, apparent recently in the range of drama series, consistently evident in news and current affairs – all that must be relentlessly sustained and even enhanced on ITV 1. The second-rate, all let's-get-by-with-this-series-as-cheaply-as-we-can-while-the-real-effort-goes-into-the-showy-blockbuster, all that sad stuff, from whatever source, must be ruthlessly eliminated. From now on, every-thing that ITV does it must do with all its might.

ITV asked for a second channel, has deserved it, has all but got it. But it has to be supplied without any diminution of quality on ITV 1. ITV companies must now provide all their programme-makers with the tools they will need to do the job: studios, equipment and staff, as well as cash. These programmes, the expansion of facilities, advertising revenue spread across two channels – all this coinciding perhaps with a severe economic depression – will for two or three years pretty cer-tainly squeeze ITV profit margins harder than for ten years past. Companies will, however, reapply for their franchises, whatever terms the Authority specifies for ITV 2, and for the good reason that their monopoly access to television advertising is prolonged and enlarged. Will all those who reapply be successful? That I cannot predict. But ITV enters the eighties with its revenue base secure, and, in spite of the current bloodletting, in good heart. The same cannot be said of BBC television.

Pilkington on BBC television: 'The BBC know good broadcasting; by and large, they are providing it.'

Annan on BBC television: 'Our general impression was that the overall standard of the BBC's television output was marginally declining.'

I agree with Annan. There has been a decline. The decline continues. The decline must be arrested and reversed.

The BBC is still the best television service in the world. But for a decade, senior management in BBC television have put on a brave face to conceal from us, from the public, and from the politicians, what is really happening. The plain fact is this: the BBC is short of money, and it shows. I am not privy to BBC housekeeping, but in this calendar year 1979 the indications are plain for all to see.

On BBC1 a marked shortage of drama for the mid-evening; on BBC1 a marked increase in the volume of imported American series of poor quality; on BBC1 and BBC2 many more repeats, and a change from a selective policy of repeats on merit, to a policy of repeating everything of dire necessity.

I understand, in fact, that BBC Television is short of £10 million in its programme budgets, that £7 million of that simply isn't there, and that £3 million, which would not otherwise be there, is made up by co-production funds injected from various foreign sources. Nothing struck me more forcibly, when I went to work in Kensington House, than the extent to which BBC producers have been occupied in raising co-production funds before they can start work on particular pro-grammes. Now this is a travesty of what a BBC producer used to do, or should be doing.

Worst of all, to get money up front, the BBC has had to sell, or anyway has sold, overseas rights, and forfeit the income from them. *Life on Earth* cost £1 million. The BBC could only afford £700,000 and, for the missing £300,000 sold all foreign rights. *Life on Earth* will still be shown around the world ten years from now. The BBC will not see a penny of the proceeds.

Sir Charles Curran, in his account of his Director-Generalship, to be published next month, *A Seamless Robe*, makes devastatingly plain that the licence fee system has been undermined, and the BBC under-funded, since BBC2 was authorised in 1962; that every increase since then has been too little too late to match commitments or keep pace with inflation; that in the seventies only the expansion in the number of colour licences saved the BBC from financial disaster; and that the BBC's efforts to manage its affairs with maximum economy, were 'at some expense to the quality of the service'. Curran denounces the one-year at a time increases in the licence fee granted in July 1977 and November 1978 as 'scandalously inadequate and politically craven'.

Now, what we have here is no less than a great national scandal. It is the BBC which sets the standard of television in this country. If the BBC is not strong the whole system is in peril. If, therefore, in introducing ITV 2, you seek 'safeguards' for British broadcasting as a whole, there is one safeguard which is immediately to hand, and wholly in your gift and that of the government; it is to grant the BBC the long-term licence-fee increase it desperately needs.

My hope for the eighties, therefore, is that BBC television will be guaranteed the funding it will need. My fear, for all of us in British broadcasting, is that it will continue to be kept on the tightest of tight purse strings. If so, it must be doubtful if, at the end of the eighties, the licence fee will survive.

But there is another question that cannot be evaded, and that is: what sort of BBC television is it that we want to preserve? The BBC feels that its claim to the licence fee must rest on a broad appeal to the total audi-ence and must reach about half that audience. Let the BBC aim at a 50 per cent share of the audience by all means, if it is a necessary condition of survival, but let that 50 per cent not become an end in itself. For attaining it cannot be and will not be a sufficient condition of our support.

We want a BBC which is proudly conscious of all the purposes of broadcasting, which risks the ratings and challenges the audience; which encourages programme-makers, writers, producers, directors, reporters, to work in an atmosphere of freedom and trust (which means dialogue down at the beginning of a project rather than reference up at the last minute); which allows the truly creative to shock, surprise and delight us with what we never saw coming for only they could have invented it, or brought it to our screen.

There is sometimes a conflict between programme quality and audience size and a genuine dilemma, therefore, for the Channel Controller. But if luck is in, the dilemma vanishes – Hancock, Steptoe, Garnett were both the critic's delight and the Controller's friends. The most popular BBC programmes have often also been the best.

My guess is that if its finances are put on a sound basis – a big if – the BBC will not find it hard in the early eighties, against ITV, perhaps with new franchise holders, coping with two channels, to achieve the audience share it seeks, and then some.

What sort of fourth channel do we want?

We want a fourth channel which extends the choice available to viewers; which extends the range of ITV's programmes; which caters for substantial minorities presently neglected; which builds into its actuality programmes a complete spectrum of political attitude and opinion; which furthers, in a segment of its programming, some broad educational purposes; which encourages worthwhile independent production; which allows the larger regional ITV companies to show what their programme-makers can do. We want a fourth channel that will neither simply compete with ITV 1 nor merely be complementary to it. We want a fourth channel that everyone will watch some of the time and no one all of the time. We want a fourth channel that will, somehow, be different.

Can all these objectives be realised on ITV 2? I believe they can.

If the channel is to have a different flavour it needs a different chef, perhaps a new unit, on the analogy of ITN, funded by the companies, answerable to a board on which they and the IBA are represented, but at a little distance from both, such a unit to plan not just the independent sector's contribution, but, in conjunction with the Controllers' Group, the whole of ITV 2. That would be my first safeguard.

Whatever method is adopted, ITV 2's budget will be provided by a levy on the ITV companies, public money if you like, a tax on their surplus of income over expenditure on ITV 1. A tax they will pay as the price for their franchises, and the continued enjoyment of their monopoly of advertising revenue.

The budget should go to commission programmes from the ITV companies themselves, who thus have an opportunity to earn some of it back, and from independent producers.

ITV 2 will be a national service.

Advertising will be collected locally.

The channel should aim at a variety of audiences and at a share of audience of just above 10 per cent.

What other 'safeguards' will the IBA impose? I suggest the following.

First a maximum contribution from the ITV majors. The majors can supply a sizeable part of the schedule but the fourth channel is for viewers', for independent producers', and for all of ITV'S, not just for the big five's, benefit. They will make money from it. They have to accept that the balance of ITV will shift, a little, away from them.

Second. A minimum contribution from the middle five, the major regionals in ITV. They have never contributed to the network schedule as of right and duty. Now the middle five should have that opportunity and that obligation. Third, a new outlet for ITN, perhaps allowing them to bring into the evening the techniques of *News at One*, the only effective innovation in news presentation on either channel in recent years. Fourth, a clutch of programmes designed to hit some broadly educational target. Fifth. ITV 2 should provide access for a guaranteed number of hours each week for genuine independent producers.

Up to now, independent producers have had a raw deal – but for a harsh and simple reason: no one needed what they had to offer. Both broadcasting systems, BBC and ITV, produced sufficient themselves to keep the schedule full. But the fourth channel will suck into television a new influx of programme-makers: the BBC will lose some good people. I wish independent producers well. I hope they will make a good living. I hope they will not all be in it only for the money. They will have to offer to ITV 2 the sort of programmes, in all price ranges, that ITV 2 needs. I see no reason why they should not offer programmes also to the BBC and to ITV 1 either on a wholly independent basis, or as a co-production. If the idea is good enough recent evidence suggests they will get a sympathetic hearing.

Independent programme-makers ought to retain full editorial control of their programmes, but they will not be allowed to work to widely different standards of taste, than those prevailing throughout ITV. One writ will run. I would urge the IBA, however, as Annan did, to allow the companies more latitude than in the last few years. I urge the IBA to be meticulous in ensuring that independents receive a fair price for their programmes, and I urge the IBA not to be meticulous in binding the hands of whoever runs ITV 2, for I do think it will be better run by an individual than by a committee, with fixed, rigid, quota obligations to all and sundry, and no flexibility whatever to improvise or invent. That way lies infanticide, instant rigor mortis.

There is one trend in programming that independent production will accelerate and which should be slowed; that is the trend to pay too much regard to the lure of overseas sales, a siren song that can drive good men bonkers. The best of British television has always been made for our own audience. Of course it is true that British audiences enjoy costume drama, bewigged, beribboned, crinolined, miles of it. But I hope that, in the eighties, those who make our programme choices will not be too easily tempted by the prospect of profit overseas.

I hope, in the eighties, to see more black Britons on our screens in programmes of particular appeal to them and aimed at us; more programmes made by women for women which men will watch; more programmes for the young, for the age group that watches television at least partly because so little television speaks specially to them. I hope to see plenty of programmes that entertain, satisfy and comfort many, and some that risk offending them. I want to see television treat the audience as adults, ready, if they choose, to enlarge their experience by watching what we responsibly put on the screen. Many more people have benefited by learning about the world from television than have ever been seriously offended by it.

I hope the competition between BBC and ITV will be competition not to grind each other down, but competition to serve all the publics we strive to reach, competition to excel. The 1980s will be the decade of the duopoly, and perhaps the last decade in which the duopoly will dominate our screens. The fear must be that, locked in competition with itself, our choice will be narrowed. But I hope the two giants will not see themselves as monoliths, but will use their power to enlarge our horizons.

Notes

1. The Independent Broadcasting Authority (IBA) was the regulatory body for the commercial sector of UK television broadcasting until 1991 when it was replaced by

the Independent Television Commission (ITC). The ITC was itself superseded by Ofcom on 29 December 2003.

2. The second commercial television channel which came on air in 1982 was eventually called Channel 4.

3. Lord Annan chaired a committee of inquiry (1976–7) to 'consider the future of broadcasting services in the UK'. The committee's report *The Future of Broadcasting* (Cmnd 6753) proposed the establishment of a fourth terrestrial television channel.

4. Sir Harry Pilkington chaired the Broadcasting Committee established in 1960 (The Pilkington Committee, reported in 1962) to consider and review certain aspects of the commercial broadcasting of television services which began in 1954.

Television Drama, Censorship and the Truth

John Mortimer*

Mortimer begins with an anecdote to introduce his argument that 'there is no clear or necessary distinction between fact and fiction, between drama and documentary, between creating and reporting'. Indeed 'one gives life to the other' and both are equally important in the search for truth. Consequently, censoring drama is as 'damaging and dishonest' as censoring the news.

Mortimer's working life illustrates this synergy between fact and fiction. His simultaneous engagement with law and the theatre prompted the discovery that while the playwright 'has to face up to the fearful truth of existence' the lawyer can exist 'in a world of pure fantasy and make-believe': the plays of 'Strindberg . . . were forced to tell the truth . . . about married life' while 'the divorce laws of England were a web of romantic fairy-tales'. Mortimer argues that truth is essential to drama and must be rooted in the reality experienced by the writer: the 'best of dramatists . . . have all dealt in worlds which are quite their own' and require them, as Proust acknowledged, to 'read the book of unknown signs within him'.

But television drama has two 'enemies': censorship and ratings. Mortimer rejects both. Censors reject material which tends to 'deprave and corrupt'. Mortimer argues that drama should shock audiences – as Dickens' accounts of the workhouse did; moreover, any 'healthy person' should expect to be 'shocked and offended at least three times a day'. Ratings also threaten drama and lead to mediocrity. Mortimer recalls being told that a television play is seen by more people than saw all Shakespeare's plays in his lifetime: a comment, Mortimer believes, which

---

* John Mortimer is an author, playwright and novelist.

proves nothing but 'the total unimportance of numbers'. The merits of drama must extend beyond pulling a crowd.

□

Sometime ago I was defending a man down the Old Bailey. Like Steptoe and Son, he was an East End totter, and he was accused of stabbing a neighbour with the knife which he used to cut up carrots for his pony. We sat in the cells under the Old Bailey waiting for the jury to return its verdict, and, as often happens between client and advocate on these difficult occasions, a silence fell between us. Then he looked at me and said, after a long pause, 'You know, your Mr Rumpole could've got me out of this, so why can't you?'

I tell this story because it shows the endless muddle between truth and invention, appearance and reality which puzzles so many people who think seriously about television. The totter had perceived something of great importance in the consideration of any art; that there is no clear or necessary distinction between fact and fiction, between drama and documentary, between creating and reporting. That one gives life to the other and that both are of equal value in the search, which must always be ruthless, fearless and individual for the truth.

And in the course of telling the truth about our life and our society, you can no more do without drama than you can do without *Panorama* or *World in Action* or the news. So to cut down on drama, to obliterate the single play, to diminish by acts of censorship a writer's meaning, or worse still to ban a play because it may cause offence and has inconvenient or painful truths to tell, may be an act as damaging or dishonest as falsifying a piece of reporting or censoring the news.

But before embarking on so ambitious an argument may I present my credentials. It may perhaps be relevant to speak of my upbringing in documentary films, 'documentary' being, of course, an area in which dishonesty is most easily concealed.

I went into the Crown Film Unit around the age of nineteen. As a fourth assistant director my job was to get the director's tea, and say 'quiet, please' before every take. As the worst fourth assistant director in the history of the movies they made me a scriptwriter where it was thought I could do less harm.

We made films in which silvery bombers were seen rising beautifully into the sky to the accompaniment of music by Dr Vaughan Williams, to drop their loads accurately on the marshalling yards of Dusseldorf and avoid touching a hair on the heads of the civilian population. But what was really wrong with the wartime documentaries was that they failed to tell the truth. All around me I noticed people who were fed up with the war, terrified of the bombs, deeply engrossed in the sale of black-market petrol or busily deceiving their husbands with Italian prisoners of war. None of this could, of course, be mentioned; just as we couldn't reveal that our bombers more often than not missed their targets and unloaded their contents on the innocent inhabitants of sleeping cities. This was not the whole truth; in many ways the war was our finest, at least, our most united hour.

It is significant that the best wartime documentaries were made by Humphrey Jennings, who had been a surrealist painter and who strove consciously to produce works of art. The failure of some other documentary directors to tell the truth about the war was failure of art, and it was a failure compounded by the demands of censorship.

When the war was over, I took up work as a lawyer and as a writer, a writer of novels, for radio and the theatre and happily of television plays. Such a life, such a split personality, does bring you slap up against the problem of the obligation drama owes to life and indeed of what life owes to drama. One of the first things I discovered of course was that while the writer of plays of fiction has to face up to the fearful truth of existence, particularly if he is a writer of comedy, the lawyer, like the politician, can exist quite happily in a world of pure fantasy and make-believe. When I started at the bar I noticed that while the plays of Strindberg, for instance, were forced to tell the truth and nothing but the truth about married life, the divorce laws of England were a web of romantic fairy-tales which make no allowance whatever for the realities of human behaviour.

What life in the law courts did teach me though was a great deal about dramatic language. Or rather about the many different languages we use in our society. One of the great achievements of television drama at its best is to write what is actually spoken in England. Such brilliant artists as the authors of *Porridge* have done much to interpret and use English as it is actually spoken by the majority of my clients. In my own experience I found the judges and the clients speaking quite different languages, which I had to do my best to interpret. There was one exquisite Old Bailey judge, the sort that used to always break off at 11.30 a.m. for a glass of cold Chablis and a nibble of cheese, who had to sentence a wildly drunken Irish labourer who had pleaded guilty to indecent exposure, insulting behaviour, assaulting the police, obscene and threatening abuse, vomiting down the stairs of Leicester Square tube station and kindred offences. As this huge, unshaven, vomit-stained man stood swaying in the dock the judge said, 'I am going to take a very unusual course with you, my man.'

'God bless you, sir, God bless your Royal Highness.'

'I am going to place you upon probation.'

'Oh thank your Eminence. May your shadow never grow shorter.'

'But on one condition . . .'

'Anything, your Royalty, any condition whatsoever.'

'You must never take another drink for the rest of your natural life.'

'Right you are, your Holiness. Not another single drop.'

'And by nothing I mean absolutely nothing,' and here the judge leant forward to emphasise his point: 'Not even the teeniest weeniest dry sherry before your dinner.'

I can't of course swear that that ever happened. It may, in fact, be a work of inspired fiction, but even if it is fiction it tells a deeper truth about the British legal system than a two-hour documentary followed by a discussion with a panel of distinguished lawyers.

So if fiction comes to our rescue and helps us to understand a real political or social situation, truth is essential to drama in television. Particularly vital to a writer of comedy, for comedy above all things must be rooted in reality before it can begin to flower. Of course the reality, the truth, is that learned and experienced by the writer concerned. In all writing the area of choice is narrow; the dramatist is bound by himself and the world as he sees it.

But within these confines the depth of discovery is infinite. The best of dramatists who have worked in television, Harold Pinter, David Mercer, Jack Rosenthal, Dennis Potter and David Hare, have all dealt in worlds which are quite their own. My own world of a writer is not a matter of choice to me. I am confined to the small, perhaps dying, middle-class professional world where I was born, with all its pretensions, prejudices, nostalgia, bewildered attitude to the future, and occasional courage. A dramatist, like a reporter, is confined to the story that faces him, although in the playwright's case it is the story only he can write; Proust said: 'A writer's only duty is to read the book of unknown signs within him.'

It's a strange fact of writing, however, that only by being most intensely, most privately yourself, by reading the book of unknown signs within you with the most scrupulous attention, that you can hope to appear to say anything of interest to a large number of other people. My father, a blind barrister, had an enormous influence on my life. When I wrote a television play about him, after his death, I included, of course, many of his anecdotes, his outrageous way of singing old musical songs, and his ruthless way of cross-examining witnesses. But I also found that I could write new dialogue for him as though he was still alive. Nowadays, when I think of my father, as I so often do, I cannot at all remember which were the things he said and which I made up for an actor to say for him. I hope and believe that both are equally true to what he was.

I suppose, if it had been a more newsworthy subject, *Voyage Round My Father* might have been attacked as 'faction': the judicious blend of fiction and fact, which is certainly as old as Shakespeare. The critics would have a field day with Richard III, which by mixing history and invention tastelessly displayed a physically handicapped member of a royal household in an unfavourable light, and no doubt caused needless offence to the Plantagenet family.

I am sure many of you will be prepared to argue that by setting out as history, a play may mislead the audience. Such arguments could be used also, I suppose, against factual newspapers which present trades union leaders as the crudest of cut-out stage villains, to be hissed melodramatically whenever they appear. I do not think television audiences or newspaper readers are as gullible as many people would believe. I think it is patronising to think of our audiences as less intelligent or more in need of care and protection than judges, politicians or television executives. And this brings me to the two great dangers that face television drama. On the one hand, it may be dismissed as unimportant because it has no real contribution to make, and, unlike the news, doesn't tell us anything we need to know. On the other hand, it may be attacked as being so powerful that it gives offence, depraves and corrupts, causes divorce, football hooliganism, the destruction of telephone kiosks and gang-bangs in Golders Green. Both the planner who sees a higher audience for *Blankety Blank* and the censor who believes that the television set is a never-silent guest in the family circle and, because it can never be switched off, must forever mind its manners, are the enemies of television drama. So I must say something about the dangers of censorship and the dangers of the pursuit of a mass audience.

The legal basis of censorship was laid down in the middle of the last century in the case of a Mr Hicklin who published pamphlets of a scandalous nature about the alleged going-on of priests with their lady penitents in the cramped area of the confessional. The test then was that that should be censored which tended to 'deprave and corrupt'. Few people have ever been produced who appear to have been corrupted by a book or a play, although at one trial the Oxford bookseller Mr Basil

Blackwell said that he felt distinctly depraved after reading a book called *Last Exit to Brooklyn*. But *as* Mr Blackwell was well into his eighties at the time, the dangers flowing from his alleged depravity seemed to be somewhat academic.

The test of depraving and corrupting is made more confusing by the enlightened action of Roy Jenkins and the late A. P. Herbert in putting a defence of artistic merit into the Obscene Publications Act. Section 4 says 'That even if a play or a book has a tendency to deprave and corrupt it shall not be convicted if it is of artistic or literary merit.' Times change. Back in the thirties the Bow Street magistrate found *The Well of Loneliness*, Mrs Radcliffe-Hall's novel about lesbian love, quite certain to deprave and corrupt. A few years ago the *Well of Loneliness* was read aloud on the BBC as the *Book at Bedtime*.

Television executives have not been content with the legal test for censorship, which indeed contents nobody: they have applied their own rules. Perhaps the least satisfactory is the form of censorship which seeks to suppress a play because it gives offence or shocks. It seems to me that no healthy person should expect to pass through life without being shocked and offended at least three times a day, and that shock is a perfectly legitimate and indeed necessary function of the television dramatist. People were deeply shocked by Dickens' revelation of the state of the workhouses and it was extremely good for them. Not only should drama shock us, but every new form of experience in the arts has been found profoundly shocking when it was first introduced. The publisher of Shelley's *Queen Mab* was prosecuted for blasphemy, and the critic of the *Edinburgh Review* was deeply offended by the poems of Wordsworth and Coleridge. Those in charge of television programmes, governments and the IBA, must clearly understand that not only is it permissible for television to shock and give offence, if this form of communication is to retain any form of vitality, it has a positive duty to do so.

So we come, of course, to violence. The first thing to be said about violence is that it has been a well-loved feature of children's stories for as long as anyone can remember. No child can read Greek mythology without meeting cannibalism and castration or Grimms' fairy-tales without encountering the most spine-chilling atrocities. This is the literary background against which we must judge the merit or otherwise of a couple of punch-ups in *Starsky and Hutch*.

To approach the problem of censoring violence in television drama it is necessary to consider whether dramatic art creates life or exposes and reveals it. After all the most sickening violence on television is to be seen each night on the news, which is no play-acting but real bombers in Northern Ireland, genuine executions in Africa and Iran, starvation and the appalling cruelties of war. Such violence is not subject to demands of censorship. We live in an age of appalling cruelty and it cannot surely be maintained that the violence is caused by television: by an overindulgence in *Kojak* or *Hawaii Five 0*.

If television drama has any value it must be to reflect the time we live in and to do so with honesty and truth. A great judge, Mr Justice Stable, said that we must be cautious of censorship because our fiction is what we rely on to be understood by future generations. Our knowledge of Elizabethan and Restoration England comes largely from the theatre; just as we know the Victorian age from Dickens and can remember just what we were like at the time of Suez by reading John Osborne. One of the vaguest, deadest areas of our history is the age of Oliver Cromwell; it was the time the Puritans closed the theatres.

It is impossible for a writer to accept that there is any aspect of human behaviour that could be forbidden to him as a subject, There can't be no-go areas in the world of art.

None of these dire warnings are meant to deny the pleasure and indeed the privilege of writing television drama. Television has one great advantage over the cinema; it is not visually exciting. As John McGrath said in the first of these lectures 'a cinema screen can flood the senses', 'a television shot is at best nice'. To expect more is to expect to listen satisfactorily to 'a symphony over the telephone'. Television is necessarily, like the theatre and radio, the place for words, where the writer and the actor must always have the most important parts to play.

However, unlike the theatre dramatist with his small middle-class audience, the television writer does have the extraordinary privilege of reaching a public as wide as that enjoyed by the Victorian novelist and the Elizabethan playwright. It's a continual excitement to know that your words and ideas can reach beyond Shaftesbury Avenue to the furthest Hebrides and the cells under the Old Bailey. Of course such an audience doesn't always listen with the concentration of theatre audiences; some of them will be making love and many may be making Ovaltine.

And this brings me to what is at once television's greatest strength and its severest limitation: its enormous popularity. And if there is nothing so stimulating as a mass audience, there is nothing so easy to use as an excuse for mediocrity.

The calculation of audience ratings is a danger to the health of television. Nothing could be more unattractive than television where the only desire is to appeal to as many viewers as possible. Opposed as I am to any form of censorship it might be a healthy development if everyone in charge of television were to deny themselves a look at the ratings. In particular those in charge of the BBC, whose pride it should be that they have no commercial reason to show any interest in the ratings whatsoever. Once television thinks it only has the duty to please the majority of the population it is lost.

Pay-TV, or choose your own satellite, may lead to more programmes, which can cater for the large minorities who will always prefer drama to panel games, thought to chat, Chekhov to *Crossroads*. But what is important is not that a television programme should be spread as widely as possible and infiltrate every home but that it must penetrate deeply and be attended to with some higher degree of concentration than the buzz of the refrigerator or the distant wail of Radio 1. When I first wrote for television I remember someone saying that a television play is seen by more people than witnessed all Shakespeare's plays in his lifetime. This is a statistic which proves nothing but the total unimportance of numbers.

I am conscious of the fact that I have said nothing about the structure of television companies, little about the franchise or the fourth channel. In discussing television I have found little to distinguish it from any other art or indeed from life itself. It doesn't matter really whether you put it on film or tape in the Bush Theatre or Drury Lane, at the Globe or the Moscow Arts, whether you sing it out at La Scala, Milan, or trap it all silently in the pages of a book. It doesn't matter if it's fact or fiction or a mixture between the two. The problem is to capture the moment of life as it is lived, to re-create it as you feel it, to say what can be said by no one else. It's a problem which can only be solved by sitting alone in a room, looking in near panic at an empty sheet of paper. After the pleasures of meeting and discussing, the excitement of argument and the joys of indignation, it is that moment alone that matters: the reading of the unknown book of signs within us all.

The James MacTaggart Lecture 1981

The Day after Tomorrow: The Future of Electronic Publishing

Peter Jay*

Peter Jay criticises the current overregulation of broadcasting and outlines a possible future organisation for what he prefers to describe as 'electronic publishing': his assumption is that the problem of 'spectrum scarcity', which provided the original rationale for regulation, has been overcome. 'Within less than two decades,' he argues, we will inhabit 'a world in which there will be no technically based grounds for government interference in electronic publishing.'

Jay sets out his vision. Every household will be connected by an interactive fibre optic link which allows 'the nation's viewers' to 'simultaneously watch as many different programmes as the nation's readers can read different books, magazines and newspapers'. The television becomes like a telephone. Viewers dial to select programmes, a meter monitors quantity and kind of programmes selected and the television set is connected to a 'central black box' which is fed with 'an indefinitely large number of programmes' and which is maintained by British Telecom. Consumers buy programmes on a pay-to-view basis.

Jay believes this future form of electronic publishing will encapsulate and reflect in its structures, the principles of consumer sovereignty, freedom and choice. It requires no regulatory laws other than the general provisions for libel, copyright and obscenity, which already govern publishing. The state may wish to continue 'to subsidise any particular categories of electronic publishing which are considered virtuous or in the

---

* Peter Jay is a journalist who has worked for *The Times*, Channel 4's *Week in Politics* and London Weekend Television's *Weekend World*; he has also been Economics Editor for the BBC. Jay was a member of a celebrity consortium which bid and won the breakfast franchise for TV-AM. In the 1970s, he was British Ambassador to America in Washington.

public interest'. The BBC would continue as a major publisher but would lose its 'self-regulatory powers'. Jay suggests that even this 'extremely compressed view of a future market in electronic publishing' illustrates that there is 'nothing God-given or immutable about the familiar duopolistic regime'.

It is a great privilege for me to deliver this important lecture at this year's Edinburgh Television Festival. I want to tackle a problem which is, I believe, increasingly disturbing in the current debate about the future of what we used loosely to call television and radio broadcasting and should now, more compendiously, call electronic publishing. The problem is the lack of perspective, both chronological and moral, in our perception of what is going on and of what we believe is about to go on. We give the impression of being constantly startled, unnerved and non-plussed by each successive revelation of the technological changes which are expanding the capabilities of electronic publishing so rapidly.

The modest contribution that I would like to make is to suggest that there is a helpful perspective in which current developments can be seen and that when they are so seen, much of the bafflement and mystification about where we are going in electronic publishing will disappear. At the same time, the basic principles which society should apply in debating the future legislative, regulatory and institutional framework within which the technological potentialities of electronic publishing should be permitted and encouraged to fulfil themselves over the next several decades, it will become very much clearer.

Let me start by inviting you to stand on its head the conventional perception in the universe of electronic publishing and ask you to consider the hypothesis that it is the world in which we have been living, for nearly a century now, which is artificial and special and that it is the world into which we are moving which will be much more properly regarded as normal and natural. Let me explain what I mean.

Why do human societies have governments? Why do they feel the need for them? The broad justification is that, at least in principle, they enable the individuals who comprise a society to live lives which are more satisfactory to them as individuals. In societies which adhere to this libertarian and utilitarian conception of government the notion that a government action could be justified because of some independent right or interest of government itself is strongly rejected.

A classic example of an activity which is normally presumed not to require government intervention is communication. Second only, perhaps, to the right of individuals to think privately what thoughts they wish comes the right of individuals to *communicate* those thoughts with one another. The historic battle to establish this right after the invention of the printing press was long and bitter. But for those who adhere to the libertarian and utilitarian tradition it is not seen as a battle between two arguable propositions or legitimate interests, but rather as a simple struggle between a sound and fundamental ideal on the one hand and dark forces motivated by interest on the other. We now regard it as axiomatic that mass communication of the *printed* word does not require any general framework of government regulation, although we may be more or less inclined to accept certain marginal constraints on this freedom for such reasons as sedition, blasphemy, libel, race relations and national security.

When wireless telegraphy became possible, the natural presumption of a liberal/utilitarian society must surely have been that this raised no new question of principle so far as the legitimate role of government in the regulation of mass communication was concerned. What in fact brought government and the law-makers into the picture was a simple fact of broadcasting technology. Since two signals could not be broadcast on the same wavelength in the same area at the same time without interfering with one another, some act of government was felt to be justified in the interests of the private individuals who comprise society for exactly the same reason that we feel government is needed and justified in imposing a 'keep left' rule for driving on the public highways.

The nineteenth-century Wireless Telegraphy Acts, culminating in the 1905 Act had this essential purpose and justification; and it has been on this very narrow and specific foundation that the whole inverted pyramid of government regulation of broadcasting has since been built. But, having once got into the act on this genuine but technical pretext, governments have moved to what is, by the standards of print communication, a massive control and regulation of electronic publishing. It is quite simply impossible, as things stand, for any individual or private institution to communicate with fellow citizens by way of broadcast radio or television unless he has been appointed by a chartered or statutory body to do so or invited by someone else who has been so appointed. Moreover, any such communication has to conform to a most elaborate series of formal and informal codes affecting the content, balance, timing etc. of such publications. My purpose at this point is not to evaluate or criticise but simply to bring out the profound difference between the framework of law, regulation and government as it applies to print publications and electronic publishing.

Against this background, let us look at what technological developments are doing to the potentialities of electronic broadcasting and thereby to our existing concepts for regulating it. When cable television, under its original guise as 'pay television' first entered the debate a decade ago, nobody doubted that this belonged squarely in the regulated area of electronic publishing. Even pay television continued to present a solid, though narrow, pretext for official involvement since the cables could not legally or practically be laid without the consent of public authority. But now we are well and truly in sight of a world in which significant parts of electronic publishing can both legally and practically take place without coming within the existing purview of the broadcasting regulators. Video is already the most highly developed form of this new wave. Cable, satellites, teletext and other innovations are all contributing to what, from the cosy perspective of the 'closed circle' of the 'authorised' broadcasters, is regarded as the fragmentation of the audience.

Quite simply we are within less than two decades technologically of a world in which there will be no technically based grounds for government interference in electronic publishing. To put it technically, 'spectrum scarcity' is going to disappear. In simple terms this meant that there will be able to be as many channels as there are viewers. At that moment all the acrimonious and difficult debate about how many channels there should be, who should control them, have access to them and what should be shown on them can disappear. But it will only disappear if we all work, indeed fight, extremely hard.

Now let me try to sketch how this wondrous emancipation can occur, if not today, at least the day after tomorrow in terms of the eras of electronic publishing. Before the end of the century, subject only to a very large initial capital outlay which could only be borne by society as a whole, it will be possible by fibre optic technology to create a grid connecting every household in the country whereby the nation's viewers can simultaneously watch as many different programmes as the nation's readers can read different books, magazines, newspapers etc. In other words, a television set (or radio) will be like a telephone in that the user selects for himself the connection he wants. Imagine each set equipped with a telephone dial on which the code number of the desired programme can be dialled. Imagine also the equivalent of a telephone meter monitoring receptions on each set, linked to the code number of the item received. Imagine finally a central 'black box' maintained by British Telecom into which an indefinitely large number of programmes can be fed.

The rest of the conditions for a free electronic publishing market, with *consumer* choice and freedom of access, fall quickly into place. No general laws are required other than those which already govern publishing (libel, copyright, obscenity, common law, etc.), though some special laws may be needed to deal with copyright in a world of satellite transmissions and cassette copying. The only necessary function of the state is to lay a duty on British Telecom to provide and operate the technology of the system, to accept all programmes which conform to the law, to collect charges from the viewing public and, after deducting its own costs and any other approved taxes or charges, to pass what remains over to the publisher of each item.

Large and small wholesale publishers will be free to establish themselves. They will arrange and finance the preparation of the programmes, set the charges for them, advertise their availability and their code numbers and reward the authors and participants under freely negotiated contracts. Individuals who wish to make their own programmes will be free to do so, though as with books they will either have to find a publisher or bear the costs and risks of publishing themselves.

There is nothing in this system to prevent the state continuing to subsidise any particular categories of electronic publishing which are considered virtuous or in the public interest. Nor is there anything to prevent any other patron or sponsor from subsidising meritorious, or indeed merit-less, productions. The BBC and the independent broadcast companies would presumably continue as major publishers on the new scene. But the IBA would disappear, and the BBC would cease to be a broadcasting authority with (self-)regulatory powers. As large independent producers the BBC and ITV programme companies would doubtless continue to set their own policies and standards; but these need not reflect any general state policy for broadcasting.

The news and party political broadcasts could be catered for either under the general provisions above or special provision. There is no reason why the news should not justify itself commercially; but, if it needs to be subsidised, this could be done by raising a small levy on all other transmissions to finance news services. Party political broadcasts should presumably be financed by the parties.

The treatment of advertising raises no insuperable problem. Either Parliament could disallow advertisement altogether. Or it could require

British Telecom to accept programme packages which included advertising, in which case the charge to the viewer would be lower – or nil. It would then be up to individual publishers to decide whether to include advertising in their programmes, while viewers would be free to decide whether they thought this interruption worth the saving in charges.

This extremely compressed sketch of a future market in electronic publishing is designed only to show that there is nothing God-given or immutable about the familiar duopolistic regime. At present cumbrous giants battle for franchises and are themselves besieged by special interests trying to steer programme content more to their way of thinking. This process in no way guarantees the maximum satisfaction of viewers' preferences; indeed, that is not even the objective of the present institutions. The addition of an extra channel, or even two or ten, would not change this essential pattern.

There are two financial questions about the scheme of electronic publishing sketched here. (a) Would the huge investment in the necessary telecommunications grid and the changeover of receivers be justified after allowing for the earnings of the other non-publishing chargeable services which could be carried on such an electronic network? (b) Would the system of meter charging for viewing, augmented by specific subsidies on merit and by advertising receipts, generate the revenue necessary to support the required level of broadcasting?

The first question is legitimate and important. The answer to it depends on many variables including, of course, the cost of the investment. It will also depend on how many other users there will be. The more there are, the smaller the specific return from sales of grid capacity to the broadcast publishers will need to be.

The question about the adequacy of the revenue to be generated is only meaningful if it is supposed that there can be a difference between what the viewing public, together with public and private patrons and sponsors, as well as advertisers are willing to pay for broadcast material and the right quantity of broadcasting. But this is not a distinction which is normally held to be meaningful in the provision of marketable services to the public, except in areas like health or perhaps housing where some measurements can be attached to the notion of the public's 'needs' as distinct from what the public will pay for. Indeed, the argument can be pressed a little further. One of the great merits of the system adumbrated here for financing broadcasting is that it generates invaluable information about the effective demand for broadcast material and therefore about the scale of resources which it is right to invest and to use in supplying the material.

This then leaves the question whether there are any good non-technological-cum-financial reasons for going on as at present. People will answer this question according to their different political and social philosophies.

In the circumstances envisaged here, there need be literally no limit to what can be published electronically, other than the general law and what the public (and others) will pay for: the only role of supervision is to prevent the publication of lawful material which the public would choose and pay for. To believe that such prevention of publication would be desirable it would appear to be necessary to believe one or more of the following propositions:

a) that a man or woman does not always know what is best for him or her to receive: that someone else does know best;
b) that free electronic publishing would in practice lead to a narrowing of choice; or
c) that economic activities, of which broadcasting is certainly one, exist primarily or exclusively for the benefit of those whose work in them, rather than for those who use their output.

It will be evident that none of these propositions makes much appeal to me. Few would defend the first proposition as it stands, but there are many who adopt positions which entail this proposition and it is better to see it nakedly for what it is: a complete rejection of the philosophy of the primacy of the individual.

The second proposition is more plausible, but only because the alternative system of electronic publishing is construed as though it were still oligopolistic publishing, but writ larger. It will be asked how in practice can indefinitely large numbers of electronic publishers afford the hugely expensive overheads which television production requires. Only the few could do it; and competition among the few leads to homogenised products and negligible choice. This is mistaken. It will not be necessary for any but the biggest publishers to have their own studios, any more than every print publisher and author has to own his own press. It will pay entrepreneurs (as indeed it already does) to provide studio facilities and to hire them out to all comers.

The argument for producer sovereignty lacks any intelligible philosophical basis. In the broadcasting industry the argument, whether deployed by executives, 'creative' staff or manual workers, is no different from the special pleading of all manner of groups – from farmers to furnace men and from opera singers to obsolete printers – to be pre-served at the expense of the rest of society in their customary way of life, irrespective of whether it any longer serves a useful purpose.

It follows then that in a world in which central supervision is not an inevitable byproduct of some broadcasting rule-of-the-road, there will be no compelling need for continued monolithic (or indeed duo-, or oligo-lithic) broadcasting franchises. Once this is accepted, it can be seen that most of the problems which preoccupy public debate about the future of broadcasting disappear. For most of those problems are problems about allocating scarce publishing opportunities between competing interest groups, whether established institutions, financial vested interests, worker vested interest, evangelical producers, Scots-men, Welshmen, Irishmen, divines, educationalists, ethnic minorities or any other form of man-in-his-organisations as against man-in-his-home-wanting-to-sit-in-his-armchair-and-watch-the-tele. Once there is no allocation to be made, there will be no lobbies and so no headaches to be suffered in arbitrating between them. At the same time, of course, the power in the hands of the great allocator is liquidated. Government will resist, but this is scarcely an argument why society should bless such an unnecessary exercise of power with spurious respectability.

In conclusion, let me re-emphasise the obvious fact that this lecture is quite explicitly and deliberately futuristic. It is, as its title states, about the day after tomorrow. It has little to say about the preoccupa-tions of broadcasters' viewers and regulators today. I certainly believe that we shall think more confidently and more coherently about the more immediate and obvious signs of the fragmentation of the system of authorised electronic publishing if we:

a) realise that these are only the modest precursors of a much more fundamental transformation of the technological base of elec-tronic broadcasting; and

b) recognise that as that transformation fulfils, the world which we will be entering will be a much less artificial one in which well-known principles of consumer and producer freedom articulated through the proper operation of the price mechanism can and should be invoked to solve problems which have seemed so recal-citrant in the world of authorised electronic publishing and which seem so baffling to those who regard the new world as merely an extension of the old world with complications.

Finally, those who care passionately for freedom in communication and publishing, whether electronic, print or simply oral, need now to gird themselves for a prolonged struggle against old habits and vested interests, in order to ensure that the new freedoms which the new technology will make technically possible are in fact translated into real freedoms for both producers and consumers under law. The belief that electronic publishing, especially by broadcast television, has mystical, hypnotic and unique powers is deeply entrenched in the political mind; and the desire to control and influence it will not be shed like an old skin simply because the technical need for a spectrum rule of the road and, therefore, for a spectrum policeman has disappeared. The battles that were fought by the great seventeenth-, eighteenth- and nineteenth-century heroes of free speech and free publication will have to be fought all over again.

The James MacTaggart Lecture 1984

The Primacy of Programmes in the Future of Broadcasting

Denis Forman*

Denis Forman argues that while technology has created the new broadcast delivery systems of cable and satellite, these developments are unimportant compared to the quality of the programming which they deliver. It is time we 'directed our attention not so much to the messenger as to the message'. It is crucial to persuade politicians, with their privatising ambitions and monetarist policies that 'the true value of our business lies in our programmes'.

The collapse of the plan to cable Britain offers testament to this view: 'not many people are willing to pay . . . for a service that . . . is made up of the cheapest television programmes'. Direct broadcasting by satellite (DBS) will eventually be a success, but the rate of penetration will be slow until 'you decide on the programme policy'.

Consequently, the future of broadcasting seems to rest 'in the hands of the duopoly'. But there are problems here: sins both of commission and omission. First, senior managers seem more concerned with profits above programming, but 'efficiency is the enemy of originality'. Second, idolatry and the worship of false gods such as ratings. Third, the sins of omission exemplified by timidity and cautiousness in programme-making. Finally, the failure to confront government challenges to freedom of expression such as the Official Secrets Act, as well as governments' increasing commitments to news management.

Forman concludes by arguing that in the field of entertainment and the arts – theatre, film and television – Britain leads the world. Managers in

* Denis Forman was Director of the British Film Institute, the inspiration behind the establishment of the National Film Theatre and Chairman and Managing Director of Granada Television. He was also Director of the Royal Opera House, Covent Garden. His publications include *Mozart Piano Concerto* (1983) and *A Night at the Opera* (1998).

broadcasting must therefore remember that the people who create programmes are the 'most important in the world – people like James
MacTaggart, a man who made programmes'. It is people like MacTaggart
that 'all broadcasting structures and all forms of technology should be
designed to serve'.

□

When James MacTaggart departed this life, in the summer of 1974, he
left a world of broadcasting unruffled by the winds of change. It was
the year of *Porridge* and *South Riding, Monty Python* and *Upstairs,
Downstairs*, and in the cinema *The Towering Inferno and Murder* on *the
Orient Express* were the main attractions. Within broadcasting, it was
still a producers' world and, outside, the legacy of consensus politics
lingered on. The future of broadcasting was in the hands of the Annan
Committee, whose wide-ranging review pondered the future mainly in
terms of only one problem, the character and ownership of a proposed
additional channel. They did not foresee any threat to the established
order until the last decade of the century.

Yet, as long as two years ago, the great cable hype spread panic and
concern among our community, which is now greatly abated; but now
we have a new phenomenon and it is direct broadcasting by satellite
(DBS) that is sending out seismic tremors of an intensity such as to make
the arrival of Channel 4 seem a very small earthquake with practically
nobody hurt.

I am going to suggest that it is time we directed our attention not so
much to the messenger as to the message; that the purpose of every messenger, no matter how fast he flies nor how sophisticated his means of
delivery, is to say something of interest when he arrives; that there is
no point in sending unwanted messages by new and very expensive
delivery services; in short, that the new technology must be there to
serve news, entertainment and the arts, and not vice versa.

The preoccupation with means rather than ends, which is inherent
in the concept of information technology, is only one example of the
influence of monetarist thought emanating from the seat of government
itself. The first problem for a simple citizen is to descry the range within
which it is deemed appropriate to apply market forces and to privatise.
Oil? British Telecom? Yes. Education and health have been mentioned
out loud, and there have been whispers about the BBC. For the monetarist sees broadcasting as an economic phenomenon. The BBC 'costs'
the licence payer £700 million per annum. ITV turns over £1,000

million per annum as part of the nation's marketing industry. Both give employment. Both save the Arts Council money, in particular the BBC's sponsorship of orchestras. Broadcasting provides the electorate with a daily stream of video material, as the gas board supplies gas. The monetarist believes that to control broadcasting in order to nurture programmes of quality is elitist nonsense. All broadcasting should be exposed to market forces: ratings should be the sole criterion.

There is an alternative view which is just as mercenary and which explains more truthfully the value of our trade in terms simple enough for the monetarist to understand. It is that in the arts and entertainment Britain has perhaps its most thriving post-war business, barring oil. To convince him of this we must put a cash value on the arts and entertainment as offered by television and, outside television, upon books, films, pictures, music, our heritage of great houses and the like. We know the market value of a Turner to be £7 million plus; Chippendale and the Beatles are also comparatively easy to value. But what about Sir Christopher Wren and George Friederic Handel? Each item and each author must be given a capital valuation, measured in terms of profitability or return on capital employed. Yesterday's popular art became in time the posh art of today; jazz, once despised by any cultured person, has now itself became a cult; *Romeo and Juliet* becomes *West Side Story* and, conversely, Bach's Air on a G String sells cigars.

Our political masters will never see broadcasting as an end in itself until we can persuade them that the true value of our business lies in our programmes. Currently they value it mainly as a means of financing the leap from the old to the new technology, but it is now clear that the first phase in this plan, the plan to cable Great Britain, has aborted. The reason is simple; not many people are willing to pay something like £12 a month for a service that, except for feature films, is made up of the cheapest available programmes, mostly old American repeats, pop videos and the sweepings of the television and entertainment industries. Thus there is likely to be little or no significant increase in the number of British homes using cable within the next ten years unless cable is given government support to develop its interactive role, as it is in most other European countries.

Similarly, alone among the EEC countries, the UK is preparing to launch the direct broadcast satellite from the broad back of British broadcasting, with a little help from its friends but with no government subsidy. Once again it is worth noting that the programmes which DBS will carry have scarcely been mentioned.

To see the dilemma DBS poses to our present system of broadcasting it is necessary to indulge for a moment in a fantasy. Suppose the mighty engine takes to the air punctually in 1988, firing on all transponders and emitting every promised watt, and suppose then that the whole of BBC1 and ITV were switched from terrestrial to satellite transmission. No *Coronation Street*, no *News at Ten*, no *Dallas* or *Dynasty*, not a single *Ronnie*, unless you spend £20 per month to rent a dish and a black box. If the brute force of the duopoly were used in this way, leaving 20 million terrestrial clients with BBC2, Channel 4 and the Open University, while there might not be rioting in the streets there would, I think, be some grumbling. But penetration would be terrific, matching the penetration of ITV, colour and VCRs.

Now let us take a more realistic view; namely, that nothing new is shown on DBS except feature films, which would be only a little newer, more numerous and more accessible than at present on off-air broadcasting. The other channels would carry repeats of 'the best of ITV' and 'the best of BBC'. Then penetration would be slow. Delete the feature films and you will only penetrate the thin layer of technological buffs who like to spend money on quadraphonic sound or on tracking space shots from the potting-shed.

There is, however, a middle course which would avoid the cries of 'No deprivation!' and which would not breach this principle so rightly engraved on the heart of the BBC. This would be to show programmes other than feature films first on DBS. Supposing *The Thorn Birds* and *The Jewel in the Crown* were first shown on DBS, scheduled harmoniously on separate days, and repeated on BBCI and ITV a month later? Supposing *Coronation Street* were shown on Sundays and Tuesdays from the sky and on the present statutory Mondays and Wednesdays on earth? Suppose you could have discovered who shot J.R. a week before your neighbour? Surely such privileged information would rate equal in the Surbiton social scale at least to the ownership of a jacuzzi?

The truth is that you cannot sensibly calculate the rate of penetration of DBS until you first decide on the programme policy. To speak of 3.6 million penetration in ten years is vain; this figure could be reached in one year or never depending upon programme policy.

I believe that, unlike cable, DBS will take wing, sooner or later. Logic supports the idea that, sooner or later, all broadcast signals will emanate from a source in the sky rather than be toted over hill and dale by hundreds of little bits of Meccano stuck on the earth's crust. But there can be no point in embarking on this £500 million enterprise if DBS is going to offer repeats of the same stuff we now transmit on earth, plus an earlier view of some feature films. Traditional real-time events – Wimbledon, Trooping the Colour – cannot be moved without deprivation. Series, serials and comedies can. Add to these the many real-time events which are not now covered by television at all and which viewers would pay good money to see. Add news, perhaps in large quantities, and you may have the basis for a programme service that would begin to justify the big spend.

It should be noted in passing that the spend-per-hour presently proposed for DBS is derisory: an average of £8,000 per hour for a programme service for which the client will have to subscribe £20 per month. This £20 compares with under £4 a month for the current terrestrial licence fee, which delivers four channels upon which an average of some £35,000 per hour is spent. So the DBS client will be asked to spend five times as much for programmes that are made for almost one-fifth of the cost.

At this point in the developing story of DBS, both the programme philosophy and the financial equation look wrong. In typical British fashion, the management shortly to be appointed will inherit a project which appears to be committed to hardware that is unnecessarily expensive and upon which £50 million of development money has already been spent, and with no viable programme plans. There are at the moment twenty-one runners lined up for the DBS marathon: fifteen ITV companies, five independents at one remove from broadcasting and the BBC.

The future of broadcasting appears to be placed more securely than ever in the hands of the duopoly. There are signs of some internal problems. If one listens carefully outside the confessional boxes frequented by the managing directors of the ITV companies and the BBC board of management, one can overhear indications that several sins are currently in commission, none of them deadly but which, when compounded one with another, may well pose a threat to the future as great as cable, DBS or Rupert in the sky with the gems of yesteryear.

The first sin, as yet only a peccadillo, is the increasing relish shown by programme-makers for what one might call the O&M department of television. To do well in councils and committees is becoming as much a measure of success as the making of good programmes. 'Sorry to postpone the programme meeting,' a weary-voiced executive will say, 'I've got to get my paper on Channel 4 offers ready for Controllers so that Council can give a view before the next PPC.'

If the top people in broadcasting become organisation men, if they are solely interested in profit or in efficiency, they will fall. For the laws governing the production of good programmes are mysterious and demand from time to time that efficiency should take second place. Efficiency is the enemy of originality and it can smother talent, which is of its nature nonconformist.

My next sin is that of idolatry, the worship of the false god, ratings. They are taken as gospel, the gospel according to St Barb, by the large and influential industry that has set itself up around the purchase and sale of television advertising time. It is natural for Fleet Street to whip up excitement by proclaiming triumph or disaster for BBC or ITV, but why should we join in?

Since vision and enterprise are generally counted as virtues, it may be fair to see their opposite qualities – timidity, overcautious, what you will – as sins, at least as sins of omission. There are those who would say that the BBC's greatest present problem lies in its lack of financial resources. The BBC has said it could not afford the cost of *The Jewel in the Crown*. The facts are that the direct cost of fifteen hours of *Jewel* was £5.5 million. Before £1 million was spent, an almost equal amount had been received from pre-sale. During its run the total direct cost of the series was recouped from UK transmission and overseas advances. Today, six months later, there is a total profit of £1.5 million, with two or three sizeable markets still to sell. This kind of operation is open to the BBC, and it is more productive than cost-cutting. The most hard-bitten among us, if he be honest, must succumb to admiration when he surveys the BBC's huge output of good professional programming, and, in the light of this, the support it gets from overseas finance seems modest and may indicate that this is perhaps where BBC enterprise (or Enterprises) is lacking.

Not so Channel 4, who have adroitly called in the new world to redress what would be a negative balance had they stuck to the old system. We must all rejoice in the success of Film on Four and of the independents generally, whose collective budget has been enlarged by taking world sales into account in advance, although I believe there is often some debate as to where the benefit should fall.

A further sin of omission is in our failure effectively to challenge the current threats to the freedom of expression. During the last decade the opposing forces have made great advances. The protection of government has become undiscriminating and obsessional, with the resulting suspicion that frequently the motive is not so much to protect the security of the state as the political comfort of ministers. Section 2 of the Official Secrets Act stands inviolate on the statute book and a Freedom of Information Act seems farther away than ever.

Similarly, we must be vigilant in resisting the increasing proclivity of governments to manage news. We should be aware that broadcasters are pushed insensibly to favour the government in power. Because the minister is at the controls he will always get more time than his opposite number, who, at least temporarily, is a backseat driver. It is not only that. Support for the government is often born of a patriotic desire to see certain government policies succeed, to see the nation prosper. More venal motives alleged against the broadcasting establishments, such as the desire for a higher licence fee or a lower level of levy, are, of course, false. However that may be, the mild socialist breeze that was stirring in the media world fifteen years ago has quite died away and there is now a brisk wind rising from the opposite quarter. This is not yet felt so much on screen, but in the draughty corridors behind it. It carries with it a coarsening of the perception of society and a more ready acceptance that might must be right, and it seems to enervate the resistance of some broadcasters to the pressures that come filtering down from most employers in ITV and most top people anywhere. The Establishment will always believe that the first duty of broadcasting is to support its view.

So, to return to the Establishment, the economic establishment, how can we persuade them to support investment in the arts and entertainment and to encourage their main financiers, television, in this work? If they were to monkey about with the BBC licence fee or the ITV levy, or to throw television more open to market forces, there is a danger that they would upset the delicate balance of a broadcasting system whose financial success rests upon the quality of its programmes, and vice versa. If we were driven into the downward spiral of the network giants in America or of the popular press nearer home, British television would change its character and lose its international markets.

The government's belief that just around the corner lies an age of burgeoning prosperity for Britain, arising from her leadership as a manufacturer and exporter in the world emporium of the New Information Technology, which is opening shortly, is a pathetic fallacy, a triumph of hope over experience which no reasoned argument can disprove. But every morsel of common sense would indicate to ordinary clients such as you and me that, whereas the British genius for invention will continue to thrive, the big battalions from America and Japan will continue to take over the commercial application of our inventive power and will apply their irresistible market forces to exploit our inventions in the rest of the world.

In all respects save one we are outgunned: we have not the size of China, the military power of Russia or the industrial power of Japan, but in the matter of entertainment and the performing arts we are top dogs. British theatre, British television, British films have built a respect for British values which has an incalculable effect upon the psychology of the transatlantic relationship. It is the last field of world leadership left to us, and we neglect it at our peril. And as for us, the managers in broadcasting, we too must be mindful that for us the people who create the programmes are the most important people in the world, and it is our task to create the right conditions for them.

This lecture is not a memorial to a John Reith or to a Robert Fraser, or to any of the great architects of British broadcasting. It is in memory of James MacTaggart, a man who made programmes, and it is people like him that all broadcasting structures and all forms of technology should be designed to serve.

The James MacTaggart Lecture 1985

Reflections on Working in Film and Television

John Schlesinger*

John Schlesinger's lecture is based around a 'few observations about my time in this business' working in television and film. Schlesinger readily conceeds that he could never 'understand the difference' between 'making television' and 'making a film for television'. The one difference is the distinctive audience reaction to the two media: the cinema creates a 'special experience'.

Schlesinger began in television working on *Tonight* ('I got the sack') and with Huw Weldon on *Monitor*; the year with *Monitor* was 'among the happiest I've ever spent in this profession'. Schlesinger went to America to make *Midnight Cowboy*. On arrival, he recalls his mix of embarrassment and delight. Embarrassment which prompted him to hide with Julie Christie during the premiere of *Far From the Madding Crowd*, which flopped badly in the States; delight and irrepressible excitement at meeting celebrities – 'it is very exciting when you're at a traffic light and Hitchcock's in the next car'. Other films followed: *Gorky Park, Marathon Man, The Englishman Abroad* and *Yanks*. Schlesinger confesses to not enjoying shooting a film, but he loved 'dreaming it all up with the writer', the editing and 'the fantasy into reality when you're talking about design'.

Schlesinger regrets the move to the conglomerate ownership of Hollywood which has replaced 'crazy moguls who believed in the artist' with 'frightened committees' and 'grey-suited gentlemen . . . [who] are scared of enthusiasm and passion'. Decisions about scripts as well as funding are harder to secure now. The British film industry faces difficulties

* John Schlesinger was a film director whose works include *Midnight Cowboy* (1969), *Sunday Bloody Sunday* (1971) and *Marathon Man* (1976). He died on 25 July 2003.

but Schlesinger argues these are overstated. For his part, Schlesinger declares, 'I will carry on working where I can on either side of the Atlantic . . . I love the show. I don't think I like the biz, too much.'

□

I think that you really only learn, in our business, by doing it. I'm not really a great theorist. So I'm going to make a few observations about my time in this business, which may perhaps be of interest, or amusing or helpful.

I was very grateful for my years in television because it really was like being in weekly rep as an actor, which I'd also done. I used to be given one day to go out and make a programme for *Tonight*. We had two on the camera and I was the sound recordist. There was no time for second thoughts: first thoughts were the only ones you could do. And it taught me an awful lot about summing up what I felt about a place, or a situation, or a character. There was a kind of assembly line in the *Tonight* show, but I used to insist on finishing my films myself. I don't mean there wasn't an editor, but I found that the actual dubbing of them, deciding what music was played on them, was the only way to make anything work for me. I think you've always got to fight for what you really believe in and what you want to say: after a year, I got the sack.

Mercifully, Huw Weldon was waiting in the wings with a much better job and the year I spent on *Monitor* was among the happiest I've ever spent in this profession, even though I had always an eye on the big screen. I've loved opera since I was a child and, while we were doing *Monitor*, I wanted to make a film about a wonderful scratch company that came from Italy to play Theatre Royal, Drury Lane. A cameraman came to sum up the backstage positions at Drury Lane but said it wasn't possible to shoot there. He went back to Ealing Studios, reported this, and they said: 'You must cancel the programme.' Huw Weldon, who was nothing if not as determined as I was to break the rules, supported me. We got a renegade camera who said: 'There's such a thing as fast-step and a hand-held basher' and we made the film which got me, actually, indirectly, into feature-film-making. So I'm glad that we won that particular battle.

While I was at *Monitor*, I got my first glimpse of great stars: people like Callas. I remember her at rehearsal, wanting to see how she looked on her monitor, and so she had it moved in front of her. She sat there very imperiously and said: 'Let me see camera 1. Higher, higher – basta

. . .' as she saw her image there. Then camera 2 and so on. I saw first hand how some of the people that I've since met have known how they should look: the great stars. Years later in Hollywood when I was visiting Mae West in her dressing room, a friend of mine was photographing her and she was simply saying, 'Lower, honey, lower with the camera.' Then Mae turned to me and said, 'I'm very into ESP you know, but that's not a drug.'

It was while I was still at the BBC that I used to have permanent rows with a certain lady who was a very distinguished person. When the programme was going out we would have a discussion about the difference of attitude towards television and film. I used to make films, they were shot on 35mm, cut the normal way, dubbed the normal way, but she said, 'You're making television.' I said, 'No, I'm making a film for television.' And she said, 'No, you're making television.' And I said, 'No, it's a film being shown on television.' And I can't understand the difference and I never have been able to understand the difference.

There are a few simple rules, I think, that in television with a film you have to get your audience, quickly. Maybe you stay somewhat closer; your composition has to be simpler – you haven't much time for atmosphere. But I've never really understood the great difference that there is except what it does, perhaps, to an audience. It is quite extraordinary how familiarity with surroundings changes an audience's perception of what they're looking at. So the special experience one can get in the cinema with a lot of people and a big screen and a darkened room is very different at home. So that great pieces of work go, perhaps unrecognised – perhaps even that's wrong – but their reaction is different. Of course, nowadays particularly, people who can't afford to go to the cinema can stay at home and see films. I think great events, which are one of the great strengths of television, which we can all share now, are altered by familiarity. The first time we all got up at four in the morning, or whatever it was, to see the moon landing. The second time not so quick. Third, we were a bit bored. Fourth, it was likely to be a disaster so we all rushed back to our sets, as I remember.

I have to confess I am not a very great TV watcher. I have some likes and dislikes: I very much like the news, perhaps that's a question of age. I like documentaries; I like to see old footage; I like interviews when the interviewee is given more space than the interviewer. I'm not a great watcher of taped drama because it seems to be neither one thing nor the other. But memorable experiences I have had: they are usually to do with the human condition. One was a programme called *On Giant's Shoulders*, which seemed to me one of the very best films I've seen on television. It dealt with a thalidomide child, played by himself, and two actors who played with him – Brian Pringle and Judi Dench – so beautifully that it's something that stands out in my memory as an experience I will not forget.

I got into films through my opera film initially because I was, as it were, discovered by a wonderful Italian producer who has been living in this country for years called Joseph Ialli. Now I owe a very great deal to Joseph Ialli, as well as to Huw Weldon. The heritage that we had in the early sixties was a patchy one, I think. We've had periods of great documentaries. The Corda period, the Ealing period under Balcon,[1] which was very special when he managed to forge an image of England, both during the war and afterwards, which was something specifically British.

But I think that entrepreneurial talent is thin on the ground in this country. Joe Ialli, who was very good on script shape, knew where in the script something would need attention, but wasn't so interested in the selling of the movie. He used to take me along. It's no use making a film unless it's going to be seen, so I had a lot to do with the selling of films. I think Britain is rather embarrassed by marketing – they think it's a bit vulgar. They don't really pay too much attention to it. Balcon did. Balcon had wonderful artists design his posters – all on view right now in the Museum of Modern Art in New York, where they're running a retrospective.

I remember when Joe and I made *Billy Liar*. We went to see the posters but the head of Anglo Amalgamated had just suffered a heart attack, and the head of publicity was using this sickness as an excuse and saying, 'Don't make too much fuss . . .' So this very sick man was leaning on an easel and then started to make his presentation. And every time one more ghastly poster was flipped over, I said, 'But that's terrib . . .' 'Ssh . . .,' he'd say. And that's how I think they got those terrible posters through that day; I resolved to fight ever since.

I never thought I'd go to America to make movies. I read *Midnight Cowboy* as a book, and thought if I was going to make a film in America, this would be something that a Brit could do, since it's about somebody from out of town, with a fantasy of what New York is like. Maybe I could do that.

My arrival in the States was extremely unprepossessing. *Madding Crowd*, which subsequently became quite a success over here, opened in New York to disastrous reviews and we were all on the plane the next day to Hollywood for the premiere there. They couldn't quite cancel it. Julie Christie and I sat in a limousine saying we'd been in Dorset for months, knee deep in shit, and here we are in an even bigger mess. But we couldn't resist, as we hid in the manager's office, peering out, because they kept saying, 'Oh, Edward G. Robinson's arrived' or whoever, and of course it was my first visit there, and it is very exciting when you're at a traffic light and Hitchcock's in the next car. It's a very strange feeling.

Classics. They're dangerous to do. At a party in Hollywood after the disastrous opening of *Madding Crowd*, I met Ruth Gordon — a very ballsy lady — and she said, 'You made *Madding Crowd*, didn't you? That'll teach you to leave those fucking classics alone.' I saw her a few weeks ago — she's over ninety, wears mini-skirts and is quite remarkable. But the flop was felt. You feel a failure in America. My God you do. Because I suppose, you know, success is a god and failure is a disease. I think here, it's the reverse. The British have a slight nasty smell under their nose about anybody who's had a success. I find both equally reprehensible.

The classic belongs to you, of course. You've got your vision of how a great classic book should be turned into a movie. The literary tradition of this country is so strong that I think that's one of the reasons that we haven't got such a strong visual one. Americans have a much stronger visual tradition. You can see America everywhere. I went really finally to prepare *Midnight Cowboy* and to work on the screenplay. Everywhere in America is a place of great excitement for me — amusement, tragedy, life is lived on the streets. I like human reactions. Observation, which is one of the great tools of a director, is my hobby as well as my profession. I like to store up a kind of mental sketchbook of things that I've experienced, seen, dig them out on certain occasions to push them into film. They are extraordinary, a sort of repository of what one sees — it's very important. But I think a lot of people now, particularly young directors, are not so much experiencing what they observe, but using their reference points of what they see on television or in old movies. They don't go out and look at life. I regret the passing of that.

I think that in the process of making a film, there are certain favourite parts I have — I don't actually like shooting very much. I love dreaming it all up with the writer and the collaboration which that entails, I love the editing process, when everybody becomes 'it', I like the fantasy into reality when you're talking about design and how people live. I think that when you're creating characters, one of the things you ask yourself is 'how do they live?' Watch any of those television programmes about the Kennedys and it's extraordinary how lacking in detail, design is. And detail is what I think film is all about.

The same happened with *The Englishman Abroad*. We couldn't afford to go abroad; we had to approximate Russia in some way. *Gorky Park* approximated it by going to Finland. We went to Glasgow and to Dundee, where we could approximate a look for Russia, but the most important thing to get the detail right in *The Englishman Abroad* was to hear some Russian spoken. We went round all sorts of clubs where Lithuanian and Ukrainian people hung out and we found the most marvellous crowd of people. So we had a certain reality in that film, from all of that detail.

Now America has changed vastly in how we deal with front office. Front office is a perennial problem because everybody that we deal with is changing all the time. The musical chairs that is played in Hollywood is alarming. You send a script to one person, then the next day he's out of a job and gone somewhere else. And I'd sung 'Mammy' in front of more front office desks, I think, than I've had hot dinners, hoping to get the project off the ground. There are all sorts of A and B lists, party lists, whether you're hot or cold. Directors, writers, actors move down like a whore's drawers.

The conglomerates, of course, have taken over so many of the companies that one's no longer dealing with those extraordinary crazy moguls who believed in the artist, but with frightened committees, who are terrified of their own position. It's difficult to get a film financed anywhere, and more difficult than ever in Hollywood. I've only had interference that was directly political once, and that was on *Marathon Man*. Gulf + Western had an oil deal in Paraguay and we, in the film, state that the Nazi played by Laurence Olivier is living in Paraguay and they insisted that we changed it to Uruguay, even though Uruguay has no jungle. But what could I do?

I think the grey-suited gentlemen that we all have to deal with are scared of enthusiasm and passion, but it's something we need desperately. While I was making *Marathon Man*, Colin Welland came to visit the set and said, 'I've got an idea for a film,' which was *Yanks* but I had already committed verbally to doing *Coming Home*. Suddenly Colin's idea sparked me so enormously that I wanted desperately to come home and make a British film. To make *Yanks* was a terrible problem. No English company would listen to us. We were going out singing 'Mammy' so often either in Los Angeles or New York trying to inject enthusiasm into United Artists and Universal that they finally succumbed, provided that we had some other money in. And the other money that came in was Deutsche Marks from dentists and doctors in Germany. So there was this ironic situation of the Germans and the Americans financing a film about wartime Britain. But we got it made.

British artists, I think, are allowed much more easily to move from one media to another. There is no stigma attached to moving from television, the theatre, the fringe to any of the commercials as far as the directors are concerned. Can't do it in America. It's very important that we should do it and have experiences in all fields, because one is learning all the time, no question. And the versatility of the British is something to be treasured and celebrated. I haven't really time to go too deeply into the situation of actors American and actors British. I love both, sometimes. I think the British actor has a classical background and the American actor has a kind of instinctual background; the American actor needs to be, rather than to act. I discovered that when I was working with Olivier and Hoffman in *Marathon Man* and it was quite interesting. Hoffman needs to be: he needed a sauna by the side of the stage so he could get up a sweat, or run round the block several times, or even drink too much red wine so that he could feel out of it. Olivier would simply say, 'Why can't he just act?' and that story is true.

With *Englishman*, which was perhaps one of the happiest experiences that I've had for a long time, I was working with a script that I absolutely adored. I had dinner with my friend Coral Browne, who told me about her meeting with Guy Burgess and said, 'Do you think this would make a film?' I said, 'No, I don't,' and I said something which I wouldn't often say because I love the cinema: I said, 'I think it's an ideal film for television.' 'She said, 'Well, I've told it to Alan Bennett and he's writing it.' Alan sent it to me and I knew that whatever happened I had to do it.

It was like a time capsule going back to the BBC. Nothing had really changed. But perhaps the great thing was not working with 150 people and nobody quarrelling about the size of their caravan because there weren't any. We had three weeks and there was still time for fifteen takes. The crew were brilliantly organised. It was such a relief to work with that smallness of number and I wished so utterly that there was a way in our business of cutting down. The success was enormous for us all. I found, nevertheless, that I still missed the big screen when it was screened at the Museum of Modern Art.

Well, what now? There's a lot of talk about the demise of the British film industry, which I don't believe to be true. There is a lot of extraordinarily independent and individual work going on. There is finance of sorts available in this country. It's still a struggle. But there are people making personal statements, which is what one really wants to see, whether it's intended for a large audience, which isn't any bad thing, or a slightly more esoteric one. I think the fact that Channel 4 has financed films, both for itself and for the big screen, is splendid and more of it should happen. Why can't the BBC and ITV follow the example of ZDF[2] in Germany, who have made so many films for the cinema?

We've got to solve those problems – whether they're with technicians or actors or writers or directors or unions – that stand in the way of greater fusion between television and film. I think it's terribly important. And I suppose one has the vain hope that a government that hasn't shown itself actually particularly supportive of the arts might feel more committed to the film industry and to the television industry. But as far as I'm concerned, I will carry on working where I can on either side of the Atlantic. My knee pads may get a bit worn now and again, and if you think it's sentimental to say this I don't really care. I'm still – thank God – excited when I see lights and a camera on any street, on any building and I'm still curious to know what's being shot, whether it's a commercial or television or a feature. I don't care what it is. I still stop and look. And I hope that that will last for a long time. I love the show. I don't think I like the biz, too much.

Notes

1. Michael Balcon (1896–1977) is one of the most important figures in British cinema. While at MGM's British production unit, he made *A Yank at Oxford* (1937), *Goodbye Mr Chips* (1937) and *The Citadel* (1937).
2. Zweites Deutsches Fernsehen is a public television channel in Germany.

The James MacTaggart Lecture 1986

'Opening up the Fourth Front': Micro Drama and the Rejection of Naturalism

Troy Kennedy Martin*

Troy Kennedy Martin picks up the cudgels first wielded by John McGrath a decade earlier in his 'swingeing attack on naturalism'. He defines naturalism in television as 'actors talking in contemporary dress against a contemporaneous background' intended to offer 'a replication of real life. In dramatic terms it is the mediation of story through dialogue'; he concludes that naturalism is 'basically phoney'.

Kennedy Martin proposes to open up a 'fourth front' alongside plays, series and serials, which would deal with 'micro drama' composed of 'dozens of fragments of drama, shards of experience made and put out very quickly'. Micro drama should embrace three key elements of advertising commercials which contrast sharply with television drama. First, ad copywriters condense information while playwrights tend to expand it. Second, in television drama the budget contracts with the length of the piece but in adverts there is no necessary connection between cost and duration. Finally, adverts reinforce their message through repetition whereas in television drama a repeat is a failure to provide something new. Kennedy Martin envisages a number of advantages to these micro dramas: repetition reinforces impact but also defrays costs. But the micro dramas should also employ similar styles 'in which time itself is altered and naturalism goes out of the window'.

Kennedy Martin offers an illustrative exemplar: a drama about unemployment and the closure of the shipbuiding industry in Sunderland. The

* Troy Kennedy Martin is a television screenwriter, director and producer who created the television series *Z Cars* (1962–5). His other work includes *The Edge of Darkness* (1985), *The Sweeney* (1975) and *Diary of a Young Man* (1964), with John McGrath.

options are (1) to commission a writer, director and cast and shoot the drama over two years, or (2) commission ten four-minute dramas from ten directors and transmit within six months. The brief for the small dramas is to make sense of the human suffering consequent on mass unemployment. They should capture 'images that will stay in the retina' wrapped in ideas which are capable of being repeated at least twelve times. Kennedy Martin suggests that these 'small dramas' should complement not replace existing dramatic forms and serve as 'a conduit for unrepresented forces'.

□

Ten years ago, at the first MacTaggart, John McGrath made a swingeing attack on naturalism. It was doomed to failure, because he attacked without a viable alternative. Although, he did mark the ground for a future assault (which is why I am here this evening). And twenty-five years ago, Jimmy MacTaggart, after whom this lecture is lovingly called, set forth from Glasgow to join me in London on a similar quest. We were going to destroy naturalism, if possible, before Christmas. We were, like the Blues Brothers, 'on a mission from God'.

We didn't understand the nature of the problem. That in attacking an aesthetic structure, we were challenging deep-rooted cultural assumptions, both on the right and on the left. It was an age of media innocence. In his MacTaggart Lecture, John said of us, 'What Jimmy and Troy did was to create a method of writing, directing, designing, sound plotting and lighting, specifically for the lens of the television camera and not for the Opera House . . . And there were other exciting features,' he went on to say (in a rather flattering way). 'The liberation of the medium meant that a lot of other sources of entertainment, pleasure, even of art, could be put to use. (By allowing a character to narrate his own story, and to relate it to images, you could actually write with a bit of verve.) Music: not for background, but as a statement. Or animation cartoons helped to say what happened. Or movement – stylised actors' movement.' In fact, many of the techniques which we were trying to develop at that time are now commonplace in commercials and pop videos.

Of course, it could be argued that in our loony way, we were trying to anticipate film, trying to insert into our Heath Robinson, pre-production process, the kind of items which would have been at the tips of our fingers in any facility house today. And this is true, but we were also trying to work out specific ways of dealing with and exploiting the limitations of the medium. We were, in the words of Tarkovsky, 'trying to appropriate time'. We were trying to deconstruct it, mould it, sculpt it, with very inadequate tools.

The live studio world in which we lived was a world of innocence because in it we could dream of the magic we would create when the equipment became available to do so: to dub, edit, pre-record and split screen. Sooner or later we knew those facilities would be invented and they would be ours. When Ken Loach and Jimmy MacTaggart and Peter Duguid and John and myself finished *Diary of a Young Man*, I did think that we had set the agenda for the next ten years. But it was not to be; it was the naturalism of *Z Cars* and the realism of the *Wednesday Play* which was going to do that.

I ought to explain at this point what I mean by 'naturalism' and by 'realism'. There are many complicated definitions which relate to the nineteenth-century novel, but at the risk of sounding foolish, I think I can define naturalism in television as actors talking in contemporary dress against a contemporaneous background. Their purpose being to make you feel you are watching a replication of real life. In dramatic terms, it is the mediation of story through dialogue. Naturalism is basically phoney.

No one who watches a naturalist play today can possibly fool himself that he is watching real life. I suppose that, years ago, in grainy black and white, with northern accents, it looked real enough. But today naturalism is essentially fictional. But it's never allowed to admit it, because if it did, like Catch 22, its credibility would collapse and it would cease to be naturalism.

Television naturalism comes from the theatre; television realism is a product of film. It sets out to do the same thing as naturalism – to make you think you are watching a replication of real life – but without the emphasis on dialogue. Fifty years of silence taught film-makers to speak in images and the images which film craftsmen produce of reality looks less artificial than the naturalist counterparts.

But naturalism does occur in film, when the images become generalised and lose their specific quality and the actors begin to talk too much – the kind of formula we now expect from Hollywood TV series. And the great watershed which was to divide TV between pre- and postproduction also divided two types of naturalism, the first coming from theatre and the second from a diluted version of the Hollywood movie.

So the great battle in television in the sixties was not between realism and naturalism, but between naturalism and non-naturalism. In those days, when naturalism stood for plot, dialogue and character, the antithesis was the novel, which stood for narrative and interior development.

While in the eighties when naturalism is now represented as a watered-down version of the Hollywood movie, the antithesis lies in the images of pop videos and the post-modern collages of commercials.

And these events which took place around 1965 signalled the end of the era of post-production. It coincided with the arrival at the BBC of Sidney Newman and the creation of the *Wednesday Play*. And although the *Wednesday Play* was produced by Jimmy, who did some of his most imaginative work there, it soon became the focus of oppositional writing and in time came to be identified with the realist school of Loach/Garnett/Allen and, later, Gordon Newman.

While the *Wednesday Play* went from strength to strength, series and serials went down the drain. There seemed to be an unconscious pact between the two departments, in which plays took on all the radical drama and series became middle of the road. Thus for fifteen years the most powerful weapon in the writers' armoury, the series, was left in the hands of the centre right. And while the Plays Department was barely out of the news in its confrontations with Mrs Whitehouse, the Series Department manufactured year in and year out, a pre-Thatcherite pap which began to cover the country in a mantle of male monotony. *Barlow*, *Maigret* and *Colditz* littered the pages of the *Radio Times*, and people like me were no longer welcome in the new offices.

Furthermore, as a result of the new post-production techniques, at least some of the writers' input could now be done by producers and script editors; any mistakes could now be rectified in the cutting room. A new media-ocracy began to develop: the creation of stories gradually became the responsibility of committees. Thus the miracle of post-production, which was going to bring such magic to television, became an institution which blunted talent and hid the incompetence of management and essentially reinforced the safe, the conservative and the bland.

It was against this background that John McGrath gave the first MacTaggart Lecture. He was deeply unhappy about the all-pervasive presence of naturalism and particularly critical of *Days of Hope* and *Bill Brand* as two political series which he felt had become blurred and defocused by the use of the naturalist idiom. I think what he failed to realise at the time, and what we can see with hindsight, is that these two series were not the end of the road for a genre which had begun with the *Wednesday Play*, but the first sign of a revival in series which over the next seven years was to give us such pieces as *Rock Follies*, *Gangsters*, *Out*, *Pennies from Heaven*, *Law and Order* and the *Boys from the Black Stuff*. These original drama series moved in to fill the vacuum caused by the crisis in single plays, a crisis which John had correctly defined, although he was unable at the time to suggest what could be done to solve it. And it is this which I wanted to address during the rest of my allotted time.

On the four-month shoot of *Edge of Darkness* the unit worked in some of the worst areas of unemployment in the north and in Wales.

In one Welsh industrial estate the design team decamped just before dawn to build a set in one of the deserted sheds, when they were surrounded by a ghostly wave of about a hundred men who stood in silence watching them work. They were unemployed and they were angry that their workplace had been reduced to nothing more than a temporary set for a BBC series. It struck me that there was no longer a connection between what we were trying to do and what these people were going through. And that even if there was it could no longer be sustained by the odd series.

And I began to think there must be another kind of drama series with scaled-down crews, living off the land who will bring back some kind of understanding of what is going on in those places.

I also thought we should open a fourth front, alongside plays, series and serials, which would deal specifically with micro drama, that is it should consist of dozens of fragments of drama, shards of experience made and put out very quickly, time being an important element of this operation.

Just over a month ago, Desmond Christy in *The Guardian* reviewed a BBC2 studio play and said, 'It's a shame that after so much hard work, the result should be so unmemorable. The usual explanation given is that it has been so tastefully made that it has lost any individuality. But I have another reason,' he said. 'Television, cinema and pop videos have speeded up our ability to absorb what we see. And in consequence, there are many of us who now find some thirty-second advertisements more interesting to watch than a 55-minute play. 'Perhaps we should review the television ads,' he said. They are – absurd as it may seem – the real plays of today. I don't want to see commercials masquerading as plays, but I would like to use them as a reference point for the development of this new kind of micro drama.

I would also like to look at commercials and pop videos for a moment and note three differences between them and TV drama. First, the copywriter is in the business of condensing information while the playwright, one often feels, is in the business of expanding it. Second, if we look at resources, we see the same contradiction. The rule in television drama is that the shorter the piece, the less the budget. In commercials, cost and length are not commensurate. Finally, if we look at reinforcement, in order to be effective, the ad has to be seen again and again. This runs counter to the conventional television view which is that a repeat is a sign of failure to provide anything new.

I think micro drama should embrace all these three advertising principles. They must be capable of being repeated time and time again. Not only does this reinforce their impact, but it is the only way in which cost can be defrayed and they should employ similar styles in which time itself is altered and naturalism goes out of the window.

Given that the technology, the talent and the resources are available, what would happen if they were used to construct short bursts of energy, micro dramas, in which the content was not dictated by the need to sell music or beer, but reflected an exuberant social, political or aesthetic point of view. Is it possible to reflect through them something more of reality than that which is currently available? Would it lead to new ways of looking at ourselves?

There are two provisos I wish to make before answering these questions. First, I do not envisage these micro dramas broadcast in isolation. In the normal run of programming, they would have zero visibility. That is what happened to Mike Leigh's little playlets ten years ago in the BBC. Ideally they should form part of a flow which would enhance their qualities and be buttressed by other similar pieces. To begin with that would involve some kind of showcase – probably late night. Later it might include the whole evening. Second, I think the channels are going to change, are going to become faster, more segmented, because younger people will take over who are not in awe of the great taboos which today invest news and current affairs. And when I consider the drive of all these young film-makers to deconstruct the framework (of reality) which is being imposed upon them like a great cage, then I think that these short charges of drama will have great effect. Antibodies in a machine which is prone to misleading us, winding us up, cheering us up, giving us hell, reaching parts of our experience that other programmes cannot reach. Yes, I think they have a lot to offer.

Let me try and construct a notional example. And I will stay with oppositional drama forms for a moment, although it is by no means essential to my argument.

Let us say that BBC drama have found a new Bleasdale in the northeast. He has come up with a six-part series about the destruction of the shipbuilding industry in Sunderland as seen through the eyes of a family, which is itself breaking up. The Series Department want to assign a top director and hope to assemble a great cast, and shoot it in the autumn of '87 for transmission in '88.

Meanwhile Channel X have commissioned ten four-minute dramas from ten directors. The brief is to find ways of making sense of the human suffering, dislocation, bewilderment caused by mass unemployment in the north. The Channel wants images. Images which will stay in the retina, wrapped in ideas capable of being repeated, Channel X are looking for at least twelve showings of each piece. So Channel X hope to get 480 minutes of programming going out against the 300 minutes of the BBC. Furthermore, unlike the BBC, they will transmit within six months.

A way of harnessing the shows has not yet been devised. But it is hoped that they can be fed into the showcase which they intend to run every night – post ten o'clock over the winter period.

The ten little films savage the trade-union movement, the Labour Party and the Tories, the local councils, the City of London and Parliament, but they do more than that. They reveal a world beyond politics, which is hard, frightening and burning with anger and frustration, but also with determination and life. They are transmitted after the dickens of a fuss and are slipped into the general flow of the other programmes, which are equally strong in their own way and which also generate flak. They continue to be repeated over a period of two or three months bringing a cohesive reinforced picture of the north back into the national consciousness, one which is difficult to erase.

Meanwhile, the new Bleasdale, equally forceful, is continuing on its way, looking for co-production money and scouting locations. They don't expect any repercussions. Because by the time it comes out, a Labour government will be in power and they can blame years of Tory misrule.

Now I want to underline that I am not suggesting these small dramas as a replacement for any of the existing drama forms, but as additional and complementary, as a way of relieving pressure, as a conduit for unrepresented forces. I think they have to be seen in terms of the increasing pressures, on popular channels during the next ten years, for faster and more fragmented shows.

If we look into the future I can see a bifurcation coming. On the one hand, a small screen with a segmented, fragmented post-modernist style. On the other, the wall screen in which television reaches its optimum size, bringing it in line with cinema, with spectacle, and with Peacock.[1] Down this latter road will go all the co-production money to give us the same kind of stuff we've been getting in the past but in bigger and more expensive packages. I think that one of the perennial problems we have had to face every time that we have been confronted with a situation which calls for *imaginative change* is that we are let off the hook by new technical developments which allow the old way of doing things just a little more life. So we started in the drama studio with black and white, then went on to colour, then out into the streets with mobile tape, then film, then super-16, then faster film, then 35-mil, now we have Wall television. At each stage, when the process should have been thrown back onto the virtuosity of its creators, the new development allows the Establishment to keep pumping out the same old naturalistic tune.

When Jimmy MacTaggart came to London, television was small, stood in the corner of the room and broadcast in black and white. In ten years time it will fill our bedrooms and be in colour. But in terms of drama, it will not have changed that much. But hopefully somewhere in the house there will still be a standard television, an Information Provider as it will then be called, whose programmes will have been allowed to develop on the lines which I have just suggested so that its style will be so singular, idiosyncratic and purposeful, that it will continue to attract viewers despite all the goodies that Sky and the other spectacle spinners will be beaming in our direction.

Note

1. A reference to Alan Peacock, the economist appointed in 1985 by the Thatcher government to examine the financing of the BBC, especially the suggestion that the BBC might be funded by advertising revenues. The Peacock Committee suggested that such a shift might undermine the quality and range of programming on BBC services and argued for a gradual transition to a system based on subscription. Report of the Committee on Financing the BBC (1986), London: HMSO [Cmnd 9824].

The James MacTaggart Lecture 1987

Power and Pluralism in Broadcasting

Phillip Whitehead*

Phillip Whitehead opens his lecture with the suggestion that the British broadcasting industry is suffering the most severe and sustained attack he can recall in the last twenty-five years. The assailants include politicians, government policy, new technology, free-market economics and even broadcasting regulators. The 'buzzword' informing policy change has been 'choice' measured by the number of available services. But diversity, Whitehead suggests, 'has to be fostered'.

Whitehead argues that Annan articulated the principle of a genuine 'regulated diversity' promoted via different authorities protected by separate sources of finance: a smaller BBC; local radio cut 'adrift' from the BBC and IBA; ITV as a truly regional service and regionally based network; and a new publishing channel commissioning independent production. Ten years on, the BBC has become closer to the model Annan espoused, but the fifteen regional companies of ITV are 'now bought and sold with little regard to their region'; the diversity of programming produced in the regions is being lost. By contrast, the independent producers have brought 'a quite new pluralism to British television', although this may be compromised by a 'Peacock afterthought' which threatens to change advertising arangements at Channel 4 and may result in a loss of 'innovatory zest'. Similarly, ITV may be 'dragged down' by its investment in satellite and cable if these innovatory services fail in the late 1990s.

* Phillip Whitehead has been a Labour MP and MEP, an author and television producer and editor of *This Week*, *Panorama* and *Gallery*. In 1987, he was Director of Brook Associates, a television production company.

But the 'real answer' to secure diversity and pluralism in broadcasting is a system of European-wide regulation 'which is protective as well as prohibitive' so that regulatory control can be exercised on those who have 'nothing to offer but long purse strings, low standards and competitive triviality, porn or violence.' Whitehead concludes, 'To sum up. Markets aren't enough.'

◻

I want to talk about power and pluralism. One, of the very last things Jimmy MacTaggart said, to a group of striking production assistants in the week of his untimely death, was this: 'Never underestimate the power of the other side. Unless you want it more than they do, and are stronger than they are, you'll lose.' I would only add, to this gathering, never underestimate their popularity either, or exaggerate your own. I do so as one who has recently realised that the instinctive assumptions people like me have made about public service broadcasting have a hard time with the new philosophy of the market place.

The power that comes from cashpoint and credit card are going to be as dominant in choice of media for information and entertainment as anywhere else as programmes become commodities, to be hoarded, speculated against, sold as futures, intermingled with the admass.

Those who believe that the only true regulator is the sovereign market loathe the protected duopoly and the statutory regulators of public service broadcasting. There are more people out there who think we are poseurs in sharp suits, pointy-headed intellectuals, effete snobs, pinkoes and perverts, than we care to recall. Every time we praise our own programmes without facing up to how much they cost, or how long they were delayed, or attempt plausible justifications of bad research, management cartels and union restrictive practices, we feed those dislikes. In twenty-five years of television – half of its entire history – I can never recall our industry under such sustained attack.

We should not be surprised that some have buckled in the heat. The BBC Governors initially collapsed when told by the last Home Secretary, that they should not broadcast *Real Lives*. The IBA has seemed at times demoralised. Its Director of television has gone so far as to say that the very phrase public service broadcasting will have to be replaced since it now seems tainted with overtones of a smug elite, as unrepresentative as any select vestry, doing what it thinks best and not what the viewer wants.

It is time for us to be more robust. Concepts may change, words may become pejorative. The cult of individual choice may sweep the field. But other truths should still be self-evident. There's a verse of Kipling which ought to appeal to Mrs Thatcher: Keith Joseph often used it. It runs like this:

As I pass through my incarnations in every age and grace.
I make my prostrations to the Gods of the Market Place.
Peering through reverent fingers I watch them flourish and fall.
And the Gods of the Copybook Headings, I notice, outlast them all.

It is time for us to take note of the Copybook Headings once more. They're as old as Gresham's Law,[1] as new as yesterday's bankruptcy. What they tell us is that state censorship is not the same as regulation; that many individual choices can sometimes be less than the sum of the public good, whether on a waveband or in a green belt, that while there must be markets to assess public demand, that choice will be wider if there is intervention in the market to help diversity along. That every act of deregulation, such as takes place daily now in European broadcasting, needs to be followed by regulations of a different kind. That the most powerful forces in the market place tend towards dominance, which has its own irresistible logic for them.

Because this is almost the last industry we do well with, our combination of an early start, a strong cultural base and the English language, we tend to agree with those foreigners who say to every committee of enquiry which goes abroad, why would you want to change a system which we envy? The answer, of course, is that we can't stop it. Britain's protected place in a European system, tightly regulated and far more heavily dependent on licence income than our duopoly has been, will soon be overrun.

The problems posed by the pace of European deregulation have been compounded by the contradictions of government policy here. The record of the past eight years has been a shambles. At a time when we are spending £1,491 millions on TV set rental and purchase and at least £1,600 million on VCR rental, purchase and software, the government chose to set up the Peacock Committee to find alternatives to the horror of a TV licence for a little over £1 per week. A study for the Home office in response to Peacock concluded that it was 'really cheap' to get four channels for a licence fee of £1 per week – a sixth of what they paid for access to their cable. It could be that the more viewers know about pay-per-channel, the more they respect the crude form of it which the licence fee represents.

So the last few years have seen a variety of different initiatives often because a particular technology became available, with little thought about how they might all fit together. The buzzword has been choice, measured in quantity, with the promise that the hand of authority over ownership and content will be relaxed. Unfortunately many of us find it hard to square the Home Secretary's call for a lighter system of regulation with the higher level of interference. The Conservative manifesto talked of stronger and more effective controls of sex and violence, which seem to usurp the functions of the regulatory authorities: backbenchers queue to offer us catchpenny definitions of obscenity. Those who argue that the public should see what it wants rather than what public authorities provide wrestle with their own dilemmas. Are we to enter a time when controls on private ownership and public obligation will be abandoned, but those on content simultaneously tightened? Our confusion comes from the fact that we don't trust the regulatory tools we have. They seem too tight for the age of consumer sovereignty, too inadequate for content, we fear. It's time to go back to the Copybook Headings.

Ten years ago the Annan Committee tried its hand at writing them down. In what seems like a different universe now, we unveiled our principle of regulated diversity as the way forward from the duopoly. I cannot claim that we got everything right, but our central point still holds. We thought that genuine diversity, instead of a multiplicity of material mainstream in appeal, and monopolist in editorial control, would come from different authorities, each protected by a separate source of finance. The authorities were not then objects of odium and we assumed that they would be both neutral and widely recruited – not least after some sour memories of the Wilson/Hill era. We wanted a smaller BBC, no longer claiming corporate universality under the theology of an all-powerful Director General. We wanted to cut local radio adrift from both BBC and IBA, exploring every method of finance, including negative rental from a new local broadcasting authority, which would also run cable. We thought ITV should be a truly regional service, though still networked, with fresh opportunities later for a fifth channel. We wanted a publishing channel, living off the land and commissioning independent production. That, at least, in Channel 4 we got. We also got a Broadcasting Complaints Commission,[2] but we were rebuffed on a proposed Public Inquiry Board with the power to instigate research and public hearings at the request of either the authorities or the government.

Ten years on many of these proposals are on the agenda again, but, randomly, not as part of a pattern. There may be something like our enquiry board, but set up in the wake of the clamour over violence: moral panics are not the best moment for dispassionate enquiry. And the BBC has at least acknowledged that it cannot do everything. It will always be more exposed: it draws the lightning for the rest of us. I remember previewing a fairly innocuous current affairs programme last year, a senior BBC official said to me, 'We couldn't put this programme on.' Brian Wenham's query whether the BBC would be able to screen *Spitting Image* makes the same point. We are all less free if the BBC is not free to put these programmes on. Or thinks it is not. We can be settled with later.

That is why many of us who wish the BBC well are uneasy about the spirit of Leatherhead Revisited which now seems to be creeping across its reworked news and current affairs output. Of course, careful programmes of analysis are needed. of course the inheritance of film, the dominance of the particular and the emotional over the general and the dispassionate, can inhibit understanding. But there are a good many uneasy Girondins at Shepherd's Bush who fear a new directorate which fits all their diverse output into one common mould. Diversity has to exist within big organisations as well as around them. My memories of the BBC twenty-five years ago are of an extraordinary diversity which bred confidence in those long sessions in Sanger's 35. [Huw] Wheldon and [David] Attenborough, [Ned] Sherrin and [Christopher] Ralling, [Donald] Baverstock and [Alasdair] Milne, were all in a state of Grace. Grace[3] herself was often in a different kind of state. She feared no politician and I once saw her order the government's chief law officer, Manningham-Buller, out of a hospitality room because he had got at the plastic chicken too early. Norman Tebbit would have had no terrors for her.

Diversity has to be fostered. It includes the right to fail, and the right sometimes to go out not knowing if your story will stand up, whether it is on recycling international debt or the misfortunes of John Stalker. Specialists can become co-opted, dissent dismissed as mere opinion. Governments of all parties would not mind that. It's the wild cards they can't handle.

If the BBC has now become more as Annan envisaged it, the same can hardly be said for ITV. The IBA to its very great credit has prevented outright changes in ownership of the two market leaders, resisting the Carlton bid for Thames and the Rank bid for Granada. But as publicly quoted companies in a lucrative field TV-AM[4] and the fifteen regional are now bought and sold with little regard to their region, which may be only a small part of the group interests in which they are now involved. ITV's networking system is under sustained attack, its monopoly advertising revenue is no longer seen as the safety net for an unbalanced regional system, where some have always had an immense return on capital, or as justified by the subvention that runs Channel 4. The government has accepted the argument for a tranche of independent production, and flirts with the idea of auctions for franchises next time.

Any organisation with many competing power centres is slow to react to such a succession of challenges, but the response of their ITV companies to their critics has been at times lamentable. Yet the questions multiply. Should the biggest ITV companies attempt to become vertically integrated international media groups, to stay in the satellite ring? What public stance is to be taken on the franchise auction? Then there is the question of the fifteen disparate regions. Might the IBA now be preparing the ground for changes here? We have to talk about these things. Waste and restrictive practices are issues for ITV, even if the Murdoch and Maxwell papers[5] have their special reasons for highlighting them. Relationships between staff, freelance and independent production teams have got to be eased too.

I've seen it said that the 25 per cent campaign has been carried away by its success in getting the ear of the Prime Minister and Lord Young. And where's the public service in that? The independents will wake up, we're told, to find that they are offered bland commissions, diluted by ITV and BBC staff turned out to grass with a contract, and unable to build an asset base of their own, because their principal role will be as cost cutters and casualisers – the famous 'Trojan ponies' of Gus Macdonald's phrase. It's true that you can make a better living inside than out. It's true that some independents forget the invention of double-entry bookkeeping, let alone audience measurement. But they have brought a quite new pluralism to British television because they have access to a market in which their independence and their very lack of vertical integration is an asset and not a crippling disability.

It's worth noting the element of regulation in all this. The small companies are dependent on the IBA and the BBC to see fair play when commissioning. There are restrictions on foreign ownership proposed, at a time when the Cable Authority is begging in its annual report for such restrictions to be lifted. And the fact that we already have a vigorous independent sector is due to Channel 4 itself. All that may now be changed. Another Peacock afterthought was the floating of Channel 4 as a separate company selling its own advertising in competition with ITV. A commercial Channel 4 run like some up-market TV-AM would soon lose its innovatory zest, which needs to be rethought anyway, now it is no longer the only broadcasting publisher in town.

The challenge of satellite and cable are ITV's possible nemesis in the late nineties. The participant companies might be dragged down by a spectacular failure of BSB, whereas its success if the sale and the rental of dish aerials takes off like that of VCRs eventually did would dent terrestrial audiences and ITV ad revenue. Will it happen? We see here the shape of a familiar pattern. The early risk-bearer finds its financial backers lose their nerve. Panic sets in. It happened in the first days of ITV. It happened with London Weekend and TV-AM. It may be happening with Super Channel. If there is then a collapse it is not the early-risk bearer, but those who buy out its losses – or often those who buy *them* out, who wins this game. The big players will be there on the day. The fact that we are many and they are few is our commendation, but it may not be our salvation. International medium power satellites controlled by groups who have the resources to hang out there for ten years can wait until people buy their dish aerial, or pick up the national high-power satellites when they go bust. By the late 1990s they'll have the audiences, and the ad revenue, to smash any medium-sized national audience, or force it into the abject flattery of imitation. Like RAI with Berlusconi.[6] Who says we don't need regulation?

There are two things we can do about it. The first is for the IBA to make it clear that it would not allow holdings in BSB by foreign investors, and to encourage the service to look for its revenue to subscription. The second, hand in hand with our pluralism, is to see that our biggest players – some ITV companies and the BBC – remain big enough, and in effective control of their product, to stay in this game.

The real answer is a European policy on satellite communications, embracing both EEC and the Council of Europe, so that regulatory action can be taken which is binding on all and satellites are not taken over by those who have nothing to offer but long purse strings, low standards and competitive triviality, porn or violence. We can't beat them without Europe-wide regulation which is protective as well as prohibitive. Satellite havens, like tax and pollution havens, are a problem Europe has to address.

Who will carry our case in Europe, and oversee the new kinds of regulation which a system of wider choice will still require? The time has come to accept that technical initiation and continuing regulation should go together. We need a proper ministry of communications and a proper communications policy now. It should be a ministry which can combine an enthusiasm for the potential of the technology with an overview of its use, which can ask the question 'how?' but also the question 'why?'

To sum up. Markets aren't enough. We need regulation as much as in the world of half a dozen radio manufacturers. We need hands-off authorities who understand that their proper function is to protect the viewer, and that that sometimes means protecting those who serve the viewer, and standing up to governments too. We need a ministry which can build on what we have, and distinguish between fads, fashions and first principle. We need lots more broadcasters, able to flourish along-side old interests, and sometimes to diminish them, and we need civil courage, a lot of it when we get stuck between the hidden hand of the market and the mailed fist of government.

Our successors will work in a world of far greater diversity. Some think that will mean the end of universally available services, to which the sense of public services can be attached. It will all be just like the print. If that is true something will have been lost for the viewer as citizen. We know from the take-up patterns of VCRs and cable that these are the heaviest for those who like the high seriousness of British television least. Supporters of consumer sovereignty will say that this proves their point. Those of us who want to test the mind as well as the maker think that information and education, as well as entertainment, should be on call, even where it is rejected for a less demanding diet. The social act of watching television, and discussing it, will remain our best method of helping those who still view, in their separate homes, so that we remind them how they interact with each other, and of the needs of strangers.

Notes

1. Gresham's Law, attributed to Sir Thomas Gresham, states that when two kinds of money having the same denominational value are in circulation, the intrinsically more valuable money will be hoarded and the money of lower intrinsic value will circulate more freely until the intrinsically more valuable money is driven out of circulation: in short, bad money drives out the good.
2. The Broadcasting Complaints Commission (BCC) was established in 1981 to adjudicate complaints from individuals concerning any invasion of their privacy or any unfair treatment in programming. The BCC was merged with the Broadcasting Standards Council in 1997 to form the Broadcasting Standards Commission (BSComm). The BSComm ended with the establishment of Ofcom in December 2003.
3. A reference to the formidable and much admired Grace Wyndham Goldie, who was a major influence in UK television for more than twenty years, especially in her role as Head of BBC Television Talk and Current Affairs. She was involved in establishing significant programmes such as *Tonight*, *Panorama* and *That Was The Week That Was*. Significantly, Grace Wyndham Goldie helped to shape key elements of broad-

casters' relationships with politicians and the presentation of politics on television, including the development of party political broadcasts, the protocols governing the televising of general elections and the emerging conventions concerning a more robust style of political interviewing. Her book *Facing the Nation: Television and Politics, 1936–76*, London: The Bodley Head, 1977, reports much about these developments in an autobiographical style.

4. TV-AM was the company that held the franchise for the breakfast programme broadast throughout the ITV network. TV-AM lost the franchise to rival GMTV in 1991 in the first round of bids using the franchise auction established by the 1991 Broadcasting Act.

5. A reference to the willingness of newspapers such as the *Sun*, *The Times* and the *Mirror* to be highly critical in their editorials of both the public and commercial sectors of television.

6. RAI is an Italian television company which was judged by many UK broadcasters to have moved rapidly downmarket following the deregulation of Italian television in the 1980s; Mr Berlusconi is the prorietor of RAI.

The James MacTaggart Lecture 1988

Ethics, Broadcasting and Change: The French Experience

Christine Ockrent*

Christine Ockrent's lecture explores and analyses the ethical consequences of rapid change in the French broadcasting system. She details
the shift at TF1 Network from a public-sector organisation run by 'miserly,
incompetent civil servants' to a private-sector broadcaster, owned by a
civil engineering company which believes there is 'no reason why a TV
station should be run differently from a pipes factory' and whose ethical
'code of behaviour' includes 'simple mottos' such as 'Kill the enemy, the
competition, the weak'. Ockrent believes that this subject will interest a
British audience because 'in many ways the French situation epitomises
the fears which many of you nourish about deregulation'.

Ockrent makes three key claims. First, while deregulation may be a pre-
requisite for the expansion of broadcasting, it is 'inevitably damaging to
standards'. Ratings have become the key consideration with game shows,
sitcoms, American series and films dominating French television schedules resulting in 'conformity and uniformity'. The paradox which emerges
is that 'we have more channels . . . but we seem to have less consumer
choice'. Standards of news programmes have also declined as 'some presenters . . . imitate entertainment shows' and 'what is interesting has long
since overrun what is important'.

Ockrent's second argument is that whatever its dangers, expansion is
essential if the broadcasting system is to survive and compete internation-
ally. This will require large capital investment of the kind Murdoch has
made in the UK to develop satellite and cable channels in France. Finally,

* Christine Ockrent is a broadcaster and programme-maker. She concludes her MacTaggart Lecture
by announcing her recent appointment to a position with the French broadcaster Antenne 2.

Ockrent argues that it is necessary to develop a new set of regulatory arrangements adapted to the requirements of the increasingly international character of broadcasting. What is necessary in France is 'a more coercive system' even though this 'call for regulation may sound weird to . . . British ears'.

I have chosen tonight to tackle the broad and complex issue of ethics in a changing broadcasting scene. Not that I see the need to convince any of you that our trade cannot blossom without an ethical dimension. Yet it may prosper without it and it already does in some parts of the world. The more technology hastens the pace of change, the more the market place calls for vertical and horizontal integration and presents it as an alternative philosophy, the greater the challenge that we, professional broadcasters, have to face in order to protect and yet develop our own set of values and principles.

Don't get me wrong, I don't want to bore you with personal anecdotes about a professional itinerary which some unkind souls may easily label as ambulatory naivety if nothing worse. I don't want either to sound like an obsolete crusader fighting the religious war, the holy public service against commercial decadence; indeed, such somehow simplistic if convenient views do not happen to be mine. I understand the British broadcasting system, long the envy of the rest of the world, is about to undergo drastic structural change. I certainly do not feel qualified to comment on your domestic quarrels and struggles, but feel there is a continuity and indeed a community of concerns which brings us all together. There are three main points which I would like to argue here tonight.

First, deregulation if necessary to the expansion of our broadcasting industry is inevitably damaging to its standards. Second, expansion is mandatory if we are to meet the economic, as well as the cultural, challenges which technology keeps raising. Finally, what is necessary in my view is a new set of regulations, adapted to the growingly hybrid nature of our business and its increasingly transnational structures.

Broadcasting has become too important as a business to be left to broadcasters alone. By broadcasters, I mean all those producers, programme-makers, journalists and even accountants who have decided among themselves to define and run broadcasting in what appeared to be in the general as well as in their own interests. Such is the theory which more and more people in our countries put forward to justify their own ambition to take over the business. The French Revolution, I feel, is a case in point.

Until a few years ago, the French broadcasting system consisted of only three channels, state run, if not government controlled. Most of the time, they were run by miserly, incompetent civil servants. Then the system exploded, not so much from internal tensions, as from political will. In 1985 the then socialist government, which had already authorised a pay TV-channel, Canal Plus, allocated a new commercial channel to Mr Berlusconi. In 1986, the new conservative government went further by creating another commercial channel, by selling off the oldest and largest of the French networks TF1,[1] for the staggering sum of six billion francs: more than £600,000,000. A new regulatory body, the CNCL,[2] with greater powers succeeded the existing authority established in 1982. What is interesting, a little more than a year after the privatisation of TF1, is to assess its impact on the broadcasting scene and to try and assess the practice of the owners and managers of TF1.

The major shareholder who actually runs the company is a civil engineering group. They won over Hachette, the publishing conglomerate, on the grounds that they would invest more in original production and would be less threatening to pluralism than a multi-media company. This is how engineers landed on this strange planet of ours: awed by it and yet so self-assured. They tell you there is no reason why a TV station should be run differently from a pipes factory. That talent is disposable and replaceable, that people, who don't fit in preconceived computer-like patterns, have to make rules for others who do.

TF1 certainly needed to put its house in order to improve efficiency, to lift the apathy, engendered by so many years of bureaucracy and limited resources. But this is a trade where imagination matters and creative processes cannot be measured by numbers alone. Company ethics do not make up for the lack of any: there are criteria other than budgets and ratings. So seasoned professionals were rather taken aback by the new code of behaviour. Its motto is simple. Kill the enemy, the competition, the weak. The new breed that seek financial and managerial control over broadcasting, have goals, but no standards. Programmes are not discussed in terms of quality, but in terms of commodities and figures, judgement comes in with the ratings the following morning.

The social and cultural role of a network as ancient as TF1 is not to be mentioned, such vocabulary belongs to the *ancien régime*. The rules set by the CNCL, the broadcasting authority, are only there to be circumscribed. Current affairs, no prime-time stuff, so many hours for documentaries, they'll do well after midnight. It is enough they think to have to maintain an expensive news division with so many journalists who seem to do nothing but read newspapers. Do they have to read newspapers during working hours? Management is only paying lip service because it is compelled to: there is no pride, no specific responsibility, no civil role.

When David Zarnoff or Bill Pailey created and built the two most powerful American networks, they behaved like profit-minded capitalists, but also like responsible, almost enlightened citizens, proud of the power, the status and also the duties they carried in the public eye. When I started at CBS, the news division was under the authority of a lawyer, each recruit was handed a booklet on behaviour which to this day, in spite of all the infringements, prices and cuts, made for the proud memory of what used to be CBS News.

In this latter part of the century, I am afraid entrepreneurs seldom behave like enlightened patrons. There are all sorts of explanations for their attitude, including that our overall system of checks and balance is at fault. Public opinion, the press, the various bodies meant to express common values in our society do not weigh in sufficiently: the CNCL has little power.

The other problem in France, of course, is money. There is too much of it; the stakes have become too high. Consider TF1: buying price over £600,000,000, annual budget over £450,000,000, advertising income over £480,000,000, necessary share of the audience to generate profit 45 per cent. The licence to operate the channel is valid for ten years. Those among you who are good at figures can easily make out what kind of net income TF1 should generate each year to prove a good investment. 1988, however, has been a brilliant year for for the channel. But predictably, investment in production has been less than promised. Programmes with appeal for large audiences have been imported or copied locally. Movies, the backbone to prime-time programming in France, have reached staggering prices: more than £600,000 for one showing of *Rambo*. Operating costs have soared and so has advertising: over £100,000 per minute on prime time. But the maximum time allowed for commercials is twelve minutes per hour. The room for manoeuvre had thus proved to be narrow indeed to the well-meaning engineers who have taken hold of the networks. Would professionals from another media culture less foreign to broadcasting have done better or would they have performed differently? It is as if the whole system is now spell-bound under increasing commercial pressure.

Look at the public sector, where advertising accounts for as much as 70 per cent of the budget of Antenne 2, the most powerful of the two public service channels, with a budget of over £280,000,000. Antenne 2 has sustained this year about 28 per cent of the audience, any less and advertisers would flee. So what do we see? Precisely the same as on the commercial channels: games, sitcoms, American series and movies. But there has been more investment in original production and more time and energy devoted to news. In many ways, the French situation epitomises the fears which many of you nourish about deregulation: We have more channels than we used to, but we seem to have less consumer choice. Conformity, uniformity settle in with their usual justifications. This is what the public wants, look at the ratings. Ratings terrorise the industry as all channels tend to aim at general audience targets. At a slower pace and a smaller scale, the erosion in quality and diversity is the same that seems to affect the aching American networks. Erosion affects news standards as well. What is interesting has long since overrun what is important. Some presenters of news programmes although journalists imitate entertainment shows: where is the borderline? Isn't the Princess of Monaco more attractive than the Third World debts?

The French broadcasting system has indeed expanded from three to six channels and it could not have done so without deregulation. But for the time being, it has not found its balance yet, between a private sector gulping down advertising revenue like fresh air and the public sector trying to do the same.

The second point I would like to make, is whatever its dangers, expansion is necessary for our broadcasting system to survive and to thrive. Economics command it as well as technological progress. To us, the Murdochs and Maxwells of this world are British exports. The problem with us is that there is simply no French company which combines the financial scope and the professional expertise to face the existing and forthcoming international competition. The problem with you it seems is that you have one too many. When the publishing group Hachette tried to get hold of TF1 its ambition was to grow into a multi-media company by European standards. Examples in Britain, Italy and Germany show that control over a broadcasting medium is indispensable to big-time operators. The prevailing legislative approach in France has been to consider concentration as the most critical issue: pluralism does not blossom when the system is out of balance with too many operators struggling for short-term financial survival. Also big investment capacity is needed to face the medium and long-term challenges of the markets which satellites and cable have yet to develop. Multi-media groups now aim at an international dimension but there is no French group in this race, which explains why Maxwell and Berlusconi were able to buy into the French market. Transnational broadcasters may not even need to speak French, which is worrying for the commercial viability of our production and therefore for the vitality of our culture.

France doesn't have a clear view or a clear strategy about satellites. Various governments including the current one have not found a way out of the quagmire created by overly ambitious technological choices but little economic viability. Cable is even less developed in France than it is in this country and has not found yet its economic or even cultural rationale so far. But there are some promising signs elsewhere. The latest trends in the American media industry show that French markets are profitable, a fragmented audience does exist, an interesting product and worthwhile money can be made and they are sometimes compatible. We are not there yet and one of the many paradoxes of the European situation is that our very wealth in terms of culture and talent may be an obstacle rather than an impetus.

There is, however, one key issue on which I would disagree with what seems to be the prevailing mood in some circles in this country and this has to do with Europe. Europe hardly exists as far as television is concerned. Our audience seems to prefer American trash to things European yet foreign. Notwithstanding or perhaps because of this intense Americanisation of our culture which television has bought about, language and cultural barriers remain strong. National regulations vary a great deal and will be difficult to harmonise by 1993. Yet, and that is the real problem, Europe is already a reality for all those industrialists, financiers, media entrepreneurs, not to mention politicians, who take an active interest in our expanded trade.

I believe broadcasting is too important a sector to be left to those people alone. There are standards which we as professionals share beyond our cultural and traditional differences. This is why I believe it is time to try to define a new set of rules and regulations adapted to the hybrid nature of this business and its increasingly international structures. This is my third and final point. Democracy obviously cannot live by freedom alone. Its genius is to devise rules which make the best of the contradictions between individual and collective interests. The same applies to broadcasting. Free-market forces do not blossom in the jungle, but in a system where regulation ensures an overall balance to the system.

It is interesting to note that, eighteen months after deregulation, the Executive Director of TFl claimed in an interview for *Le Monde*, 'One can let market forces follow their course and wait for some channels to sink, but can the state be satisfied with sheer economic logic?' Now irony set aside, it is true that the French situation does show the many pitfalls of deregulation: all the channels aiming at a national all-purpose audience have scheduled virtually the same type of programming at the same time. The cost for the limited amount of programmes available have soared, bumping money into purchases but not in production. The commercial channels 5 and 6 are in trouble. TF1 struggles in spite of its weight and its attractiveness to advertisers. Antenne 2, the leading public channel, finds the competition impossible without relying heavily on advertising income and the increased sponsoring of programmes.

It strikes me that the most valuable asset you have in this country is the balance between the public and the private sectors of broadcasting and the guarantees given to independent production. What needs to be done in France is to revitalise the public channels so that they can better their own identity. It means more money from public taxes, rather than advertising. But this is a delicate mix which you have on the whole succeeded in doing. We are still searching.

Entertainment should not be the province of commercial channels alone. News, education and culture should not be for public channels only. What is called for in France is a more coercive system. Not only quotas of original production to be financed and aired by commercial channels, but also minimal scheduling rules so that TV trash does not profit from Gresham's Law anymore. Every channel in an expanding system cannot be all purpose, general audience orientated. Every channel cannot and should not be vertically integrated so as to generate its own productions. There should be incentives as well as penalties to make sure that new outlets become a breathing space for independent innovative production.

Whatever its status and its duration, a licence to broadcast originates from the public domain and is therefore subjected to specific constraints. This is what the philosophy of the market place in my view has to understand. Phillip Whitehead raised the right question when he asked in this lecture last year, 'Are we to enter a time when controls on private ownership and public obligation will be abandoned but those on content simultaneously tightened?'

Well, I am afraid that recent months have not brought about an easy answer, either here or in France. There, controls have not been abandoned, but they are not adequate. The quality of programmes is at stake and also the quality of news. In broadcasting, rigid guidelines imposed by an outside body do not fit in a democracy, but internal guidelines can only stem from a strong tradition of independence. In this respect, French channels have little to be nostalgic about. But private ownership should not be without a sense and a code of civic responsibility. It is not only a question of scheduling newscasts at regular hours, it has to do with investing in the news, with expanding its role and its ambition.

I understand how this call for regulation may sound weird to your British ears, but I believe that some of the problems we are going through across the Channel also point to the necessity of better harmonising between European countries. There is no protection any more resulting from splendid isolation: not for our economies, our culture, our television systems, or ourselves. As we are privileged enough to be the flesh and blood of this industry, I believe it is our task to work on the global problem it now has to face. We have as much right to do so as anybody else but much more responsibility.

Notes

1. Télévision Française 1 was the first television channel to be launched in France (8 December 1935). It was the first channel to carry commercial advertising (1968) and was the first public service channel to be privatised in 1987.
2. The Commission Nationale de la Communication et des Libertés (CNCL), a regulatory body for broadcasting, was established in 1986 to oversee (paradoxically) the deregulation of television broadcasting, following the election of a right-of-centre government. The CNCL replaced the HA (Haute Autorité de la Communication Audiovisuelle) established by the 1982 Communication Act. CNCL was in turn replaced by the Conseil Superieur de l'Audiovisuel in 1988 following the election of Michel Rochard's left-of-centre government.

The James MacTaggart Lecture 1989

Freedom in Broadcasting

Rupert Murdoch*

Rupert Murdoch offers a highly contentious and critical assessment of public service broadcasting, denouncing it as an ideology deployed by 'propagandists' to protect the interests of a narrow broadcasting elite, but with debilitating consequences for British broadcasting. Most significantly, public service broadcasting and its 'guardians' militate against the prospects for viewer freedom and choice. Such restrictions 'are not compatible with a mature democracy'.

This ideology of public service broadcasting is a form of 'special pleading' which misrepresents an economically inefficient, paternalistic and unaccountable broadcasting system, as the only organisational structure capable of delivering quality programmes and encouraging creative risk-taking in programme-making. Murdoch's argument rests on a 'simple principle'. Namely, 'in every area of economic activity in which competition is attainable, it is much to be prefered to monopoly'.

By contrast public service broadcasting is nowhere clearly defined, although Murdoch redresses this problem by suggesting that 'anybody who, within the law of the land, provides a service which the public wants at a price it can afford is providing a public service' (subsequent MacTaggart lecturers have contested this definition). Consequently 'if in the years ahead we can make a success of Sky Television, that will be as much a public service as ITV'. Murdoch offers a number of examples to illustrate his argument that the market-led American system has been substantially more successful in creating greater quality and diversity of

* Rupert Murdoch is Chief Executive of News International.

programming than British television informed by the principles of public service broadcasting.

◻

What I want to address tonight is no more than an interim stage on the way there. It is a transition in which British television will come of age, reaching maturity by breaking out of its self-imposed duopoly and entering a time when freedom and choice, rather than regulation and scarcity, will be its hallmarks.

For fifty years British television has operated on the assumption that the people could not be trusted to watch what they wanted to watch, so that it had to be controlled by like-minded people who knew what was good for us. As one of these guardians, my distinguished friend Sir Denis Forman, explained a few years ago, even so-called commercial television in Britain 'is only an alternative method of financing public broadcasting, and that method itself has depended on the creation of tightly-held monopolies for the sale of advertising and programme production'. So, even though the lure of filthy lucre was to become part of the British television system with the advent of ITV from the mid-1950s, it was done by subordinating commerce to so-called public service. And it was done in a way which was very appealing to the British Establishment, with its dislike of money-making and its notion that public service is the preserve of paternalists. Even then, many of the 'top people' in British society bitterly opposed commercial television in the 1950s, and commercial radio in the seventies. Much respectable opinion seemed to see nothing wrong in retaining a government monopoly of television and radio, making broadcasting by anybody else a criminal act.

Such restrictions on the freedom to broadcast, of course, are not compatible with a mature democracy, though much of the British Establishment did not seem to realise that at the time, just as those who fight to restrict choice to the current duopoly do not appreciate how fundamentally anti-democratic their attitudes are. The arguments of the anti-ITV lobby thirty years ago seem absurd today, just as the arguments of the pro-duopoly lobby will sound ridiculous only a few years hence.

I start from a simple principle: in every area of economic activity in which competition is attainable, it is much to be preferred to monopoly. The reasons are set forth in every elementary economics textbook, but the argument is best proved by experience rather than theory.

Competition lets consumers decide what they want to buy; monopoly, or duopoly, forces them to take whatever the seller puts on offer. Competition forces suppliers to innovate continually, lest they lose business to rivals offering better, improved products; monopoly permits a seller to force outdated goods onto captive customers. Competition keeps prices low and quality high; monopoly does the opposite. Why should television be exempt from these laws of supply and demand, any more than newspapers, journals, magazines or books or feature films?

The consensus among established broadcasters, however, is that a properly free and competitive television system will mean the end of 'quality' television and that multi-channel choice equals multi-channel drivel – wall-to-wall *Dallas* is the sneering phrase most commonly trotted out to sum up this argument. Put aside the fact that the BBC is happy to run *Dallas* at prime time (and to repeat it as well); put aside, too, the simple economic truth that if fifteen channels were to run it wall-to-wall, fourteen of them would quickly go bust. I want instead to concentrate on the assumption that is behind the established broadcasters' case: that only public-service television can produce quality television.

There are real problems of definition and taste here. For a start I have never heard a convincing definition of what public-service television really is, and I am suspicious of elites, including the British broadcasting elite, which argue for special privileges and favours because they are supposed to be in the public interest as a whole. Such special pleading tends to produce a service which is run for the benefit of the people who provide it, rather than the viewers who watch it, sometimes under duress, especially late at night, because there is nothing else to watch.

My own view is that anybody who, within the law of the land, provides a service which the public wants at a price it can afford is providing a public service. So if in the years ahead we can make a success of Sky Television, that will be as much a public service as ITV. There remains, however, widespread scepticism in this country that a largely market-led system can produce 'quality' television. This view was perhaps best put by my colleague, Simon Jenkins, writing in *The Sunday Times* of 18 September 1988, when he wrote that 'to run a free market television company in Britain will be a grim, remorseless business, as it is in America'. He went on to accuse the government of 'dismantling a system that produces reasonably good television in favour of one which, on every scrap of available evidence, will produce incomparably worse television'. Well, so much for the monolithic Murdoch press!

But quality is in the eye of the beholder, or, in the current debate in Britain, the propagandist. Much of what is claimed to be quality television here is no more than the parading of the prejudices and interests of the like-minded people who currently control British television. It may well be that, at its very best, British television does produce what most viewers would regard as some of the world's best television.

Examples have been given to prove the case, though the fact that the same examples are trotted out all the time, and they are all getting a bit long in the tooth, suggests to me that the case is weaker than generally believed. Moreover, the price viewers have had to pay for these peaks in quality has been pretty high. The troughs of British television, such as much of the variety, situation comedies, sporting coverage and other popular fare, are not particularly special by international standards. In any comparison of the most popular programmes on both sides of the Atlantic, the British television system does not come out well.

The American weekly top ten list is dominated by an excellent current affairs show, *60 Minutes*, several situation comedies thought of sufficient high quality to be shown on Channel 4 in this country and some well-produced, high-budget series, representing the best of quality popular television. By comparison the British top ten is dominated by several mundane, low-budget soaps both home-made and imported. Whatever else can be said about public-service broadcasting, it cannot be said to be raising the overall viewing standards of the British public. In terms of quality television, the most-watched programmes in the US are far more impressive than the most-watched shows in Britain.

Much of what passes for quality on British television really is no more than a reflection of the values of the narrow elite which controls it and which has always thought that its tastes are synonymous with quality – a view, incidentally, that is natural to all governing classes.

But this public-service TV system has had, in my view, debilitating effects on British society, by producing a TV output which is so often obsessed with class, dominated by anti-commercial attitudes and with a tendency to hark back to the past. What I have in mind is best illustrated by many of the up-market costume soap operas which the British system produces, in which strangulated English accents dominate dramas which are played out in rigid, class-structured settings. They pander to an international desire, particularly to those Americans who watch PBS,[1] to portray and freeze Britain as a museum. This obsession with the old Britain is combined with constant sneering at the new Britain. As a result, in the values it exudes, British television has been an integral part of the British disease, hostile to the sort of culture needed to cure that disease.

The fact that those who control British TV have always worked in a non-market environment, protected by public subsidy and state privilege, is a major reason why they are innately unsympathetic to markets and competition. The new breed of television businessmen are portrayed as greedy, power-hungry thugs, while the current broadcasting elite comes out as something akin to Plato's Guardians.

People often say to me, however, that the current British system encourages creative risk-taking, and that a market-led system would not fund all manner of excellent programming currently on show. 'Without public-service television, there would be no Dennis Potter plays on television' was how the argument was put at a recent seminar organised by the Broadcasting Standards Council.[2] Of course, a Potter play is very much part of the cultural values of the broadcasting elite, and whereas it is true that the market-led American television system does not produce the US equivalent of a Potter play, it cannot be a serious criticism of American TV that it does not do things that are very much the product of British cultural values.

My argument, however, is not that television can be left entirely to the market. In a market-led TV system there is still room for a public service element to provide programming that the market might not provide such as the Potter plays. What I am arguing for is a move from the current system of public broadcasting, in which market considerations are marginal, to a market system in which public broadcasting would be part of the market mix but in no way dominate the output the way it does at present.

In the United States the programming of the Public Broadcasting System has added to the choice of American viewers. PBS has helped enrich the American TV scene just as the BBC will no doubt continue to do in a more market-led British TV system, even if it will find it hard to justify the compulsory poll tax that finances it when its charter comes up for renewal in the multi-channel world of the mid-1990s. So I do not dispute that there will be a future role for public broadcasting, though in a scaled-down form. But I suspect that the market is able to provide much more variety, and risk-taking, than many of you realise.

This brings me to my next point. Contrary to conventional wisdom in this country, there is much to admire about American television. I want to dwell on this for a moment because America provides the best example of a market-led television system and because it has been so disgracefully misrepresented by propagandists in this country.

We are told, for example, that all the new channels promised for Britain will be doing nothing but reruns. But in the United States that is clearly not true of Cable News Network, Financial News Network, C-Span's[3] two channels on public affairs and Headline News, which are all original, and live. Nor is it true of the sports and film channels, which feature original material. Nor is it true, increasingly, of most cable channels. A channel called the USA Network, for example, has this year commissioned twenty-four original made-for-cable movies. TNT[4] is doing the same. The Arts and Entertainment Network this year will co-produce 104 hours of drama, documentary and the performing arts. And 70 per cent of the Discovery Channel consists of programmes never seen before in the United States.

And of course there is much more than wall-to-wall *Dallas* on American television. Take current affairs and factual programmes. In Britain the ITV network for the year ending April 1989 ran an average of nineteen hours fifty-five minutes a week. That is exceeded by one programme alone on CBS *Nightwatch*, which broadcasts twenty hours of news programming a week; add on to that the three hours a week of prime-time programming on factual affairs on CBS; add on to that another twenty hours or so for non-prime-time news and factual programming and it quickly becomes clear who is being better served. And that is without taking into account the other networks, independent terrestrial broadcasters, the Discovery Channel, CNN, Arts and Entertainment, C-Span and ESPN.[5] Clearly, when it comes to news the market system is providing the better public service both in quantity and quality.

Take the ethnic and racial minorities. How are they served? In Britain, by one or two token programmes, usually in the wee small hours. But in the United States, 80 per cent of Hispanics have access to at least one Spanish-only channel; most have access to two. There is a Black Entertainment Network and there is National Jewish TV. In New York television alone, there are 10 hours each week of Korean, Chinese and Japanese television. The diversity of multi-channel television is real.

I watch television regularly on both sides of the Atlantic; when there were only four channels on this side, I was regularly frustrated by the lack of choice, and given the quality of much of the prime-time programming it was always difficult to believe that I was tuning into a cultural citadel which had to be preserved at all costs. These are, of course, my personal views, views with which the shapers of British television in this hall will differ. I don't ask you to accept my judgement as against your own, though I can guess whose side the Saturday night TV viewer would take. But I do believe that the people should be allowed to decide, and that the choice should be put before them.

At News International, we stand for choice. I say this aware of the fact that some of our critics accuse us of stifling choice in the media because we are supposed to own so much of it. That, I contend, is non-sense. Consider first, newspapers. We have three daily and two Sunday national titles, some serving the quality market, some serving those who prefer the tabloid format. Some profitable, some unprofitable. Every one of our readers is free to choose between our newspapers, other national newspapers and provincial newspapers owned by pow-erful chains. This is as it should be in a democracy.

As in newspapers, so in television; our role is that of a monopoly destroyer, not a monopolist. At present, we have less than 1 per cent of the TV audience. The truth is that, even by the time Sky is in several million British homes and becomes a commercial success, it has no pros-pect of dominating the medium. For just as Wapping so lowered the cost of newspaper production as to enable *The Independent* and others to enter, so Sky has paved the way for non-Sky channels. By leasing transponders of the Astra satellite system and by investing heavily in persuading viewers to equip themselves with receiving apparatus, we are opening the door for other organisations to seize the opportunities to become national broadcasters at a fraction of our cost.

So we see ourselves as destroyers of monopoly power and as creators of choice. In Britain cross-ownership of media is a force for diversity. Were it not for the strength of our newspaper group, and our human and capital resources, we surely could not have afforded to have doubled the number of television channels available in Britain from 5 February. We could not have created Sky News, which has become a third force in British television news alongside the BBC and ITN.

We began this decade with television in the hands of two powerful groups which shared the same values and objectives; we start the new decade with the possibility of enormous diversity, with monopoly control blown apart by market forces. It is a revolution with huge pos-itive benefits for society, above all in the realms of freedom and educa-tion; for a multi-channel broadcasting system in the hands of a diversity of owners is a bulwark to freedom and not susceptible to the sort of state control that has dogged British television throughout its life.

As British television develops, governments will increasingly lose their influence over it. Public-service broadcasters in this country have paid a price for their state-sponsored privileges. That price has been their freedom. British broadcasters depend on government for protection; when you depend on government for protection, there will come a time when that government, no matter its political complexion, will exact a price. The pressure can be overt or, more likely, covert. The result is the same either way: less than independent, neutered journalism. I cannot imagine a British Watergate, or a British Irangate, being pursued by the BBC or ITV with the vigour that the US networks did.

British broadcasters are now constantly subject to inhibiting criticism and reporting restrictions. BBC staff have even been vetted by government security services. But if, like the BBC, you're dependent on the government to set the licence fee, you think twice before offending powerful politicians.

But this kind of government control will become increasingly impossible in the new age of television. The multiplicity of channels means that the government thought-police, in whatever form, whether it is the benign good and the great in Britain, or the jackboot-in-the-night elsewhere, will find it hard to control more and more channels.

Across the world there is a realisation that only market economies can deliver both political freedom and economic well-being, whether they be free-market economies of the right or social-market economies of the left. The freeing of broadcasting in this country is very much part of this democratic revolution and an essential step forward into the Information Age with its golden promise. It means freeing television from the lie of spectrum scarcity; freeing it from the dominance of one narrow set of cultural values; freeing it for entry by any private or public enterprise which thinks it has something people might like to watch; freeing it to cater to mass and minority audiences; freeing it from the bureaucrats of television and placing it in the hands of those who should control it – the people.

Notes

1. The Public Broadcasting Service in America.
2. The Broadcasting Standards Council (BSC) was established as a regulatory body in 1988, but given statutory recognition by the Broadcasting Act 1990. While the major thrust of broadcasting policy under successive Thatcher governments was essentially deregulatory, the BCS enjoyed a particular brief to monitor portrayals of violence and sexual behaviour in programming.
3. Cable Satellite Public Affairs Network is a cable channel, established by Brian Lamb, which broadcasts gavel-to-gavel coverage of the proceedings of the US Senate and House of Representatives.
4. Turner Network Television, an American cable network.
5. Entertainment Sport Programming Network is an American cable network.

The James MacTaggart Lecture 1990

Deregulation and Quality Television

Verity Lambert*

Verity Lambert addresses the question 'What can we do to preserve quality?' in the context of a broadcasting system experiencing deregulation, reflecting both government policy and the emergence of multi-channel broadcasting. Lambert begins with definitions but acknowledges that the notion of 'quality' is contested. She suggests that money is central since it allows high production values, well-researched programmes, a good programme mix and funds innovation, risks and the occasional mistake. Lambert claims 'you may not know it [quality] when you see it, [but] you certainly know it when you don't'.

The inclusion of a 'quality threshold' in the Broadcasting Act 1990 is a significant amendment, but, additionally, the ITC must hold ITV companies to their programming commitments, especially the production and airing of documentaries and current affairs in prime time and the BBC and Channel 4 must 'not lose their nerve' when confronted by falling ratings.

Lambert concludes by considering the role of programme-makers (in-house and independents) in sustaining quality: her focus is on independent production. Establishing an association for independents would help eliminate the fragmentation and competition between them which can reduce programme quality. Independents also require ownership of the rights in their programmes, an independent mechanism for evaluating a fair price for programmes and guaranteed access to the network. If deregulation and a freer market are to co-exist with quality programming it will

* Verity Lambert is a well-known writer, producer and director who has worked at the BBC and ITV. She was working as an indpendent producer in 1990.

require programme-makers to refuse 'to compromise or lower standards' but also to 'seize the opportunities that are there'.

◻

What I want to talk about tonight is: what can we expect from deregulation and what can we do to preserve what is best from regulated television? What can we do to preserve *'quality'*? Of course, quality is a word that is in great danger of being removed from the official language of television, because the only thing everyone agrees on is how difficult it is to define. Let me attempt to define it for you.

To begin with, let me give you some examples of programmes that *I* believe reflect quality: *An Englishman Abroad*; *Edge of Darkness*; *Traffik*; *World in Action*; *Death on the Rock*; *The South Bank Show*; *Only Fools and Horses*; *Yes Minister*. I'm glad to say that I could go on and on. But will I be able to do this in four years' time? I've come to the conclusion that one definition of quality is money. Spending a lot on a programme is no guarantee of excellence, but money does mean that high production values can be attained and that projects are properly researched and developed. Money means that there will be a good mix of programmes in the schedules. Money means that programme-makers can be innovative, and, most important, that the occasional risk can be taken – even that the odd mistake can be made. Money also means that dramas and documentaries about domestic subjects can be made, fully financed from the domestic market.

It is essential that we continue to make programmes on domestic issues because another aspect of quality is our awareness and understanding of what is going on not just globally, but at home as well. Preserving our national identity is important. Not in a chauvinistic way, but in a way which reflects the diversities and contradictions in our own society.

So that's my definition of quality. You may not agree with it, but as I've already said it's one thing that we seldom agree on. So, if you're busy disagreeing with me about my definition, I'd like you to remember this. When somebody asks you to define a Stradivarius, you don't reach for your dictionary, you play a violin.

A further point about quality is that although you may not know it when you see it, you certainly know it when you don't. And the television audience that we aim to serve, and please, still wants to know whether or not it's going to see it in the 1990s. Well, one thing is certain, in the next two years we're all going to see a lot of it. It's no news to anyone that the current franchise-holders are, as usual, pulling out all the stops in the run-up to the franchise applications. We are going to have beautifully crafted – and expensively made – high-quality dramas, documentaries, arts programmes and so on, the like of which we haven't seen since the last round of franchise bidding. So stay in and watch – it may be your last chance.

The apologists of multiplication and deregulation will tell us that more means better. This isn't a new observation – there's an old Scottish proverb dating back to 1721 which says, 'Quality, without quantity, is little thought of.' Rupert Murdoch, in rubbishing the concept of public-service television, went so far as to say that for him, anybody who within the law provides a service the public wants – at a price it can afford – is providing a public-service. That makes the *Sunday Sport* a public-service newspaper. And Strangeways a public-service prison.

Sometimes we are so busy complaining about what we are losing that we fail to notice that all is not lost. We should remember that what we are entering is *not* a totally *free* market, but a free*er* market.

The IBA and other groups have succeeded in getting various amendments to the Broadcasting Bill, notably the 'quality threshold'.[1] But we must not be complacent. For although the Bill is nearly in its final form, there is still more we can do to safeguard standards.

Firstly then, the IBA, which will become the ITC, *must* insist that within the franchise applications there is not only a commitment to *make* documentaries and current affairs programmes, but also a commitment to *schedule* them in peak time. Some people in this room will say that what I'm asking for is public-service television – I'm not. I'm asking for television that *serves* the public.

So, what is the ITC going to do to keep the new franchise-holders up to the mark? If, as the IBA claims, the ITC will have the power, in the final analysis, to take *away* a franchise if necessary, we'd like to think they will do it. There are, however, many of us who, from the IBA's past performance, have justifiable doubts on this score. A recent article in *The Independent* suggested that George Russell[2] had 'lots of clout'. Well, I'd like to see him use it.

Secondly, what about the new franchise-holders? They will be for the first time publishers, as well as broadcasters. Well, the first thing they can do is to keep the promises they make in their franchise applications. Are they going to give programme-makers the support and the money to make programmes of quality? To be original and innovative?

From my experience the best and some of the most successful programmes have been made because someone had the guts to ignore the rules. When I Joined Thames in 1974 as their Controller of Drama, Jeremy Isaacs was the Director of Programmes. I was determined to make innovative contemporary drama. As luck would have it, I was presented with two ideas which seemed to me to fall into that category. One, from Stella Richman, was a series about a radical Labour MP written by Trevor Griffiths. The other, from Andrew Brown and Howard Schuman, was a non-naturalistic and highly original drama series about a female rock group. Feeling very pleased with myself I took these ideas to Jeremy and told him that these were the first two new series I wanted to put into production. Jeremy's face fell. 'Don't you realise,' he said, 'the two most difficult things to sell to the network are dramas about politics and show-biz?' However, he did sell them to the network, and because of his trust and support *Bill Brand* and *Rock Follies* were made – two series of which I'm very proud.

So, the franchise-holders need executives with courage to back their programme-makers. They also need to schedule with courage. I know this is an obvious statement, but when there are many channels to choose from the ratings fall. Some years ago, if a programme didn't achieve a rating in the mid- to high thirties, it was pulled instantly. Nowadays, providing the programme is reaching its *targeted* audience, it is considered successful with a rating in the mid-twenties.

Reaching a targeted audience is what the industry calls reaching the right demographic group. For the purposes of advertising the public is divided into groups from A to E categorised by the kind of jobs and income people have. Groups with greater purchasing power buy *different* products to those with lower purchasing power. *Coronation Street*, which gets an audience of seventeen million, delivers a smaller number of high-purchasing group viewers than a programme like *World in Action*, which only gets a rating between five to seven million – so that from an advertiser's point of view *World in Action* could be as valuable as the higher-rating programme, because they can still target their commercials to the audience that they know will be there. It all sounds complicated, but what it means is that documentaries, current affairs and some minority programmes need not be seen as an inevitable loss to revenue.

I've talked about programmes and schedules, but what about finance? I hear so many moans, about how difficult it's going to be, to make programmes *and* make money, that I sometimes wonder, why anyone wants to own a franchise at all. So, how to make the money go further? New franchise bidders will be able to learn from past mistakes.

Over the years the ITV companies have grown unwieldy. Overstaffing, restrictive practices, inefficient management – we've seen it all. But the reality is (as Channel 4 has proved) that it is more cost effective *not* to produce programmes in-house. I believe that in order to be profitable, the future franchise-holders will produce less and less themselves. Getting rid of staff is both expensive and emotive. Sooner or later, this is going to have to happen. It's not going to get any less expensive, or emotive, so why not do something about it now?

If the franchise-holders have conviction, stick to their promises, and are prepared to take risks, then all is not lost. One thing is for sure, if Channel 3 (as ITV may be called), and Channel 4 and the BBC go down market in order to try to attract larger ratings, the audience will *not* have diversity of choice and eventually they will switch over – or switch off.

And now to the programme-makers? What can *we* do? There is *one* problem common to all of us, whether we are working for the BBC or ITV, in-house or as independents. Money, or the lack of it, or the seeming lack of it.

If you're working for the BBC there definitely is a shortage of money. The licence fee is inadequate. This is very discouraging, because there is a genuine desire on the part of the programme executives to look for innovative material. There is still an air of adventure, which is not apparent in *some* of the ITV companies. If you're working for an ITV company the picture is not so clear. You are told that money is very short. But, the profits of the five major companies, and some of the larger regionals, don't look unhealthy at all. Under these circumstances, complaints of a lack of money become a bit difficult to swallow. Now, projects that have been gathering dust for a number of years because they were too expensive are suddenly being taken down from the shelves. A cynical thought crosses my mind. Could it be that there is plenty of money to be spent on winning a franchise, but not much to be spent on giving the public quality programmes thereafter?

Another problem common to us both is whether or not BBC1 and Channel 4 will stand firm and not panic when confronted with falling ratings. The BBC *say* they will continue to make and schedule programmes which cater to minority interests. But make no mistake, informal meetings to discuss the new BBC licence fee have already taken place and the BBC will have to convince their political masters – or mistress – that although its share of the audience will fall, its reach to its audience will still be maintained. Once the franchises have been awarded, the BBC is going to need all the support it can get from programme-makers and the public. In addition, Channel 3 can certainly help Channel 4 by cross-scheduling programmes.

Programme-makers working in-house have advantages which they can use. Some of you will have been an integral part of a franchise-holder's successful bid. You will have been put there because of your track record – the quality of the programmes you have made. So you have some clout, you can lobby constantly. Life in the independent sector is more complex. So why *did* I go independent? Because I wanted the freedom to develop ideas. I wanted to control my own destiny. That, I realise, is something of an illusion as we are always dependent on someone else's enthusiasm for our ideas. Also, to be honest, I wanted a more permanent reward for my work in making those ideas into successful, and yes, quality television programmes. Okay, I wanted to make money as well. Well, the making money bit has yet to come. Most independents have to concentrate on just making a living.

'Oh dear,' I hear you all groan. 'Here comes the yearly Edinburgh whinge from the independents.' Well, here's the point. If an independent is offered a commission at a certain budget, regardless of whether it is adequate or not, most of us are not in a position to refuse. So what do we do? We use our ingenuity – but we also cut corners, and before we can say 'Never mind the Quality Feel the Width', standards have gone down the drain. Independents are fragmented and, more importantly, most of the time are in competition with each other for commissions. The independent sector is not going to be able to realise its *full potential* until it has a viable financial base.

There is a large and varied independent sector, how can we, the independents, have some influence on the quality of programmes? One way would be to combine ourselves into groups. An association would provide protection by reducing overheads, and the combining of several independents could result in a more diverse programme package. This, in turn, would make it more attractive to distributors or other sources of finance. Working outside the system can be a very isolating experience, so another advantage of combining would be the possibility for programme-makers to interact with one another.

Combining ourselves into groups is all very well but there are other important factors to be taken into consideration. First, the question of ownership of rights. The government with its Broadcasting Bill has created a legalised monopoly situation. Under the terms of the Bill the franchise-holders are publishers, broadcasters, producers and distributors. The question that has to be asked, and I hope the IBA is listening, is: 'Is this right?' I'll give you my answer to that question: 'No, it isn't.'

A further point: we need to control the rights in the programmes we make, in order to attract financing to meet the budget deficit. If an independent is able to bring finance to a programme, it is as much to the franchise-holder's advantage as it is the independent's. It means that the franchise-holders do not have to find that part of the money, nor do they have to take all the risk. We need to control the rights so that we can make sure that they are exploited properly and to their full potential. And apart from *individual talents*, the control of rights in the programmes we make, are the assets which will go towards making the independent sector financially self-supporting.

We also need for there to be an independent external system of evaluating a fair price for our programmes. At the moment some of the ITV companies are putting a lower price on programmes made by independents compared to what they have to pay in-house. Leaving aside the morality of this kind of transaction, how is the independent going to retain quality in this situation?

Then there is the question of guaranteed access to the network. Andrew Quinn, Managing Director of Granada TV, has said that an 'overpowering reason for removing guarantees is that a peak time network schedule will only succeed if serviced by an *open* system of supply of programmes of *merit*.' I agree with him. I do believe that once the 25 per cent quota for independents has been *genuinely* reached, it *should* mean that the independent sector is healthy and self-supporting. Then, *and only then*, the 25 per cent quota could wither away, provided that the franchise-holders had *no guaranteed access* to the network either. I believe that we, the independents, are prepared to be judged on our programme-making merits, so long as the franchise-holders are prepared to be judged in the same way.

The industry has been in some disarray since the mid-1980s when Alan Peacock was first appointed to examine the BBC. If deregulation and the freer market are going to work – while still providing quality and diversity of choice – it will depend on how *vigorously* the ITC are in implementing their powers; it will depend on how *scrupulously* the new franchise-holders will be in keeping the promises they make in their applications; it will depend on the BBC and Channel 4 *not losing their nerve* in the face of falling ratings. And it will depend on us, the programme-makers, refusing to compromise or lower our standards, and seizing the opportunities that *are* there. Resisting change is one of our more maddening British characteristics. *Don't* let's go backwards into the future.

Notes

1. The idea of a quality threshold was introduced as an amendment to the Broadcasting Bill 1990. It required any company bidding for a Channel 3 licence to persuade the regulatory body – the Independent Television Commission (ITC) – that the programmes to be broadcast would meet certain benchmarks specified in legislation (the new Broadcasting Act 1990). This set of programming requirements was the quality threshold.
2. The first Chief Executive of the ITC.

The James MacTaggart Lecture 1991

The Future of Television: Market Forces and Social Values

David Elstein*

David Elstein's concern is to explore the Thatcher legacy to broadcasting which, he argues, is characterised by a shift away from social values to market forces as the key engines driving broadcasting. The Peacock Committee initiated this 'sea-change' by introducing notions such as consumer sovereignty and competition into programming considerations. Significantly, the Peacock Committee exceeded its brief by largely ignoring the BBC, while proposing 'the groundwork for a powerful attack on ITV'.

Elstein argues that the 1988 White Paper (*Broadcasting in the 1990s: Competition, Choice and Quality*) and the subsequent Broadcasting Act 1990, with their requirements for the allocation of ITV franchises by auction, the financial restructuring and sale of ITN, the separation of Channel 4 from ITV and the creation of Channel 5, will have damaging effects on the commercial sector of broadcasting and lead to the 'demise of those high-cost, high-quality programmes like *Poirot* [and] *Who Bombed Birmingham*?'

Elstein concludes that only the BBC is 'currently immune to these commercial pressures' but he queries 'will it remain so?' He suggests the licence fee will continue to provide funding for the BBC although his preference is for subscription, which he argues provides 'the safest,

* David Elstein has been a producer of current affairs programmes such as *This Week* and *Week in Politics*, has held senior positions at the BBC, Primetime Television and Thames Television, was Head of Programming at BSkyB from 1993 to 1996 and subsequently became Chief Executive of Channel 5. He has been a visiting professor at Oxford and Westminster Universities. In 1991 he was Director of Programmes at Thames Television in the wake of the *Death on the Rock* controversy.

most socially equitable, most politically insulated form of funding the BBC'.

□

I am delighted to have been asked to deliver this year's MacTaggart Lecture. I want to reflect on the remarkable sea-change that has taken place in the way that the structure of broadcasting is perceived: the shift from social values to market forces. The Thatcher premiership may be over, but the Thatcher legacy to broadcasting has yet to mature. This August might well be an appropriate moment to reflect on the significance of that change, and the portents for what is to come.

It was also in August, 27 years ago, that I joined the BBC, soon after the publication of the Pilkington Report. This had awarded the third television channel to the BBC, concluded that ITV fell 'well short of what a good public service of broadcasting should be', and offered a remarkable disquisition on the purposes of broadcasting. Reading through all the previous committee reports on broadcasting – Sykes, Crawford, Ullswater, Beveridge – as well as the debate surrounding Pilkington, what was evident was for how long and how successfully commercialism had been kept at bay intellectually as well as politically: in the process, allowing most European countries to follow the BBC rather than the American model for organising broadcasting.

The Peacock Committee was appointed in 1985. In July 1986, three months after I became Director of Programmes at Thames, the Peacock Report was published; the job I had taken changed beyond all recognition. It was not just that Peacock introduced the notions of consumer sovereignty, extraction of monopoly rents, the pursuit of efficiency and competition in programme supply. The new Thatcher administration allowed the Treasury and the Department of Trade and Industry to invade the Home Office's broadcasting preserve.

Into this new context has been injected a rich stream of governmental hostility towards the broadcasting establishment. Politicians have long resented the fact that television is more trusted than they are by the public. That resentment has been fuelled by television's willingness to expose awkward facts and nag away at apparent miscarriages of justice. The agonising summer most incumbents are enduring has been perceived by some as an explicit piece of political revenge – a death on the rack to make up for *Death on the Rock*.[1] Is that so far-fetched? If we look back over the Thatcher years, from Carrickmore[2] to the parliamentary roasting of Alasdair Milne during the Falklands war,[3] from

Norman Tebbit's feud with the BBC over the Libya bombing[4] to Leon Brittain's intervention in the *Real Lives* affair,[5] a pattern emerges of a somewhat manufactured degree of political outrage at broadcasters performing a fairly straightforward news/current affairs/documentaries function.

Whatever the rights and wrongs of the conflicts between broadcasters and politicians in the 1980s, I have no doubt about which side initiated hostilities. Indeed, the appointment of the Peacock Committee was openly flaunted at the time as a means of disciplining the BBC. It was a profound irony that the Peacock Committee – the most blatantly packed of any of the seven such committees of enquiry over the decades – failed to offer up the BBC to the advertisers. By way of consolation, Peacock spectacularly exceeded its terms of reference (which exclusively referred to the BBC) by proposing the groundwork for a powerful attack on ITV, which was made all the easier by ITV's own internal divisions over network access, and the rocketing success of the independent producers' lobby in its critique of ITVs internal and external uncompetitiveness. Even so, when the White Paper was published in late 1988, it was hard to miss the element of spite in the government's proposals.[6]

More serious evidence of governmental prejudice is the plight of ITN. The recent financial destabilisation of ITN may have had deeper causes – managerial incompetence, a swathe of major stories giving full scope to high-tech, high-cost reporting, competitive investment in news by the BBC – but the painful politicisation of the ITN board, diverting so much energy and attention from the main functions of the organisation, must have been a substantial contributory factor. Again, the White Paper offered no rationale for the forced sale of a majority of the shares in ITN – how could it, when the whole proposal had been cooked up in a private arrangement between 10 Downing Street and an ITN employee or two operating secretly behind the backs of fellow board directors?

The decision to separate Channel 4 from ITV may not have been explicitly designed to damage ITV – indeed, it is in practice much more likely to damage Channel 4 – but there can be little doubt that the prime movers behind the change were the people who felt most frustrated by ITV's monopoly right to sell Channel 4's advertising. Those who had campaigned unsuccessfully for advertiser access to the BBC were clearly not to be denied the consolation prize Peacock had promised.

The highest-bid tender system is, in the eyes of many, the most distinctive element of the legislative package.[7] Although in principle it would be hard to object to the government extracting the most from the ITV companies they could afford, it is impossible to believe that what we have already begun to see in the outcome of the licence round is what the government intended. How can the market be said to be operating efficiently if Central and STV secure their licences for less than a million pounds a year each – potentially depriving the Treasury of £400 million over ten years – whilst TVS (assuming they survive the process) pay out £54 million a year for an equivalent right to broadcast? Or is this the national lottery with which Mrs Thatcher so often flirted?

We have already seen the bathetic version of pass-the-parcel to which the first national radio licence auction has been reduced with high bidders failing to come up with their equity at the last moment. Applying such hit-and-miss methods to a delicate federal system like ITV is fraught with risk. If there are licensees who have bid to the limit, how will they be able to respond if competitive pressures require an increase in the network budget? Are we now playing blackjack? Twenty-one is a win, twenty-two is bust?

Conversely, if Central and STV are confirmed as having bid the minimum, how long will it be before their workforce demand a share of the loot that's been saved? It would be ridiculous if a system designed to deliver competitiveness actually engendered gross distortions in wage rates instead. We may end up with the worst of all worlds – a market-forces system where the market forces don't work. But while shares in STV and Central soar in expectation, and those in other companies drop far below their stated asset value, we are surely entitled to ask whether, for 'market forces', we should read 'market farces'.

For the record, I would not want this lecture to be perceived as anti-Conservative. Labour's record on broadcasting and civil liberties is scarcely spotless. Only the 1979 election spared us from having political commissars in the BBC, and an unworkable Open Broadcasting Authority running Channel 4. Sadly, the next election will come just too late to give hope of saving ITV and Channel 4 from the dangers they now face. The damage is already being inflicted on the industry. Whilst we await the October ITC outcome, ITVs commissioning process is virtually paralysed. This, combined with an advertising slump which will automatically affect Channel 4's spending power, has severely affected the independent production and facilities sector. ITVs own workforce, already battered by de-manning and a decline in real income, is deeply demoralised by the realisation that all that pain may still not guarantee them any long-term future.

The timetable itself is a problem. The ITC has given itself six weeks from announcing awards to the signing of contracts. Yet it has also made clear that it will try to include in those contracts detailed programme and financial commitments. If these commitments go beyond the basic requirements set out in the Act and the Invitation to Apply, there might well be resistance, or even withdrawals. The ITC, having announced its chosen licensees, would have some difficulty in changing horses in mid-stream.

In the bare six weeks available, the successful bidders that are plc's (the majority) will presumably need to secure shareholder approval before they sign their licences. Some, of course, with six months' further evidence of the decline in ITV revenue since submitting their high bids, may think better of them, and – as with the radio auction – mysteriously fail to come up with all their equity at the crucial moment. And losers will be considering judicial review. On balance, I discount the likelihood of any judicial review, because it is so hard to imagine successfully establishing that the ITC has acted *ultra vires*.

But even in the absence of judicial review, and even if the contracts are all signed on time, there are many hazards. The first is if one or more current major supplier of FM programmes is dislodged. There can be little doubt that the BBC would move swiftly to establish an output deal which might secure it such plums as *Blind Date* and *London's Burning*, or *Coronation Street*. Would the successful bidders – particularly incumbents – sit quietly watching? According to the ITC's timetable, they should be gathered round a table earnestly discussing future net-working arrangements, and the remit for a central commissioning system. But it is hard to believe that they would passively allow some of ITV's prime assets to be snapped up.

I have not begun to address the other threats to ITV that the new commercial environment will present. One such is the likely demise of those high-cost, high-quality programmes like *Poirot*, *Who Bombed Birmingham?* and *A Murder of Quality* that contractors have over the years delivered at a loss, for broader strategic reasons.

The only crumb of comfort for ITV at the moment is that the recession could not have come at a worse time for BSkyB, which depends for its survival on selling dishes and subscriptions to consumers with no disposable cash. The one area where satellite poses an early threat to ITV is in children's programming. As dishes spread, ITVs children's programming will be under pressure from advertisers to compete in kind; in due course, the pressure will knock on to BBC1. What we will lose is home-grown drama, entertainment and information programmes specially made for children. That is the nature of the new market forces. Of course, the arrival of satellite owes nothing as such to Tory broadcasting policy, except insofar as the artificial exclusion of BSkyB from ownership restrictions shows the degree of political spin in the legislation. Although Labour has promised to end that exemption, by the time they are likely to get a chance of doing so, BSkyB will either have become profitable or gone bust.

As for Channel 4 I would not expect its share of commercial viewing and revenue to start failing until 1994. That is because ITV, for at least the next two years, will be too preoccupied with internal issues to formulate a collective competitive approach towards it. This may therefore be Channel 4's last chance to marshal its programme resources, and shape the independent production sector so that it delivers what the channel needs by way of reliable comedy and drama. Hitherto, Channel 4 has allowed the independent sector to remain fragmented, and spent too much of its cash on funding low-budget feature films. That may win plaudits from the film industry, but is not a survival strategy in a competitive market place. Also, Channel 4 will no longer be able to afford the luxury of commissioning in isolation from the schedule. The loose structure of the channel will surely become much more commercial in its operation. Channel 4 may also find some of its main audience-winners either rising in price or unavailable if ITV eventually chooses to compete head on: American films, comedy and drama are currently picked up cheaply off the back of ITV deals, while athletics hand-overs and ITV comedy repeats are interesting features of Channel 4's current strong audience performance. I would hate to see ITV attacking Channel 4 directly – after all, the long-term outcome is much more likely to be a change of remit than a commercial collapse – but it is a scenario the new Act makes possible and market forces may make inevitable. If it happens, and it leads to a marked narrowing of the range of our terrestrial programme service, let us not forget this was a risk deliberately run by a government too much influenced by advertisers, too little by viewers.

Channel 5, I am sure, has been built into the business plans of all the ITV licence applicants: whether it actually captures a 10 per cent, 12 per cent or 14 per cent share of advertising revenue, as variously predicted, remains to be seen. I would only offer one comment. Channel 5 is the first additional terrestrial television channel to be created with no public inquiry.[8] Why was there no debate? Had the market forces philosophy so completely won the field that those who might have questioned the social purpose of a new channel simply could not gain a footing? Perhaps. But I think a major contributory factor was the neu-tralisation of the most radical elements in the broadcasting community.

Despite the huge expenditure – and human distress – inflicted on ITV by the process of de-manning and ending old working practices, it was undoubtedly overdue and necessary, and I have no argument with that part of the Tory attack on the broadcasting establishment, despite its occasional hyperbole. What nearly seventy years of experi-ence has shown us is that broadcasting is not just a series of transac-tions between producers and consumers. Of course, social values have not disappeared from the commercial sector. But no objective observer could now seriously expect this to be anything more than a holding operation, with the ability of ITV and Channel 4 to hold on to their current programming policies heavily dependent on the success – or failure – of the new satellite services and Channel 5.

Only one broadcasting system, the BBC, is currently immune to these commercial pressures, but will it remain so? There is no one in ITV who fails to understand that the bedrock of quality television in this country is a securely funded, well-managed, broadly ranging BBC. The BBC keeps ITV on its mettle: whatever the pressures from satellites, as long as BBC1 can sustain a strong audience share with a schedule that contains peak-time factual series, ambitious drama, authoritative news and reporting, and home-grown children's programmes, ITV must compete in kind.

Although, for obvious reasons, ITV has talked up the audience lead it has established recently, I do not believe the BBC faces any ratings crisis. Schedule performance is not, except in the very short-term, a BBC problem. Far more important is the next phase of the financial reor-ganisation. Every indication is that the BBC will want to keep the licence fee, and that a post-Thatcher Downing Street will permit this. My own view remains that subscription is the safest, most socially equitable, most politically insulated form of funding the BBC. The BBC has argued that subscription would end universality, which only holds true if you believe licence evaders are entitled to watch BBC television. Resistance to subscription strikes me as more than just financial: the BBC seems just not to want such a direct relationship with the viewer.

All that said, if the BBC concludes that it wishes to continue the licence fee, we should unhesitatingly support it. And just as important as the BBC's funding is the principle that it covers the full range of tele-vision programming. For the BBC to retreat into a public affairs ghetto might temporarily enrich ITV, but it would permanently impoverish the nation's viewers. If the market-forces argument won by default in the 1980s, with all the consequential risks we now face in the commercial sector, let us ensure that in the 1990s, there is a full public debate about the BBC, and the social values it embodies.

How do we define such values in the future? We cannot turn back the clock. Any new concept must incorporate the new ideas of the eighties – value for money, independent access, multiplicity of choice. Reith's paternalism could not survive the substitution of active consumer for passive viewer. Similarly, concepts of public service from the 1960s and 1970s, resting heavily on universality and the licence fee, are no longer relevant when dish technology can put 95 per cent of the population within reach of dozens of free or pay channels. Range is crucial, and not just because viewers should be able to enjoy a mixed diet of drama, comedy, sport and multi-cultural programming. It is equally important that this range be seen to offer a rounded picture of the viewer as citizen, with television as society's prime source of information, entertainment and cultural stimulation in the broadest sense.

To deliver such range, and to generate so much in the way of new ideas and new production, requires the BBC to have ambition, competence, size, secure funding, creative talent and room for experiment and failure. As I list these characteristics, I cannot help but note that they are currently all present in ITV, but all at risk in the next few years.

However odd it may seem for an ITV Director of Programmes to be urging an audience of disaffected independents and producers to rally round a BBC not immediately threatened, perhaps Edinburgh is as good a place as any to stand back from immediate preoccupations, and to acknowledge that we collectively failed to offer a coherent statement of the social purpose of broadcasting when faced with a government policy that explicitly placed competition and choice ahead of quality. In doing so, we may yet emerge with a refined and toughened concept of the social value of broadcasting in the nineties. If it is too late to correct the mistakes of the eighties, at least let us resolve at this Edinburgh to learn from them, to set about defining what we truly value in our broadcasting system, to state those values boldly and clearly, and fight for them. I know that's what Jimmy MacTaggart would have done.

Notes

1. *Death on the Rock* was a programme broadcast by Thames Television about the three members of the IRA shot by the British Secret Service on Gibralter. The programme contested the government's suggestion that the three IRA members had intended to detonate a bomb and that they had been given a warning before the British person-

nel opened fire. The Windlesham–Rampton Report cleared Thames Television of the government allegations of bias and partisanship but No. 10 never acknowledged the credibility of the report.

2. In 1985 the BBC programme *Panorama* broadcast pictures of an IRA road check at Carrickmore which seemed to enjoy the co-operation of local people.

3. A number of senior ministers suggested in parliamentary comments that the case for Britain was not being sufficiently stressed and supported in the BBC's reporting of the Falklands war.

4. Norman Tebbit, when Chairman of the Conservative Party, ordered a party enquiry into what he alleged was bias in the Corporation's reporting of the bombing of Libya in 1986.

5. Home Secretary Leon Brittan asked the BBC Board of Governors not to broadcast a programe in the *Real Lives* series which featured Republican and Democratic Unionist politicians. Mrs Thatcher, who had not seen the programme, wished it banned because it offered 'the oxygen of publicity' to terrorists.

6. *Broadcasting in the '90s: Competition, Choice and Quality* (1988), London: HMSO (Cm 517).

7. The franchise auction established by the Broadcasting Act 1990 requires companies who wish to secure a licence to broadcast in one of the ITV regions to submit 'blind' bids detailing the sum they are willing to pay the Treasury annually throughout the life of the licence. The procedure was intended to introduce competition into the broadcasting market, but in the initial auction in 1991 triggered substantial over-bidding in some regions (Yorkshire) while other companies (Central) secured the franchise uncontested for the minimum bid of £2,000.

8. Channel 5 was given a statutory remit in the Broadasting Act 1990, although, because of technical difficulties and the lack of broadcaster interest in bidding for the franchise, the station did not eventually begin broadcasting until 1997.

The James MacTaggart Lecture 1992

The Future of the BBC

Michael Grade*

Michael Grade's MacTaggart Lecture, widely interpreted as an application for the job of Director General of the BBC, analyses the finances, management and programming of the BBC following a period of robust clashes with the Thatcher government and in the run-up to the Charter renewal in 1994. Grade argues for the significance of programmme quality and standards at the BBC for the wider broadcasting industry. 'It is the BBC,' Grade famously remarks, 'which keeps us all honest.'

Grade identifies a number of key problems confronting the BBC. First, the BBC has adopted a policy of 'political appeasement' in its relations with government which can only result in 'terminal decline'. By contrast, in-house management at the BBC has adopted a 'sort of pseudo Leninist style' which relies on 'central control' and promises the spectre of 'editorial dictatorship'. Grade concludes that the Governors cannot be both managers and regulators, and consequently advocates a single new regulatory body – 'Let us call it the British Television Commission' – for all television services.

Second, Grade is troubled by the impoverished vision of the BBC held at the highest levels and exemplified by Michael Checkland's opening statement as Director General that the 'BBC is a billion pound business.' The BBC has become preoccupied with cuts, savings and making money rather than programmes; the BBC is haemorrhaging talent.

Finally, there is a the problem of the licence fee which empowers governments against Governors and can encourage the latter towards political

* In 1992 Michael Grade was Chief Executive of Channel 4, having been Head of Programmes at the BBC. Since 2004 he has been Chairman of the BBC Board of Governors.

compliance (see Dyke's discussion of the 'culture of dependency' in 1994). The BBC must escape the 'poverty trap of a licence fee' by establishing a long-term formula which ends the Corporation's status as a 'supplicant'.

◻

The main item on my agenda tonight is the future of the greatest broadcasting institution in the world, the BBC. You might ask why I have chosen this subject tonight. Why bother? The fact is that the BBC is once again the object of intense political scrutiny. Its future is being weighed in the balance and, I suspect, like everybody in this gathering tonight, I care deeply about the Corporation and its future direction. It was Douglas Hurd who, as the then Home Secretary, described the BBC as the cornerstone of British Broadcasting. It certainly is. An impoverished or marginalised BBC would lower the standards of all UK broadcasting.

The logic behind that statement is simple. Where you have strong, benchmark public-service television channels driven to produce excellent, home-grown programming of all kinds for its domestic audiences, then all television has to aspire to the same quality in order to compete and gain share of viewing. In Britain this is certainly true. It is the BBC which keeps us all honest. With the competition growing in the market place, that makes it even more vital for the viewers that the BBC has a secure future.

So what I want to try to do is to offer a reasonably informed analysis of the difficulties the BBC faces. I believe many of them to be of their own making. I will argue tonight that the licence fee which has underpinned the Corporation for over fifty years is in danger of becoming a dwindling asset, but only because the BBC itself seems prepared to pay too high a price in return for the Charter and licence renewal and the legislation which makes payment compulsory. I want to argue that the BBC Governors have adopted a policy of political appeasement. They have set the BBC on a course which can only lead to terminal decline.

About five years ago, two events subtly and fundamentally changed the Corporation. These events signalled, I believe, what I might call the 'brutalisation' of the BBC. The first was the sacking of the then Director General, Alasdair Milne. Presumably, the reason he was so publicly and brutally dispensed with was to mark the new regime in control: *pour encourager les autres*.

To set it in context, I need to remind you of the mood of the government at the time. Mrs Thatcher had clearly and openly signalled that she thought the BBC was out of control. Carrickmore, Falklands war coverage, *Real Lives*, *Tumbledown*, *The Monocled Mutineer*. Row after row — dutifully fuelled by the rabid elements of the Tory press and led for the most part by the News International titles.

In response, the Governors determined to throw themselves at the mercy of a government that had shown the BBC no mercy at all. They decided that the only way to win back government support, and there-fore safeguard future levels of licence fee increases, was to try to catch up with the political mood of the times and be seen to be taking charge. More and more they encroached on the day-to-day management of the place. Given the amount of time the Chairman[1] and the Vice Chairman[2] spent in their own offices at Broadcasting House, you could be forgiven for mistaking them for full-time executives — not part-time 'non execu-tives'. The Chairman and the Vice Chairman sat on the appointment boards which chose today's channel controllers. The fortnightly Governors' board meeting agendas were full of decisions to be taken on detail, rather than strategy.

This leads me to my first, logical conclusion that the Governors, by involving themselves so deeply in the management, can no longer be arm's length regulators of the service as well. I therefore whole-heartedly support the recent proposal of Sir George Russell, Chairman of the ITC, that there should be a single regulatory body for all terrestrial television and cable. Let us call it the British Television Commission, whose job it would be to license and regulate Channels 1, 2, 3, 4 and 5 and cable.

The second of the events I believe changed the BBC was Michael Checkland's opening statement on being appointed to succeed Alasdair Milne. He said, and I quote: 'the BBC is a billion pound business'. That represented his vision of the BBC, and the vision of the Governors, since they appointed him. Was that moment of public identification with business the moment when the BBC abandoned its heritage? I suspect it was. Because what has followed has been a continual series of initia-tives and pronouncements from the top that unrelentingly echo the jargon of commerce not culture.

Ten point plans, efficiency initiatives, task forces, positioning in the market place etc., etc. They sound more like IBM or BP than the BBC. The latest jargon inside the BBC speaks of 'downsizing', 'de-layering' and 'out-sourcing'. That's closure, redundancies and dark studios to you and me. I am all for cutting back on wasteful bureaucracy, most of which is to be found in the corporate centre of the BBC. I would have attacked that first before I laid a glove on the production end.

Producer Choice[3] may well serve to flush out any waste, or empire building in the resource areas, but it carries with it some dangers. If

Producer Choice led the BBC into becoming solely, or mainly, a publisher contractor, buying in the market place and putting nothing back in the way of training and development, the case for public funding would seem to disappear altogether. We must also consider what the end cost of Producer Choice might be. A sudden surge in demand from the BBC for private-sector facilities might not be met by the supply and then the costs of those facilities will surely rise – for all of us.

Listening and talking to people at the BBC (my sources must remain anonymous), one is left with the conclusion that programmes are to become commodities. So many units of resource for a sitcom, so many units for a drama etc. This seems to me to be a denial of everything the BBC stands for. The house style of the BBC is made distinctive and distinguished by production values, and by the love and attention that are dedicated to serving the producer's vision. This is supplied by individual, in-house crafts people with specialist skills, people with an almost inflated pride in their work and what the BBC stands for.

But in its headlong rush for the myth of demonstrable and measurable efficiency, the Governors [of the BBC] have forgotten that dramatic weight reduction induces giddiness. The staff are punch drunk with change. Riding a roller coaster may be an exhilarating experience for a short time at the fun fair, but it is not a condition conducive to sound judgement, clear-sightedness and responsible risk-taking. And that's what good programme-making needs. The in-house production base is the foundation of the BBC. It is also the foundation of the whole British television production industry. If you dismantle the BBC's own resources, you remove another crucial justification for the licence fee.

That's enough about resources. Let me now turn to programmes. No one at the top of the BBC seems to have much good to say about them. Any recent public utterances have mostly been negative. All news and current affairs pre-1988 have been written off publicly as a bad job. Nearly a whole generation of BBC-trained journalists have disappeared in the recent news and current affairs revolution.

Present editorial policies are subject to death by a thousand whispers. Creative talents can no longer look to the top of the BBC for support when they most need it. Dennis Potter's *Blackeyes* was publicly rubbished by the Chairman of the BBC. Win, lose or draw, surely you must publicly support your creative people, particularly such a talented bunch as Verity Lambert, Julia Smith and of course Jonathan Powell. They have delivered brilliantly for viewers in the past and will deliver again. A public message of support from the top would not come amiss – it would also give the hierarchy some credibility. As and when the show does come good, they'll be the first to say, 'we always knew it would'. Second-guessing is second nature at the top of the BBC.

What has been forgotten, or not understood, is that the BBC has always prided itself on its record of staying with shows that weren't instant successes, like *Dad's Army* and, yes, *EastEnders*. It must never look like a place where safety first is the rule, where instant success is demanded of popular entertainment.

The Chairman recently said in the annual report: 'as the market place fills with new traders, the BBC must ensure its wares are quality wares and are not being sold at the next stall'. Underlying this statement is the implication that if the private sector is providing it, the BBC should not bother. This is a curious position to hold because some of the greatest successes in the BBC's history have come from taking talent and ideas from other channels, applying its own creative criteria and adding value, to use the jargon. Think, for example, of Morecambe and Wise, the gang that created Monty Python (poached from Rediffusion), the Two Ronnies (poached from LWT), Sir Robin Day (poached from ITN), Victoria Wood (from Granada), Harry Enfield, French and Saunders, Ben Elton etc. (from Channel 4). The list goes on and on. The market provided them, but the BBC improved them.

What about programme types? The market-stall argument dictates that if Survival Anglia is doing penguins, then penguins are out of bounds to the BBC. But the BBC has a genius for taking what others have and developing it into programming that the viewers value even more. Why throw that brilliant tradition away for the sake of yet another designer slogan with which to dazzle the free marketeers? It's an Alice-in-Wonderland policy that will only deprive the viewers and threaten the licence fee.

The high-ground policy carries with it other dangers. It smells alarmingly like programming by prescription – the enemy of all good works in my experience. I learned very early on as a young director of programmes at LWT that ideas prescribed from the top usually turn into disaster on their way on to the screen. All the best television and radio programme ideas are a combination of the creative management team and the production force – both trusting and supporting each other. That sounds a long way from the direction the BBC is headed.

It also sounds rather arrogant, to my ear, that you will only commission 'distinctive' work. How do you know it will be distinctive? And who decides and on what criteria? Who, honestly, could have read the first *Goon Show* script and pronounced: 'This will be a benchmark in British comedy?' It must have read like gibberish. You don't – you just back your hunch, back the talent and hope the audience verdict will be favourable.

And why should the BBC be dismissive of the bought-in series it acquires from overseas? ITV could have bought *M*A*S*H*, *Dallas* or *Neighbours*. They saw them all, but passed. The BBC bought them and the public were suitably entertained. It is all very rum, indeed, that some kind of 'distinctivity test' will be applied to all programmes before they are commissioned.

The general public, on the other hand, look to the BBC in the first place to entertain them. This is a truth the Governors ignore at their peril. Think back, if you will, to 1956, the year the new ITV really took off and BBC television was reduced to a 27 per cent share of just two channels. If the BBC hadn't responded with popular programmes to redress the balance of share nearer to 50–50, does anyone seriously believe we would be sitting here in 1992 still talking about a licence fee? The public certainly wouldn't have supported it.

The Governors need reminding that if the popular parts of the schedule are working well, it has a buoyant effect on the ratings for all programmes, arts, documentaries, news, current affairs, education and, yes, religion. If BBC television becomes a cultural ghetto, a high-minded, elitist service it will certainly lose its claim to its two, precious terrestrial channels. Without the courage to remain popular in the widest sense, that clear channel choice for viewers would blur, and, with it, the justification for hanging on to two channels. The high-ground policy is simplistic nonsense. It will marginalise the BBC, reduce choice and erode the public's willingness to pay.

From what I know of the BBC, they seem to have adopted a sort of pseudo Leninist style of management which relies on the exercise of central control. Even more serious than managerial dictatorship is the spectre of editorial dictatorship. In a national, public broadcast institution, the public interest demands plurality of editorial voice and tone. The BBC, even in an expanded market of many channels, will still, I hope, command a significant share of audience attention – most particularity in the area of news and factual programming. Nothing *is* more dangerous than for the BBC to present a view of the world which is so narrowly focused, so filtered, that it denies plurality. This is *not* an argument for unbridled licence to say anything. It is an argument for a BBC which represents the views of the people who pay for it.

The handmaiden of central control is secrecy, the BBC is also more secretive than ever it was. And so, as the great BBC debate unfolds, the institution itself is silent. The so-called task forces reported over a year ago but still there has been no BBC mission statement: the silence is eerie, almost ominous. The staff are afraid to speak publicly unless every word has been cleared with the BBC's own thought police. The BBC is no longer a leaking boat; it is more like an airtight fortress from which no stray opinion, no unauthorised conviction, no judgement about public-service broadcasting unsanctioned by the Board or the so-called policy unit is permitted to escape.

We all know that there are people alive and thinking in there – amongst them, some of the cleverest and most imaginative characters I have ever known. But there comes a point where iron discipline is virtually indistinguishable from brain death. And the worst consequence of all this is on the morale of the staff who speak disparagingly of their managers – but behind their backs. In the middle of all this, good programme-makers trying to make good programmes begin to look outside. The independent sector is now full of ex-BBC talent, at all levels, people who decided enough was enough. To paraphrase Ted Turner, the BBC is haemorrhaging talent.

So, the big question is, why have the Governors put the BBC in this position? For the answer, we come back to the licence fee. Because of the funding relationship, the balance of powers is tilted massively in favour of government. It grants permission to broadcast, grants the funds and these days sets the level of funds on a regular basis. Government holds all the cards. It follows that there will always be the potential for unequal conflict between government and the BBC, and this is of course reflected in the editorial differences – programme rows and accusations of political bias. Worse, the BBC's editorial decisions will always be seen in the light of their relationship with government at the time any controversial decisions are made.

BBC staff used to say that ITV might be rich, but the BBC were bold. But in recent years that boldness has been replaced by an enervating caution which starts at the top and quickly becomes the culture of the whole organisation. There's talk inside of the 'pre-emptive cringe' but only in private. But can anyone in the hall see the BBC in its current mood even making, let alone transmitting *Death on the Rock*? The BBC hierarchy would have 'referred' the programme out of existence.

The Charter renewal is a golden moment of opportunity for the BBC to settle a major issue of principle, and I don't mean whether or not to privatise the graphics department. I mean the issue of extricating the BBC, once and for all, from the poverty trap of a licence fee. Let us be clear. There is no alternative to the licence fee. The BBC knows that, we here know it and, in its heart of hearts, the government knows it.

What the BBC should now be fighting for is a long-term formula that eliminates the all too frequent and debilitating funding negotiations with Downing Street. It has no future as a continued supplicant. It is not even in the politicians' interests that the independence of the BBC should go on being questioned as a result of the government's funding arrangements. If it is not truly independent, and seen so to be, the BBC is no use to anyone. The whole point of this debate must be to ensure long-term security, not a quick fix.

I have talked a little tonight about the BBC's imperfections. But when you love an institution, you'll forgive it anything. There is an army of supporters ready to speak out on the BBC's behalf. All they need is a sign – not from heaven, just from Broadcasting House. The government needs to feel the full weight of the argument for a strong, independent BBC so it can continue as the cornerstone of our broadcasting. The people prepared to speak up for the BBC will do so with a passion, commitment and objectivity that no government can ignore.

Notes

1. Marmaduke Hussey was the former Chief Executive and Managing Director of Times newspapers; he was in post during the twelve months of *The Times* closure due to an industrial dispute.
2. Lord Barnett, previously Joel Barnett, a Labour politician and ex-Treasury minister.
3. Producer Choice was a budgeting system for the funding of programmes which was devised by John Birt (see his lecture 'A Glorious Future', 1996) and formally stated in BBC (1993), *Responding to the Green Paper*, London: BBC. Producer Choice offered producers control of their programming budgets and allowed them to shop outside of the Corporation for facilities for programme-making. The intention of Producer Choice was to introduce a competitive market into BBC production and thereby to refute suggestions by government and others that the BBC was overly bureaucratic, inefficient and costly.

The James MacTaggart Lecture 1993

Occupying Powers

Dennis Potter*

Dennis Potter begins his eloquent lecture by warning his audience that he does not wish to be kind or gentle: his ambition is to 'land a few blows on some of the nastiest people besmirching our once-fair land': especially on that 'pair of croak-voiced Daleks' (John Birt and Marmaduke Hussey) who head the BBC. Potter argues that the BBC is currently under attack and 'driven on to the back foot' by an ideologically motivated and malicious government, aided and abetted by supine managers at the BBC who have responded by taking 'several more steps backward'. The creative culture of the BBC is being replaced by 'management culture', articulated via a 'dogma-driven rhetoric'.

Television which used to offer a 'window on the world' has been 'ripped apart' and reassembled by politicians and cost accountants who now decide 'what we can and cannot see on our screens'. Potter argues that we must build defences to protect broadcasting and democracy from the occupying powers of business, bureaucratic management and politicians. There must be regulation to control the growing concentration of ownership and the expansion of cross-media ownership. This simple act of 'public hygiene' might temper abuse, widen choice and maybe even return 'broadcasting to its makers'. Potter concludes by announcing, with tongue planted firmly in his cheek, his intention

* Dennis Potter was a distinguished and controversial television dramatist. His plays for television include *Vote, Vote, Vote for Nigel Barton* (1965), *Pennies From Heaven* (1978), *Blue Remembered Hills* (1979), *The Singing Detective* (1986) and *Lipstick on Your Collar* (1993). *Karaoke* and *Cold Lazarus* were broadcast in 1994 shortly after Potter's death. His play *Brimstone and Treacle*, which was banned by the BBC, was shown at the 1977 Edinburgh International Television Festival.

to apply for the post of Chairman of the Governors of the British Broadcasting Corporation.

☐

I am giving the melodramatic title 'Occupying Powers' to this year's James MacTaggart Memorial Lecture so that I can reflect behind the barricade of metaphor about what it really feels like for many others besides myself who sell their services and some of their passions to the strange new generations of broadcasting managements and their proprietors.

Quote: 'Broadcasting is at the heart of British society. The structure and composition of the broadcasting industry, the purpose and motivation of broadcasters and the programmes and services they offer are vital factors in reflecting and shaping that society' unquote. The quotation is certainly one which James MacTaggart would have taken for granted.

Jimmy was my first drama producer at the BBC. He was in charge of *Vote, Vote, Vote for Nigel Barton*, the first play of mine to be hoicked off the screen without so much as a by-your-leave on the very day it was scheduled to be broadcast. Back in those good old days there was a bureaucrat in every cupboard and smugness waiting with a practised simper on the far side of every other door. I recall these things in order to offer up at least one small strip of sticking plaster for the suppurating wounds of the poor wretch who is the present Director General.[1] I haven't made this long journey in order to be kind and gentle, but I think it is only fair to tell him that the fear and loathing now swirling jugular-high around those same circular corridors do have some antecedents, and it always was possible to measure the distance between so-called management and the so-called creative by the time it took for a memo to go in one direction and a half-brick to come back in the other.

It is a wretched thing to have to say, but there are legions of troubled and embittered employees at the BBC who can scarcely understand any of the concepts of the new 'management culture' which the present Director General tries to enunciate. I have just this week finished a co-production with the BBC and it was during the making of *Midnight Movie* that I came to see just how deeply and how seriously the demoralisation, the bitterness and, yes, even the hatred had bitten into the working lives of so many hitherto reasonably contented and undoubtedly talented BBC staff.

I tell you now, it was impossible not to wonder how on earth those currently and I hope temporarily in charge of the BBC could have brought things to such a miserably demeaning condition. My impression was that there is now a one-way system of communication, and that the signals being sent down the narrowed track were so laden with costive, blurb and bubble-driven didacticism that they were more than half perceived as emanating in a squeak of static from someone or, rather, something alien and hostile. And you cannot make a pair of croak-voiced Daleks[2] appear benevolent even if you dress one of them in an Armani suit and call the other Marmaduke.

When making *Midnight Movie*, and watching and listening to what is going on at the BBC as it trims down its staff almost as fast as it loses its viewers, I was struck – and not for the first time – by how much the shifts and turns which seem particular to any one large institution can in themselves be seen as a model for the wider society in which all of us live. Any virulently new management culture can be studied as scrupulously as one might examine the bacteria proliferating around a wound. Both are the response to previous damage made worse by infection picked up from the outside world. The ideas in the unclean air, so to speak. The glories of privatisation and the brutalities of the unshackled market – as unleashed by Mrs Thatcher and her successor ideologists – were always likely to rattle a few of the professions, and sometimes rightly so. This iconoclasm fractured many old attitudes, many old bonds, and even many whole communities. And the deep hatred of any other claim, any other way of seeing, of anything other than the forces of law and order in the public domain, was always going to be arrowed with poison-dipped barb at the slow, decent, stumbling and puzzled giant run from Broadcasting House.

And thus it is in model form that the turmoil, the distress, the dogma-driven rhetoric, the obtuseness and the spluttering aggressions at and around the BBC can also be picked up in similar shapes, cries, contortions and an almost identical bluster – from *both* sides – in so many other areas of our national life. We have been at war with each other, and some of our fellow citizens have felt that bits of their very brain and fibres from their very soul are being crunched with the other, apparently all-important numbers in the computer.

The reason I am speaking in this way on this occasion is not simply because my fists are already clenched, and not just because I really do want to land a few blows on some of the nastiest people besmirching our once-fair land. No, tis because I object to the manner in which too many of us too much of the time half hide behind the anonymous, the over-smoothed, over-soothed and anodyne. Even as we quietly rot or noisily spin, and even as the disaffected, the dispossessed, the poor and the more than half-mad surge almost necessarily unnoticed at the littered edges of the gutters, even then, even then, the normal, polite meta-language of Britspeak and its halfway decent conceptual evasions, modulated only by a whine, choke off enough of the pain or sufficient of the venom. But then we are left emptied of almost everything except a numbing bewilderment, a paralysis of the spirit, and that long, aching, nearly inexpressible sense of loss which is I feel – what's the current phrase? – the Hidden Agenda lurking behind so much of our public discourse.

I would not dispute for one wayward whistle or crackle that the BBC of my childhood was not paternalistic and often stuffily pompous. It saw itself in an almost priestly role. But at a crucial period of my life it threw open the 'magic casement' on great sources of mind-scape at a time when books were hard to come by, and when I had never stepped into a theatre or a concert hall, and would have been scared to do so even if given the chance.

Of course, the characteristic media ploy of separating the 'popular' from the 'serious', yes, that process had already begun with the split between the Home Service and the Light Programme. But such a parting of the ways was nothing like as rigidly mapped out as it is nowadays, where listeners are presumed to be walking about with one of the digits one to five tattooed like cattle brands on their high, middling, low, lower and yet lower brows. On the old Light Programme you could suddenly, maybe reluctantly, collide with a play or a discussion or an embryonic drama-documentary. The now totally pervasive assumptions of the market place, which have stiffened into something close to Natural Law, had not by then removed the chance of being surprised by something you didn't know or – better still – by something you didn't know that you knew. It would be graceless of me not to acknowledge with an open heart the significant part the BBC had played in my life. Millions of our fellow citizens feel the same way, for there have been all too few British institutions of any size of which one could say with hand on heart that they truly work, that they are 'the best' that is.

I place quotation marks around 'best' because the potential vices of any form of moderated paternalism are all too clear, and were too often demonstrated in the old BBC monopoly, first and for longest in radio and then for many years in television. Paternalism has been defined as power with a conscience, and it can also be arrogance without a banana skin. This-is-what-we-think-is-good-for-you.

The dangers of the older view of how to run radio and television are, unless faced and redefined, sufficiently troubling to leave enough space for someone such as Rupert Murdoch to drive a golden coach and a team of wild-eyed horses straight through the gap. His James MacTaggart Lecture here a few years ago was little short of a masterpiece of apparently libertarian rhetoric. Indeed, it was the kind of peroration I would like to hear him deliver from the scaffold.

The insecurities and contradictions of the BBC's only half-digested and half- shamefaced self-definitions lay like rubble spread in inviting heaps in front of the supercharged, savage toothed JCB of his unslaked appetite. The Corporation has already been driven on to the back foot by the ideology-driven malice of the ruling politicians, and its response has been to take several more steps backwards, with hands thrown up, and to whimper an alleged defence of all it has stood for in the very language and concepts of its opponents. This palpable ambivalence and doubt, where you pretend to be the commercial business that you cannot be, has led to the present, near-fatal crisis where it seems to be thought that the wounds (often self-afflicted) can only be staunched by shuffling about word-processed words about a new 'Management Culture'.

Management of what? Management for what? Management. Management. Management. The word sticks in one's interface. Please excuse me if I dare to laugh, but I know that each age, even each decade, has its little cant word coiled up inside real discourse like a tiny grub in the middle of an apple. Each age, even each decade, is overly impressed for a little while by halfway-bright youngish men on the make who adeptly manipulate the current terminology at precisely the right moment to make precisely the right impression on those who are a little older, a little less intelligent and considerably less alert. Ah, me! Which one of us here this evening has not fallen into one or other of these categories, and perhaps into the wrong one at the very moment we thought we were in the other. Life in the media business can be a hoot.

As a writer who needs to clutch his pen as though it were a lifebelt, I have to admit that I have nevertheless improved many a shining hour with a probably untransmittable little playlet about one of the more intriguing encounters of our time. I was not there when Fortnum met Mason, Laurel met Hardy, or Murdoch met Mephistopheles but I would have given my old thesaurus or my new sequence of Reader's Digest Prize Draw Numbers to have been a hornet on the wall at that surely entrancing, fascinating and maybe even comical occasion when dear old Marmaduke first met dear young John and each of them sort of half-discussed what was sort of half-wrong with the greatest broadcasting organisation the world has ever seen. Where, I wonder, did they meet? Who was the first to smile – lethally? Who said, um, 'structural walk-through' as he ordered the mineral water, and did the waiter say 'Pardon'?

My invention has not run out, but the temptation to dish back what has been so wantonly dished out must be resisted. It is too easy to accuse others of betrayal when you are not ready to acknowledge your own. I remember the way in which I made the journey up the tick-tick-tick examination ladder, all the way to Oxford. Teachers love to get their hands on a bright and pliant child, and they do not consciously give wing to the invisible worm that flies in the night, bringing the blight of an especially English type of betrayal deep into the oh-look-at-me! folds of the most precocious bloom. You are first made to feel a little different, and then you *want* to be different, and although you know what you gain with your little Latin and less Greek, you do not for a long time realise what you have lost.

'Only connect,' said E. M. Forster. What a good word: *connect*. The verb which far better than the merely technical transmit is if not actually, certainly what should be the defining activity of all television – especially that threatened and peculiarly self-threatened section which has no need, and indeed no remit, to package up A, B, or C-defined groups of the allegedly passive on behalf of predatory advertisers. The section of broadcasting which, above all else, and quite separately from any temporarily dominant political language or so-called 'Management Culture' must continually remind itself that it is not a business trying to distribute dosh to its shareholders, not owned by its current administrators, not a company entitled to build Chinese walls around its momentary practices, but something held in trust and in law for every citizen of this misgoverned and too-long abused group of nations we, for probably a few decades more, call Great Britain and Northern Ireland.

I have already described with real gratitude how the radio days of my childhood widened the horizons, and sometimes made them shimmer. Those plummy voices spoke as though from another land, and yet they did not seem to be trying to make one a stranger in it, let alone a shopper. I think, even, that they were trusted, unlike virtually all the other manifestations of power and authority. But perhaps this was partly due to the fact that you could not see the pictures, and radio people too often quote with pride the child who so famously said that she preferred the radio to television 'because the scenery is better'.

Television could scarcely resist calling itself 'a window on the world', as it did in its early days, even using the subtitle on *Panorama*. But windows have frames, and the frames are part of a structure that has already been built.

Our television has been ripped apart and falteringly reassembled by politicians who believe that value is a monetary term only, and that a cost accountant is thereby the most suitable adjudicator of what we can and cannot see on our screens. And these accountants or their near clones are employed by new kinds of media owners who try to gobble up everything in their path. We must protect ourselves and our democracy, first by properly exercising the cross-ownership provisions currently in place, and then by erecting further checks and balances against dangerous concentrations of the media power which plays such a large part in our lives. No individual, group or company should be allowed to own more than one daily, one evening and one weekly newspaper. No newspaper should be allowed to own a television station, and vice versa. A simple act of public hygiene, tempering abuse, widening choice and maybe even returning broadcasting to its makers.

The political pressures from market-obsessed radicals, and the huckster atmosphere that follows has by degrees, and in confused self-defence, drawn the BBC so heavily into the dogma-coated discourses of so-called 'market efficiency' that in the end it might lose clear sight of why it, the BBC, is there in the first place. I fear the time is near when we must save not the BBC from itself, but public-service broadcasting from the BBC.

Thirty years ago, under the personal pressures of whatever guilt, whatever shame and whatever remaining shard of idealism, I found or I made up what I may unwisely have termed a sense of Vocation. I have it still. It was born, of course, from the already aborted dream of a common culture, which has long since been zapped into glistening fragments by those who are now the real, if not always recognised, Occupying Powers of our culture. Look in the pink pages, and see their mesh of connections. Open the *Sun* and measure their aspirations. Put Rupert Murdoch on public trial, and televise every single second of it. Show us who is abusing us, and why. Ask your public library – if there is one left – to file the Television Franchise Applications on the shelf hitherto kept for Fantasy, Astrology and Crime bracket Bizarre bracket.

I was exceptionally fortunate to begin my career in television at a time when the BBC was so infuriatingly confident about what public-service broadcasting meant that the question itself was not even on what would now be called the agenda. The then ITV companies shared much more of this ethos than they were then willing to acknowledge. Our profession was then mostly filled with men and women who mostly cared about the programmes rather than the dividend. And the venomous hostilities of the small minority who are the political right – before its wholly ideological transformation into the type of venal, wet-mouthed radicalism which can even assert without a hint of shame that 'there is no such thing as society' – before those people had yet launched their poisoned arrows. Clunk! They go Clunk! Clunk! And, lo and behold, we have in the fullness of such darkness been sent unto us a Director General who bares his chest to receive these arrows, a Saint Sebastian eager for their punishing stings.

The world has turned upside down. The BBC is under Governors who seem incapable of performing the public trust that is invested in them, under a Chairman who seems to believe he is heading a private fiefdom, and under a Chief Executive who must somehow or other have swallowed whole and unsalted the kind of humbug-punctuated pre-privatisation manual which is being forced on British Rail or British Coal. But I do not want to end on a malediction. I first saw television when I was in my late teens. It made my heart *pound*. Here was a medium of great power, of potentially wondrous delights that could slice through all the tedious hierarchies of the printed word, and help to emancipate us from many of the stifling tyrannies of class and status and gutter-press ignorance. We are privileged if we can work in this, the most entrancing of all the many palaces of variety. Switch on, tune in and *grow*.

I hope it is clear by now that I happen to care very much about the medium that has both allowed and shaped the bulk of my life's work, and even my life's meaning. However, I do have the odd hour or two in each day in which to pretend to be a Saint George rather than a Saint Sebastian. I therefore hereby formally apply, in front of witnesses of substance, here at the Edinburgh International Television Festival, for the post of Chairman of the Governors of the British Broadcasting Corporation.

Notes

1. This was John Birt.
2. A reference to Marmaduke Hussey, Chair of the BBC Board of Governors, and John Birt, the Director General of the BBC.

The James MacTaggart Lecture 1994

A Culture of Dependency: Power, Politics and Broadcasters

Greg Dyke*

Greg Dyke attacks what he describes as the 'culture of dependency' in UK television which subjects broadcasters to an increasing dependence on government 'in some cases for their very existence and, in the commercial sector, for their financial success'. He argues that it is 'not the role of broadcasters to spend their time currying favour with the government' since this is antipathetic to one of the fundamental activities of broadcasters in a mature democracy: namely posing challenging and critical questions to government. But the Broadcasting Act 1990 sent a message to the ITV companies that 'being a business was more important than being a broadcaster'. The result has been a shift in power to business executives rather than managers with a background in programme-making; programming promptly loses it critical edge.

Dyke alleges it was the relationship between Murdoch and Thatcher which 'really changed the nature of the game'. This Faustian pact meant Thatcher enjoyed the political support of the Murdoch press while News International's majority ownership of BSkyB was exempted from consideration by broadcasting legislation. 'The lesson was there for all to see: lobbying . . . was clearly effective.'

But what about the BBC? Surely the licence fee provides independence of government? That was its prime purpose. The Charter lasts only ten

---

* Greg Dyke has been Director of Programmes (1987), Managing Director (1990) and Group Chief Executive (1991) of London Weekend Television (LWT). In 1994 he joined Pearson Television and chaired the consortium which bid successfully for Channel 5. In 1999 he joined the BBC as Deputy Director General and became Director General in January 2000. He resigned on 28 January 2004 following the Hutton inquiry. At the time of this MacTaggart Lecture he had just left LWT and declared himself 'the first genuinely unemployed MacTaggart lecturer'.

years, so by year seven the 'old game is back in play' and everyone has to 'keep the government happy'. In his conclusion, Dyke proposes establishing a Government Commission on Broadcasting, the appointment of more independent regulators and a guaranteed income for the BBC for ten years.

I believe that the broadcaster's ability to carry out one of its crucial roles in an advanced democracy, the role of effectively questioning government, is still in danger of being eroded. Now of course there are those, particularly some politicians, who I suspect do not believe that the effective questioning of government action should be the broadcaster's role at all.

But at a time when the power of central government grows daily, when we live in the era of the enormous expansion of government-appointed quangos, when the local democratic process has been undermined – largely because the people elected didn't agree with central government – the role of the fourth estate, the press and broadcasters is more significant than ever. And in many ways the broadcasters are the most important of all because traditionally they were more independent than most of the press and certainly reached more people.

I believe our ability to question government is one of the essential protections we have against the ability of the state to control information, manipulate funds and abuse power. My concerns are twofold and they make up the basic theme of my lecture tonight.

Firstly, that in commercial broadcasting the delicate balance of being both a business and a broadcaster is in danger of being too dominated by business and I think that this could have serious implications in the area of programming generally and current affairs journalism in particular.

Secondly, and perhaps more importantly, I fear the relationship between broadcasters and government is becoming a dependent one, with broadcasters constantly wanting favour and legislative action from government – a position which is largely of government's making, and as a result gives government far too much power in the relationship. So that's the case I intend to argue in this lecture: I will also come up with some proposals for change.

I fear there are fundamental changes taking place in the relationship between broadcasters, and in particular commercial broadcasters and the state. Changes which aren't obvious, their insidiousness is part of the danger, but changes which I fear could increasingly bring into doubt the right to question, unless we recognise them and take some action. Of course, conflict between broadcasters and government is not new: government's temptation to shackle the broadcasters is not new either.

So, what are the threats to the broadcasters' freedom to challenge to rock the boat or to expose, which I now believe we have to counter? As I have said they are not obvious. They are not Norman Tebbit openly attacking the BBC, or Margaret Thatcher ranting and raving about *Death on the Rock*. I would argue they are caused by the growth of a dependence culture, in which broadcasters are increasingly dependent on the actions of government in some cases for their very existence and, in the commercial sector, for their financial success. This is not healthy for broadcasting.

Let me explain, and let's look first at ITV. The old ITV franchise system was once explained to me as a game of pass the parcels: everyone got into trouble with the regulator or even the government at some time during the period of a franchise. The art was not to be in trouble with the regulator at the time of franchise renewal. What this meant in terms of questioning journalism was that inevitably companies were more cautious when a new Broadcasting Act was going through or franchises were up for renewal. But for the rest of a ten-year franchise period the ITV companies were largely strong enough to see off government pressure, usually with the support of the old Independent Broadcasting Authority, which was legally the broadcaster and was set up as independent of government.

Over the years I, along with most ITV executives, have moaned about the regulators. It is inevitably a love–hate relationship, but in the area of questioning journalism the old IBA had a decent record, particularly in the eighties, and was very supportive of programme-makers. Of course it was the IBA's decision, under the leadership of Lord Thomson, to support the broadcasting of the Thames programme, *Death on the Rock*, that many believe persuaded Mrs Thatcher to abolish the old IBA. After *Death on the Rock*, the IBA was seen as the enemy, even though it had only been carrying out the function Parliament had given it: to ensure fairness and impartiality, free from government interference.

In ITV some of us naively believed that once the franchises had been awarded in 1991 the old pass-the-parcel rules would reappear and we would be free from the need to lobby and 'stay close' to government, as the PR men would put it, for a decent period. Of course, nothing has been further from the truth. For a range of reasons – a combination, I suspect, of the inadequacies of the Broadcasting Act, the business ambitions of some of the ITV companies and the changing face of competition partly due to the changing face of television technology – the larger ITV companies now always want something more out of government. This, I would suggest, is a potential threat to a politically free broadcasting system and potentially gives enormous power to the government of the day.

The problem is that the 1990 Broadcasting Act effectively told ITV companies that being a business was more important than being a broadcaster. As a result, if you look around the ITV system today, in only four of the fifteen companies is the most powerful executive from a broadcasting or programme background, and two of them are in the smallest companies, Border and Channel. The rest, now, are almost exclusively run by accountants or people with a financial background. There are still outstanding programme-makers and broadcasters in virtually all the ITV companies, but there has been a significant shift in power and we should recognise that.

Now, I have no problem with ITV companies being treated as businesses. I was very proud of increasing the profitability of LWT.[1] But if you are running a broadcaster, you have other responsibilities as well and the very difficult task, in an increasingly competitive commercial broadcasting world, is going to be balance the two.

Of course, it was the relationship between Rupert Murdoch and the Thatcher government which really changed the nature of the game. The cross-media ownership rules in the 1990 Broadcasting Act were devised to create diversity of ownership, but just happened to exclude News International's majority ownership of BSkyB. It's equally clear that this exclusion was a reward for putting the full weight of the Murdoch papers behind the Thatcher government. The lesson was there for all to see: lobbying and currying favour with government was clearly effective.

So, we need to recognise that the ITV companies, for their perfectly legitimate business interests, will continue lobbying government. Last year the powerful companies in ITV wanted to change the ownership rules for their own business reasons, so they lobbied government. This year for business reasons they wanted to encourage the notion of terrestrial digital television, not just for its own sake but because they think it will probably scupper Channel 5 – potentially a serious business rival. So they lobbied government. Next year they will want to stop the government accepting the Channel 4 argument that the money transferred from the Channel to ITV – which in 1995 could be as much as 60 or 70 million pounds – should be left with Channel 4. Again for business reasons they'll be lobbying the government. At the same time the two largest ITV companies, Carlton and Granada, who now own 72 per cent of ITN between them – something which the law doesn't allow – will no doubt want, for their own business reasons, to change the ownership rules of ITN. Again they'll be lobbying government.

Now it is not my intention to stand here today and be holier than thou. If I was still running an ITV company – and who knows I might be again in the future – I'd be in there lobbying with them. But let's recognise what the possible threat is; it will take a very brave ITV broadcaster to make or broadcast a controversial programme about government if by doing so it believes it is seriously threatening its chance of persuading the government to change a particular piece of legislation. I think the companies will increasingly find themselves in an impossible position not of their own making. And of course the pressure on the ITV companies could get worse if ITV's revenue is squeezed in the second half of the decade; and there are circumstances in which that could happen.

So what about the BBC? Aren't they now safe for ten years? Can't they occasionally take on the government? Certainly in recent years the BBC does not appear to have been at its bravest. The Charter renewal process has had the same effect on the BBC as the franchise process has had at times on ITV.

Politically embarrassing programmes like Peter Jay's *Panorama* on the economy, which was due to be broadcast before the last general election, or John Ware's *Panorama* on Westminster Council, due out just before this year's local elections, were both postponed – for production or legal reasons or course: nothing, we are assured, to do with politics. But we all suspect that's not really the case. However, it's important not to be pompous about these things. If postponing a couple of programmes resulted in a long period of freedom for the BBC, it was worth the price.

But does the government's White Paper[2] mean that the BBC is now able to be a broadcaster free of the need to keep government on side? Sadly I don't think it does. Firstly, the government has renewed the Charter for ten years not the fifteen it got last time. So, by the seventh year at the latest the old game is back in play, everyone has got to keep the government of the day happy. But look closely at the White Paper and you'll discover that the government has still to make up its mind over whether or not to privatise the BBC's transmission as it did ITV's. The BBC wants to keep theirs, so there's one lever the government has.

But far more important, the government plans to look again at the means of funding the BBC after just five years. Effectively the BBC has no certainty of funding beyond the nineties. So the message to the BBC could well be interpreted as saying: step out of line and you could well lose the licence fee.

So they are the problems as I see them for all the major broadcasting organisations, but one of the important tenants of Birtist journalism at LWT back in the late seventies was that it simply wasn't enough to pose the problem. You had to come up with a solution which was intellectually credible. So it would be churlish not to make some attempt to come up with proposals for change tonight.

So use your imagination and put yourself in, say, October 1996. The Blair government has just been elected on a programme of open government. There is a short window of, say, a couple of years before the Labour government follows the paths of most governments and realises it doesn't want government to be quite so open after all. What, in that two years, do we want them to do to protect broadcasters from undue government influence and at the same time to sort out the legislative mess left by the 1990 Broadcasting Act?

What this scenario gives us is an opportunity to reverse the trend of the past decade and create structures for broadcasting which, once again, will put government at arm's length from broadcasters. It is an opportunity that must not be missed. So how do we go about it?

First and foremost, after just a week in government, I'd like to see the new Labour Secretary of State for National Heritage set up a Government Commission to look at broadcasting, with a requirement that it reports within a year. It should be a Commission made up of interesting and thoughtful people, not politicians, who hopefully are not representing a set of vested interests, who have a year to deliver their results before the Labour government initiates legislation. What ideas do we want them to look at?

Well, firstly, I think we can assume that the Blair government will go ahead with plans for both a Bill of Rights and a Freedom of Information Act, and as such we shouldn't burden our Commission with all that work as well. What is important, however, is that the Commission ensures that within the Bill of Rights not only is the individual protected against the power of the state – and, incidentally, the excesses of some sorts of journalism – but that proper, fair, questioning, journalism is also protected from the power of the state by statute, supported by an independent constitutional court.

The Commission also needs to ensure that the powers given by Parliament to the broadcasting regulators should be enacted as part of this Bill of Rights, so that the government of the day cannot simply abolish or change their role on a whim. Government would have to demonstrate that what it was planning was not unconstitutional.

Thirdly, it's important that the broadcasting regulators are appointed by, and answerable to, an authority other than the government of the day. We must never again be in a position where the government of the day can fill the Board of Governors of the BBC with their friends and placemen as the Thatcherites did in the Eighties. Nor should the chairman be the government's man as the present chairman quite clearly was and is.

Fourthly, the BBC should be given certainty of its income for the whole ten years of its Charter. This could be done by, say, giving it an annual increase of inflation minus 1 or 2 per cent. But it would be guaranteed and it couldn't be changed. This would give both certainty and freedom to the BBC.

Fifthly, the Commission needs to sort out the role and purpose of regulation of commercial television for the next decade. This will not be easy because the world of commercial television is changing rapidly, but it needs to be done. The regulator's role needs to be clearly defined, and regulation needs to be equally applied to all commercial broadcasters, which it isn't at present. The commercial system will not survive if one part of it is heavily regulated as ITV and to an extent Channel 4 are now, while other parts, like BSkyB and other satellite and cable channels, are virtually unregulated.

Sixthly, because of what could be the growing tension between some sorts of journalism and the business interests of commercial broadcasters, the commission should look closely at the viability of a requirement that commercial broadcasting organisations should have two boards – a business board and a broadcasting board. The first is there to protect the interests of the shareholders, the second to take account of the wider interests of the public. It is interesting to note that the boards of some of the ITV licensees no longer have anyone on them other than executives; there is no one to represent the wider public interest.

Finally, we have to be able to offer the ITV companies, Channel 4 and possibly Channel 5 some sort of certainty in an uncertain commercial world. We have to end the position whereby they believe they can always get a bit more from government. We have to end the unhealthy dependency culture which has grown up in the past five years. Of course, if we succeeded, we'd actually free up some cash for programmes. We could get rid of half the lobbyists, consultants and public relations officers who have proliferated in broadcasting companies in recent years. Lobbying and currying favour in Westminster would then be largely redundant.

To end then, let me turn to Grace Wyndham Goldie,[3] a woman I never met but a woman whom I admire greatly, a great woman who helped create a politically free broadcasting system in Britain. In her book on *Television and Politics* she says profoundly: 'Nowhere more than in broadcasting is the price of freedom eternal vigilance; resistance to political pressures has to be constant and continuous. But it must be realised that such pressures are inevitable, for the aims of political parties and those of broadcasting organisations are not the same.'

Wyndham Goldie wrote her book in 1977, only two years before the Conservatives came to power at the start of the longest period of one-party government this century. I suspect that period is coming to an end and, as such, we have an opportunity to start anew. Our opportunity comes not because one party replaces another. In the end, as Wyndham Goldie says, they are all politicians and their aims are different from ours.

Our opportunity is that we have two years before the next general election to persuade all parties, but in particular to persuade Tony Blair and the new Labour Party as they are likely to win the next election, that the freedom and independence of broadcasters matters, and that it can only be guaranteed in the future if they are prepared to commit in their manifesto to make changes to what has been institutionalised, and are prepared to give up some of the powers they, as a government, will inherit.

It will not be an easy task. Politicians do not like relinquishing power, but if we wish to retain a politically free, independent broadcasting system in the future, it is a battle which has to be fought and won. The opportunity is there. The question is – will we take it?

Notes

1. London Weekend Television was the company which held the franchise for commercial television services in the Greater London area following the 1991 allocation via the 'franchise auction'. LWT was taken over by Granada Television following the government's relaxation of the rules restricting media ownership in 1994.
2. The White Paper Dyke mentions is *Broadcasting in the '90s: Competition, Choice and Quality* (1988), London: HMSO (Cm 517) which recommended a 'major reform of the

transmission arrangments, giving scope for greater private sector involvement' (cited in Franklin 2001: 61).

3. Grace Wyndham Goldie was Head of Television Talk and Current Affairs and pioneered many developments in television broadcasters' early relationships with politicians: especially the development of party political broadcasts. Her book *Facing the Nation: Television and Politics, 1936–76* (1977), London: The Bodley Head, offers a largely autobiographical account of developments in political broadcasting across forty years.

The James MacTaggart Lecture 1995

Talent versus Television

Janet Street-Porter*

The theme of this lecture is the 'crisis' facing British television triggered by the departure of 'talent' – by which Janet Street-Porter means 'everyone who makes a difference to what hits the screen'. The cause of this malaise is television management, which has typically been composed of '"M" people' – 'Middle-class, Middle-brow, Middle-aged and Male, Masonic in their tendencies and, not to put to fine a point on it, fairly Mediocre.' The final problem with M people is that there have 'always been too many of them'.

The other problem with television is its structure. Senior managers, moreover, have lost any sense of purpose and have become 'conservative, risk-averse caretakers of creaky structures and out of date formula shows'. Perhaps unsurprisingly, audiences for such programming are diminishing. Talent itself has contributed to the malaise in two ways. First, by cynically linking 'commerce and crap', talent has failed to recognise that making the highest quality programmes for the most discerning audiences will generate the greatest opportunities. Second, talent seeking promotion has typically moved into management for higher pay. Structures must be put in place which reward creative people for staying in creative jobs where they can deliver most value.

Street-Porter concludes by reflecting on the irony of management reports expressing concern about minorities while ignoring the minority

* Janet Street-Porter is a journalist, broadcaster and producer. She was Head of Youth and Entertainment at the BBC until 1996 before establishing her own production company Screaming Productions. In 1995 she was Director of Programming at Live TV. She has subsequently been Editor of the *Independent on Sunday* and President of the Ramblers Association.

in their own ranks – namely women. Women, claims Street-Porter are, 'so woefully underrepresented in TV management it makes me want to weep'.

□

James MacTaggart was truly a talent worth remembering in this annual lecture. His vision not only created some of the most memorable TV for viewers, it inspired television's talent to reach further than they had done before, to follow his example. And it is the notion of inspiring our talent that I want to address today. Talent has drifted so far out of the mainstream of the TV debate that I have entitled this lecture Talent versus Television.

My theme is the crisis that British TV currently faces. Talent is leaving British TV – frustrated and fed up. We might face a multi-channel future, but the only thing multiplying is management, and it doesn't seem to have a clue what it's doing. TV is not where truly innovative ideas end up any more because TV isn't fun any more and fun is where ideas breed. Fun is the grow-more of creativity, the fertiliser the ideas factory needs. But a terminal blight has hit the British TV industry nipping fun in the bud, stunting our growth and severely restricting our development. This blight is management – the dreaded four Ms: male, middle class, middle aged and mediocre. Britain as a nation has always led the world in a number of fields, and crummy management is certainly one of them. It's so scary because we are at a major turning point in media.

We are on the dawn of the Second Industrial Revolution enabled by the technology to transport information in any form to anywhere in the world. There are currently three truly global software industries – movies, music and computer games. Together they turn over a hundred billion dollars a year. British television programming is never going to catch them. The same UK TV show will never sell around the world in the way that you can sell Sonic the Hedgehog. But there is a new market emerging destined to be a multi-billion dollar global business, which gives British TV its first – and possibly last – chance to be a global player. It's perfect for Britain because it isn't entertainment, which is already dominated by the US and Japan. It is, in the widest sense of the word, education, or, as I shall call it, 'exposition', which includes all forms of learning, training, leisure and lifestyle material, hobby-related programming as well as education itself. This market is definitely emerging, both online and in physical products. People disagree about when it will arrive, but all agree when it does it will be gigantic.

But despite this whole bunch of new media opportunities let me tell you the reality. They are already passing us by. The government's own Foresight Panel on Leisure and Learning, on which I sat, reported that 'if the UK does not establish effective means for generating high quality learning materials for the new electronic delivery systems within the next two to three years it will become a major net importer of education and training and lose its traditional export markets'. That's quite an achievement for a nation with the BBC and the world's leading educational publishers.

So why is British TV doomed? Firstly, it has been ruined by regulation where government has imposed a nanny mentality. Secondly, its structures are historical, not helpful. And thirdly, we've a forgotten that television is about talent.

By 'talent' I mean everyone who makes a difference to what hits the screen – that is the people who produce the programmes, or those who directly help them. This covers an enormous number of people within the television industry – not all of whom are usually categorised as talent. The talent usually refers to the stars, presenters, writers, directors and producers, who are perceived to have the magic touch of delivering awards and/or audiences. It's also a tiny handful of executives. However, the talent, and certainly the creativity, within British television isn't only within that group of people known as 'The Talent'. Our engineers' imagination leads the world every bit as successfully as our TV producers.

I am treating 'Television' as meaning all those people who own and/or manage the talent, as well as the TV institutions that they have created or maintain. My focus is less on the new channels than on the dear old backbone of Britain – Terrestrial Telly. That is the sector that still employs the greatest number of people, and enjoys the vast majority of the viewers. It also has the greatest number of important issues to confront to survive. It is a sick patient and incapable of self-diagnosis.

Returning to my theme of the crisis that we face. The British TV business is the worst performing of all of our creative businesses: in 1995 fertiliser sales will bring more money into Britain than broadcasting. One of the reasons that the TV business does a lot worse than the record industry is although they're both driven by creative talent, the TV industry is disadvantaged because it is better educated and more middle class. Historically, many of the dynamic ideas that made Britain a cultural force world-wide have come from working-class people. From music to fashion to computers. Many of the top people in TV management have never worked outside the system in which they started, and some not even for another employer. How can they respond to the pulsating disparate mass, the hothouse of ideas in a multi-cultural British society if they all talk in one accent which was polished at the same universities, and all end up shopping at the same delicatessens? No wonder the programmes they commission are all starting to look and feel the same – vets, hospitals, detectives. Can the public tell the difference?

British television management with few notable exceptions have always been, 'M' people – Middle-class, Middle-brow, Middle-aged and Male, Masonic in their tendencies and, not to put too fine a point on it, fairly Mediocre. The other big 'M' about British TV management is that there have always been too many of them. Name me one other business with so many layers. The inefficiencies and failures of British television started at the top, a long time ago, and it is the talent who are now being made to pay the price for years of their managers' inadequacies and mistakes.

In the past we were run by a Masonic men's club. Today we have business school graduates and accountants. But I believe that the new boys – and again they are all boys – have lost the plot. If they are so good at business, how come European TV is dominated by Germany, Italy and France, with a complete absence of UK players? How come hundreds of talented creative people have left the broadcasters to take a chance as one-person independent production companies?

British TV managers and media owners still can't cope with the world that they have created in which they no longer own the talent, but have to work with it. The notion of talent with its own career plan is alien. Stars who set up their own companies are regarded as presumptuous, and treated accordingly. British television doesn't yet understand that you have to create a place where the talent wants to come to work. And usually the wanting is determined by much more than the size of the cheque. As Bill Cotton said, 'It's the talent that pays our wages,' and he was right – it's not the other way round.

I believe it all started to go wrong when ITV bosses decided to separate broadcasting from production. This is a classic case of 'corporate think' winning over common sense. Is 'Network Centre' a term to inspire creative talent to feel comfortable with the concept of central commissioning? Sounds more like a sinister John Le Carré idea to me. But most importantly, the bosses have tried to manage production like broadcasting – but you can't treat the creative people like transmission equipment. This mentality is the least helpful for an industry undergoing the enormous changes I mentioned earlier. TV executives have been captured lemming-like by the language and mentality of the management consultant, creating a wasteland of numerically fixated, culturally barren, confidence-sapping uncertainty.

What the winning media companies have is a confidence, a culture, that nourishes and defines their employees as they work together motivated by the same set of beliefs. It is the thing that the most successful British TV companies did have, but most don't have any more. Granada did have it, but it has been smeared too thinly from Manchester to London's South Bank. Channel 4's is still very much intact, but stuck in a sixties timewarp. Once companies had identities. Now they only have cashflows as their owners care less and less about creativity. But creativity is where the long-term profits will come from.

The other main problem with British TV is its structure. It responds to legislators not talent, corporations not creativity. Our biggest British media company, the BBC, is still focused on internal British political issues – not global commercial opportunities. It believes the government is the key to its future. John Birt has made a crucial step in securing the licence fee. But there is no way that the licence fee alone can sustain the BBC into the next century. The BBC has to become a global player in order to survive.

For my long experience in TV, I know that uncertainty is the most corrupting element in any creative person's life. It starts at the top in British broadcasting where the bosses themselves don't seem to know what they are there for anymore. Although many of them used to be extremely good programme-makers they find it hard to describe what their present job is all about. Television when I joined it was all about the new – anything was possible. Now so many television people are conservative, risk-averse caretakers of creaky structures and out of date formula shows. The best thing about the bad old days of the broadcasting monopolies was they gave their programme-makers enormous freedom to take risks – and the result was often fantastic, commercially successful television. But I said I would not hark back to the past.

Let's talk about the unpleasant reality of *now*, where management has mislaid its vision of what TV is for. TV is losing its audience. Some of them are inevitably going to the satellite and cable channels, but more worryingly, many viewers are leaving TV behind and not coming back, and these are the most valuable audiences who are deserting – the young ones and those over fifty with the highest disposable income. People are just getting out of the habit of watching television, and once they have gone these are the audiences you will never get back. The fact is, the whole social contract between the audience and the visual medium is being rewritten. People aren't grateful for TV any more. Last year there were more visits to art galleries than cinemas. This requires broadcasters and producers to apply new and different thinking. Yet there are few signs that this process is underway. As I said earlier, talent is in contact with this changing world but management is not.

But talent itself is not entirely blameless. It has always been assumed by British TV talent that commerce and crap were inextricably linked. This meant that they feared anything to do with commercial exploitation, popularising work in any way, or otherwise cheapening their art. A terrible cynicism has crept into TV commissioning. It believes that if you make formula and lowest common denominator shows, you'll get the biggest audiences and make the most money, or justify the licence fee. But as you can see in every other walk of life, from Marks and Spencer to Walt Disney, it is the creation of the very best products to the highest standards, for increasingly discriminating audiences, that will ultimately deliver the biggest profits and the greatest range of opportunities. And if you make that your reputation, that is how you will become the first port of call for the best talent.

We also need to acknowledge that the best talent is not necessarily the best management material. Why does promotion have to mean a management role? Because managers are paid more. Why are managers paid more? Because the managers are in charge of the salary budget. Some programme-makers are clearly destined for management, some should be persuaded to stay doing what they do best. Structures need to be devised that leave creative people where they can deliver the most value but reward them for doing so.

The BBC must take the lead as it has the most to lose – and to gain. Why can't the BBC aim for the year 2000 by starting again from scratch and saying: here is what the audience want from us; here is the talent there is available, so let us work out the best way to serve those markets and secure our financing for the future. Channel 4's great strength was to have that opportunity to start from nothing. The BBC's difficulties can only be resolved if they take a similarly year zero approach and bite the bullet. The BBC management has, under pressure, set itself the task of increasing efficiency, assuming that the programming quality was a given. This is the wrong emphasis – the task is always programme quality with efficiency important but not an end in itself. The management should be concentrating on giving the BBC staff something to be proud of – a clear vision of why it's great to work for the BBC in the nineties.

Similarly, the BBC have also been side-tracked into exploiting the past and not looking at the future. The archive programmes on BBC television and UK Gold are good for business but not necessarily good for talent. Ultimately the BBC has got to nourish the one thing it is best at – which is producing programmes.

British TV has – up until now – been the place where a lot of the most talented young people want to work. It won't always be like that, if the young talent coming up now don't see the medium as an exciting place to express themselves. Young talent wants challenging outlets and flexible structures – not crass copying of existing formulas for less and less money.

There's a particular point I want to make about one of the most critical imbalances in the industry, which I have observed for many decades. I have a good laugh when I read all management's reports about reflecting the audience, catering for minorities, talking to the regions. Because there's a majority they've chosen to ignore within their own ranks – women. Women are so woefully underrepresented in TV management it makes me want to weep. Earlier this year I wrote that prime-time TV was full of powerful female icons, from Cilla to Bet to the Ab Fabbers to *Prime Suspect*. Women write, direct, produce and star in hugely successful entertainment. The two most powerful and influential people in the American TV industry are Oprah Winfrey and Roseanne Barr. They are huge businesses. Here we have talented businesswomen like Denise O'Donoghue, Verity Lambert, Beryl Vertue, Linda Agran, Linda James and Lynda La Plante all making entertainment watched by millions of happy viewers.

But let's get personal now. Who commissions the comedy and entertainment on British television. Fewer women than you could count on the fingers of one hand. Does managing entertainment require testosterone over and above any other talent? Does understanding what makes a good gameshow need a lot of jangling of coins in the pocket and rounds of golf with the lads? Is dealing with creative stars a task that requires a willy? Why not ask the Talent? You might get some interesting answers.

So let's sum up the way forward. I care about management because I know it could be so much better. I care about business because it makes our talent go further. We must not and cannot demean our talent by condemning it to a parochial future. For this industry to survive, management must have a vision of the role of television. This role can only be achieved through programmes, not processes, balancing immediate profits with the need to invest for the future. There are two huge prizes. First, to revitalise the position of British terrestrial TV. Second, to remove its glass walls and ceilings and re-marry management and talent so that, together, they can corner the limitless global education and information markets.

If we succeed in releasing the enormous resources of our talents – of both sexes – we can amaze ourselves by the extent to which British television can become, more than ever, something to be proud of.

The James MacTaggart Lecture 1996

A Glorious Future: Quality Broadcasting in the Digital Age

John Birt*

John Birt, then Director General of the BBC, used his 1996 MacTaggart Lecture to outline his vision for the BBC in the digital age. He began by listing the BBC's major achievements and concluded with a plea for an increase in the licence fee.

Reformulating Reith's original injunction that the BBC should 'educate, inform and entertain', Birt claimed in recent times the BBC's role has been to 'delight, educate and inform' and, by so doing, to act as 'the touchstone of quality in UK broadcasting'. Birt summarises the BBC's considerable achievements: 'we have become a major cultural patron . . . we have opened up intellectual vistas; and, at the same time . . . we have won the hearts of our viewers and listeners'.

While the digital age of broadcasting offers considerable advantages, there are a number of dangers confronting the BBC which must be overcome by government and regulators. First, the digital age will be dominated by the key players who own and control the vital gateway into the home (the 'set-top box') which carries not only television signals but potentially unlimited economic and financial exchanges. The struggle to control this gateway will constitute 'one of the great business battles shaping the next [i.e. the twenty-first] century, to rival the nineteenth-century battle for the railroad'. Second, the ready access to a global system of programming will encourage a decline in programme standards and an Americanised world culture. Resistance requires a

* John Birt worked as a producer and programme-maker at Granada and Director of Programmes at London Weekend Television (1982–87) before becoming Deputy Director General of the BBC (1987–92) and Director General of the BBC (1992–2000).

strong, well-resourced and valued indigenous broadcasting system: the BBC.

To face the challenges of the digital future successfully, the BBC must exercise 'self-help' and make whatever economies are possible. But it will also require the government to make an increase in the licence fee, if the BBC 'is to remain as creative and dynamic an institution in the twenty-first as it has been in the twentieth century'.

□

This evening I want to explain to you why Britain is best at broadcasting, for it did not happen by chance or by accident. We need to understand *why* so we can carry forward our great achievements into a very different future, the revolutionary period that lies ahead.

We owe much to John Reith, who stamped British broadcasting with a duty to put quality first. Aggressive, disliked and feared by many, all now acknowledge his far-sighted vision as he laid down the first templates in broadcasting. But Reith's BBC was an ivory cultural control tower – at times too remote and elitist. The arrival of ITV shattered the glass and in came the fresh air of competition. The BBC lost 70 per cent of its audience overnight – and was reminded forcefully that it must speak to all of the people in a voice that they can recognise and appreciate. Later, Channel 4 burst on the scene as a non-conformist broadcaster – liberated from the old, monolithic structures; breaking conventions; and shaking up the airwaves in its own innovative way. Channel 4 invaded territory the BBC had previously had to itself, and forced us to think harder about specialist and minority audiences.

Between all of us, we British broadcasters lead the world in delivering an unmatched range of programmes to satisfy a wide spectrum of tastes and needs. But as you would expect, tonight I shall concentrate on the vital role the BBC plays in acting as the touchstone of quality in UK broadcasting.

The BBC Today

The BBC at its best encourages artists, comedians, writers and programme-makers to take risks, to push back creative frontiers. We champion, succour and sustain the extraordinary creativity and variety of British talent, tapping deep into the wellspring. I want to remind you tonight of some of the glories of the BBC – how we delight, educate and inform. First the delights.

Last year Radio 3 played music by 300 living British composers, and commissioned over seventy original works. Our archives bulge with the fruits of this policy over decades in music and other areas. We commissioned works from Britten and Tippett, plays from Pinter and Stoppard. *Under Milk Wood* was a BBC commission. And we still commission new writing. This last year, for instance, Peter Flannery's mighty chronicle of our times – *Our Friends in the North* – was fresh, devoid of stereotype and full of the unexpected. A major work! For decades BBC comedy has reaped rich rewards. The surreal vision of Monty Python or the Goons expressed our taste for the absurd. Satire from *TW3* to *Have I Got News for You?* has carried forward an ancient national tradition of puncturing the powerful and the pompous.

Programmes inspired only by ratings, reworked formulae, copy-cat versions of last year's hits, never strike the authentic note of true originality. Trusting in talent pays – over and over again.

At the BBC, we not only delight, we educate. We broaden horizons with a wealth of riches stretching all the way from David Attenborough telling the story of the natural world with breathtaking illustration; to Andrew Graham Dixon's self-confident journey this year through the annals of British art. For creatively watchable information, the BBC has no rival.

So we delight and we educate but we also inform our viewers and listeners with the world's most powerful newsgathering capability, rooted in the expertise and excellence of our journalists, driven by the BBC's values of accuracy, fairness and independence of judgement. The national debate resounds across our screens and airwaves in a profoundly democratic way, unmatched in any other country.

The BBC's independence was hard won. There are many publicly funded broadcasters around the world; and most have remained since their inception in the firm grip of the state or under the close supervision of the main political parties. The BBC is a relative rarity on the world stage, as a publicly funded broadcaster, in having fought for – and slowly, gradually, incrementally, won – its independence. We broadcast not only at home, but around the world. Other global broadcasters may be tempted to make editorial compromises. We don't. As a result, the BBC's brand of journalism is not universally popular with all the world's regimes! It is not only morally right, but it is also in our long-term interest to preserve the trust of the world in the BBC's journalism.

The wonder of the BBC is that we have won our independence; that we have become a major cultural patron; that we have opened up intellectual vistas; and, at the same time, that we have won the hearts of our viewers and listeners. Almost half of all viewing and listening in the UK is to the BBC. People spend almost 30 per cent of their leisure time with the BBC. This extraordinary success is no accident but is, in important measure, a triumph of British governance and regulation. The right structures were created; wise decisions were made; and there was clear-sightedness over funding. In contrast, other countries drifted into advertising as well as licence funding to support their publicly funded broadcasters, and many of those broadcasters have lost their way. Successive British governments have shown vision, and they deserve our plaudits.

The Future

Some of the conditions which created our world are ending. British broadcasting is to give way to a brand-new and different technology – digital. The impact will be seismic.

The Digital Age

The digital age will have three key characteristics: we enter a world of plenty – where hundreds or thousands of channels and services become possible. We enter a world of interactivity – where high-quality pictures and sound will be able to move to and fro, between any two points. And we enter a global world – where services can be obtained from any point on Earth.

At some point in the future each of us will be able, on a single machine, with a ravishing wide-screen picture, and with CD-quality surround sound:

- to arrange a video party on our birthdays with a group of old friends scattered around the globe
- to access any book or reference from any library in the world
- late at night to watch a breakfast show out of Sydney
- we will be able to see any sport or major event live from anywhere in the world
- to watch any number of themed channels: golf, cartoons, business, whatever
- to call forth any programme from the BBC's colossal archive
- or to compile our own news bulletin, with individual items of our choosing, in an order we determine.

We will also be able to bank or to shop from our armchairs: moving pictures will lure us to book a holiday, or to buy a car, or a new pair of football boots. This awesome vision of a mature, interactive, high-quality picture digital future is probably ten to fifteen years away. But the digital world is already upon us, and advancing rapidly.

The digital age will bring marvellous opportunities for the BBC and for other broadcasters. But if the full potential is to be seized, if the future of British broadcasting is to be as glorious as its past, then a number of threats, dangers and difficulties need first to be overcome – by government, by regulators and by the people in this hall.

The first danger to be overcome is that the digital age will be marked not by openness and diversity but by dominance. Broadcasting will be only one among a number of competitors for the attention of the consumer in the home. The economic power of those other sectors – retail, banking and telecoms – dwarfs broadcasting. The competition for the consumer's attention will be fierce.

The vital Gateway into the home in the digital age will be controlled by those who own the wires or other means of delivery into the home; probably all contained in a single set-top box. The battle for control of this Gateway, and a share of the enormous economic value passing through that Gateway, will be one of the great business battles shaping the next century, to rival the nineteenth-century battle for the railroad or the twentieth-century battle for office software systems. These latter-day Vanderbilts must earn a fair return for a risky investment in the digital infrastructure. But no group should be able to abuse control of that set-top box to inhibit competition. The hallmark of the digital age must be full cultural and economic freedom!

We need in the UK a unified regulatory framework that ensures open and non-discriminatory access to providers on fair financial terms; and that ensures, frankly, that the Gateway controller cannot relegate BBC1 or ITV to Channel 249.

The second set of dangers we face in the digital age is that the easy availability of programmes and services worldwide will encourage the emergence of a single global culture, and that the huge increase in competition that the digital age will bring will result in a drop in programme standards. A single global culture will mean an Americanised world culture. The way to counter-act this powerful global force is to husband and to cherish our own – and other countries' – wonderful, rich and unique national cultures, identities and heritages to ensure that real choice remains strong.

The first thing we need to do – as Corporal Jones reminds us – is not to panic. In particular, ITV should not panic. We have seen in other countries that when commercial competition bites, choice narrows. ITV should continue to offer a rich mix of programmes, accessibly scheduled. And ITN should not be kept in a strait-jacket! Like any leading news provider, it should be commissioned to provide coverage of major news events. We will need measured judgement and a sense of proportion and of timing from those who control ITV to ensure that ITV's own long, honourable and distinct programme tradition survives in the rough waters ahead. But the most effective means of countering the risks of the globalisation of culture, and of declining standards – of nations ensuring that they maintain their own national cultures in the digital age – will be by sustaining their publicly funded broadcasters. In the United Kingdom, that means sustaining the BBC.

The BBC in the Digital Age

In the digital age the BBC will be freed, like everyone else, from the shackles of scarcity and the limitations of analogue technology. And the BBC will help lead the way into the digital age with a programme-led vision. We will offer better picture and sound quality; more choice; and greater convenience. The new technology will also allow us to offer exciting alternatives to the main channel schedules on BBC1 and BBC2; multiple choices varying from hour to hour: you will have access to more live coverage of major news, sports and arts events. This is a glorious prospect, and it is about to happen! We either join it or be history.

The Financial Challenge for the BBC

The digital age will present the BBC with a formidable financial challenge. I want to give everyone here an understanding of that challenge.

The recent financial history of the BBC has been miraculous. The BBC's commercial arm – BBC Worldwide – is a growing success. We are Europe's biggest exporter in broadcasting. But commercial activity still only accounts for 5 per cent of the BBC's income. The BBC is overwhelmingly – 95 per cent – dependent on the licence fee. And that is why our revenue has been basically flat for a decade. The miracle is that in recent years we have not only funded all these rising costs on a flat income but have in addition enriched and increased the volume of BBC services: this year alone we have invested another £80 million in extra programmes and services.

But actually it wasn't a miracle! It was achieved by a lot of hard and difficult work, accompanied by not inconsiderable pain, and wails of understandable anguish from this and other platforms. Funding rising pay and rights, and our enhanced and expanded services, was achieved by a massive attack on the bloated, inefficient BBC that history bequeathed us. We have freed hundreds of millions of pounds to spend on programming, and reduced the cost of production, facilities and support services to market levels. And let us be clear: we have done all this and enhanced our creativity. The Jeremiahs were wrong again. We are a BBC on song, at the top of our form. We have the most imaginative, innovative and dedicated broadcast staff in the world.

Preparing for the Digital Age

To prepare the BBC for the digital age will be a task at least as great as the transformation the BBC has accomplished in recent years. We will need to invest in: digital production facilities; digitising the archive; creating a digital distribution network inside the BBC, our own Superhighway; delivering our services by all the new means by which our viewers and listeners will receive them, including satellite. And, most importantly, we will need to invest in the extra programme services digital technology will free us to offer.

How can we afford all of this new and substantial investment? Well, in recent years, the BBC has become practised in self-help. Digital technology will allow us to make another step-change in our efficiency. Lightweight kit, desktop editing, virtual sets and powerful information technology will enable us to rethink how we make programmes and we will invest the substantial savings in new digital services. We can help ourselves further by using the new technologies to grow our commercial income, introduce a variety of new commercially funded services, at home and abroad, and to re-invest the gains in our free-to-air services. But these measures of self-help will not be sufficient fully to fund a digital future for the BBC.

The Need for a Licence Fee Increase

If the BBC is to sustain the existing level of services; if it is to remain as creative and dynamic an institution in the twenty-first as it has been in the twentieth century; if it is to innovate with high-quality services in the new technologies as it has done again and again in the old, then at some point in the future – and for the first time since 1985 – we shall need a real increase in the level of the licence fee.

I want to give some arguments in support of some real growth in our licence income in the next period of the BBC's history.

The first argument is that BBC revenue growth should bear some relationship to industry revenue growth. Over the next ten years, the television industry's finances will be transformed. This year, satellite and cable revenues will overtake BBC television revenues – an historic moment. Sometime around 1998 they will overtake ITV's revenue as well. Over the next ten years, subscription and pay TV revenues in the UK are forecast to grow by around 300 per cent. In the same ten-year period, advertising revenue will grow much more modestly, but still by something like a third.

If the licence fee remains fixed, in real terms, BBC revenues will barely grow. BBC television's share of industry revenues would drop to around 20 per cent, even though our share of audience would be far higher. If our relative financial position in the industry were to deteriorate in this way – however creative, efficient or energetic we were – the BBC's role as the national broadcaster would be diminished.

The second argument for an increase in the licence fee is to enable us to keep pace with growing consumer aspirations. As consumers grow richer, they spend more on recreational and cultural activities. They spend: 40 per cent more on leisure in real terms than ten years ago; 50 per cent more on cinema and television; £300 a year on a full Sky subscription. But all the while, remember, consumers spend less on their licence fee in real terms than they did ten years ago. In fact, the level of the licence fee in the UK is now towards the bottom end of the European league table.

The third argument for an increase is that if, as the national broadcaster, we are to remain in step with the nation, our licence income should grow as the nation's wealth grows. Over the past ten years, spend on public services in the UK has grown broadly in line with national wealth. BBC spend has lagged significantly behind.

Maintaining the BBC's Role

The BBC is the most successful cultural institution in the world, one of the great inventions of the twentieth century. Don't diminish the BBC. Let it flower; let it blossom; let it flourish; let it pioneer; let it grow!

The BBC was for many decades a monopoly; then part of a duopoly. It is not difficult to see why it became easier to bash than to revere! But as we become one of many players in a rapidly expanding broadcasting environment, I ask all of you here – whether from the BBC or from the wider broadcast industry; whether independent or competitor; whether viewer, listener or commentator – not to take the BBC for granted any more. Support the BBC; help us win the argument for some real growth in our licence fee income over the next period of our history.

Focus too on the many other challenges of the digital age: press for an open regulatory framework; hold your nerve; don't panic about competition; fight for quality. Ensure that when we return to celebrate the fortieth anniversary of the Edinburgh Television Festival, we can tell ourselves that we saw with crystal clarity the opportunities and the threats of the digital age, that we seized the opportunities, countered the threats and preserved into the next millennium the world's most varied, successful and creative system of broadcasting, with the BBC at its heart and core.

The James MacTaggart Lecture 1997

Rewarding Creative Talent: The Struggle of the Independents

Laurence Marks and Maurice Gran*

The theme of Laurence Marks and Maurice Gran's lecture is the relative powerlessness of the creative workers (writers, producers and directors) – 'the talent' – in television and the other creative industries. Establishing an independent production company provides writers with creative control over their work but even independent producers can end up being treated as little more than 'a glorified freelance at the mercy of the market' without ownership and distribution rights over programmes. It is still preferable, however, to working directly for a broadcaster such as the BBC or ITV which often involves being 'under-respected, under-consulted, [and] under-rewarded'.

In 1989 Marks and Gran established their production company Alomo: their programme credits include *Birds of a Feather*, *Love Hurts* and *Goodnight Sweetheart*. The BBC remains the most important customer for talent, but its attitude towards independent producers remains 'essentially patronising' preferring to 'concentrate their cash, care and chauffeur-driven cars on the front-of-camera talent, soap stars and celebrity chefs': both the BBC and ITV 'betray the behind-the-camera talent'. Channel 4 is little better. A creatively liberating partner, Channel 4 drives 'some of the hardest and cruellest bargains financially'.

At the BBC the problem reflects the fact that creative leaders and their ability to commission work have been undermined by 'legions of lawyers . . . and policy unit apparatchiks'. These new 'gatekeepers' have little

---

* Laurence Marks and Maurice Gran are highly successful comedy writers whose independent production company Alomo has produced popular programmes such as *Birds of a Feather* (1983–98), *Love Hurts* (1992–4) and *Wall of Silence* (1993).

enthusiasm or interest in programming and apply to television 'the same discipline they would apply to the production of biscuits . . . Like the Hitler Youth they know no other system.' Television must change and talent must be rewarded.

▭

LAURENCE
Tonight we hope to reclaim the MacTaggart Lecture for those of us who make programmes rather than policy.

MAURICE
It was talent, other people's talent, that made us want to become television writers.

LAURENCE
The pleasure and excitement of watching comedies like *Porridge*, *Fawlty Towers*, *Rising Damp*, *Till Death Us Do Part*, as well as dramas such as *When the Boat Comes in*, *Cathy Come Home*, *Boys from the Black Stuff*, *Pennies from Heaven*, *Minder* . . . You've all got your own lists, programmes you really loved, that made *you* want to be in TV.

MAURICE
These were programmes written and produced by people who cared passionately about getting exhilarating, entertaining ideas onto the screen.

LAURENCE
They showed us that on television the script was respected.

MAURICE
The writer mattered.

LAURENCE
We wanted to be part of that.

MAURICE
We were also inspired by some pretty awful sit-coms, mostly on ITV, to believe we could do better. Thus encouraged, we set out on a four-year campaign to see how many TV comedy departments we could get to reject our scripts. Bull's-eye. They all did.

LAURENCE
Then Humphrey Barclay, Head of Comedy at London Weekend, decided to chance a couple of grand of LWT's money on a pilot script

called *Holding The Fort*. *Holding The Fort* was a top ten hit. We didn't
have to re-apply for the day jobs we'd given up in the ignorance-is-bliss
belief we could make it in television. Our next TV experience was not
so thrilling.

MAURICE

We had written a script called 'Roots' about a Jewish dentist.

LAURENCE

As production proceeded, we realised we were making it with a clue-
less director, an underpowered cast, for a comedy department that was
the only genuine joke to be found at ATV.

MAURICE

We asked Charles Denton, then Controller of ATV, if he could replace
the director or cancel the show? We would repay our fee.

LAURENCE

Mr Denton told us the show must go on . . . but he was very kind to us,
the sort of kindness you show crazy people. Then he saw *Roots* . . . and
realised we weren't crazy.

MAURICE

That was when we first realised how powerless the talent normally is in
the great TV equation. We wondered if we were doomed always to place
our scripts into the hands of people who usually knew less about the
business of comedy than we did. Was there any way to get control of
our own work? Well, yes, there was a way; we went to Witzend, the
only independent comedy producer around.

LAURENCE

We only knew such things as independent production companies
existed, because a few months earlier, our agent had told us that
Porridge creators Dick Clement and Ian La Frenais (our heroes) were
returning to Britain from Hollywood.

MAURICE

They were going to set up a company called Witzend, with their
partner . . . film producer, Allan McKeown.

LAURENCE

Allan, Dick and Ian started Witzend for two simple reasons. They
wanted to make their own shows their own way, and they were determined to earn more from their success than a simple script fee. Through
their experiences in America they saw that talent, especially writing

talent, is the key to success in TV fiction, and TV fiction is the key to success if you're running a TV station.

MAURICE

What we took to Witzend was an idea for a comedy drama called *Shine On Harvey Moon*.

LAURENCE

When we pitched the idea to Witzend's Managing Director, Tony Charles, he asked if we would like to write him a treatment, but made a crucial contribution to the project: he offered us 500 quid for it.

MAURICE

Witzend and ITV got twenty-six hours of *Harvey Moon*. Tony Charles started a relationship with us that ultimately led to the formation of SelecTV. Eventually, SelecTV was bought by Pearson for around £50 million.

LAURENCE

Harvey Moon was produced under a pioneering deal between Witzend and ATV. Ironically, it was Charles Denton at ATV who had realised that his in-house comedy department wasn't cutting the mustard. So he gave Witzend a three blind pilot a year deal. Three blind pilots, see how they run!

MAURICE

And, boy, did they run. *The Other Half*, *Girls on Top*, *Roll Over Beethoven*, *Harvey Moon*, *Auf Weidersehen Pet*, all top ten hits, all proof of what a small, dedicated, talent-driven indy could do.

LAURENCE

Eventually the Witzend relationship with Central TV, as ATV had become, bit the dust, when Charles Denton was succeeded by Andy Allan. Andy believed Central could produce all its comedy and comedy-drama hits in-house.

MAURICE

In one 'Lunch of the Long Knives', Andy waved goodbye to the Witzend roster. Out went Jennifer Saunders, Dawn French –

LAURENCE

Tracey Ullman, Ben Elton, Ruby Wax –

MAURICE

Nigel Planer, Ken Cranham –

LAURENCE
Linda Robson, Pauline Quirke –

MAURICE
Jimmy Nail, Tim Spall –

LAURENCE
Clement and La Frenais, and us.

MAURICE
Then as now, the ITV big boys hated the thought of sharing their slice of ITV's output with upstart independents. As to whether Central did manage to unleash a stream of in-house comedy hits, well, we're still waiting, Andy.

LAURENCE
Independent production gave us, as writers, the chance to have real creative control over our work, whereas writers working directly for a broadcaster were often under-respected, under-consulted, under-rewarded. But in the light of the demise of the Witzend–Central pact, we realised that a production fee is all very nice, but an independent producer who does not own and distribute its shows is just a glorified freelance, at the mercy of the broadcaster.

MAURICE
With this determination to hang onto our rights, in 1989 we finally set up our own production company, Alomo, in association with Allan McKeown's SelecTV. We decided that the best place to take our shows would be the BBC. Our proposal was simple: we will supply you with hit shows, you allow us to keep our rights, build a valuable library, develop a proper business. The first show we gave the BBC was *Birds of a Feather*, an instant hit. We then gave them *Love Hurts, So You Think You've Got Troubles*, our film *Wall of Silence* and *Goodnight Sweetheart*.

LAURENCE
Has this string of hits led to our being rewarded with better terms of trade and improved fees?

MAURICE
Not yet. The BBC's attitude to independent producers remains essentially patronising. Their over-riding assumption is that if they fund your production they should own the rights. They will not come to terms with the idea that we producers of a programme should own it and benefit from it, beyond the fees – the wages – we get for making it.

LAURENCE

Some of you are probably muttering what do those two have to moan about? They aren't putting in hundreds of hours of unpaid research and development, in order to come up with one idea a broadcaster might deign to buy! No, we aren't. Because we were lucky, and because we happen to work in the one field of TV where demand always outstrips supply. As they told us when we started work at Paramount Studios, 'funny is money'. Except at the BBC, where 'Funny is only 60 per cent of the budget'.

MAURICE

But if we didn't voice the frustrations of the independent sector, you would all be slagging us off for being complacent bastards! Okay, we've gained certain benefits from our relationship with the BBC.

LAURENCE

But we are still fighting for the right to own and distribute our own shows. Fighting not to have to deficit finance our productions, far beyond the amount we could ever recoup. Arguing to gain the same on-screen promotion that in-house shows receive. And we shall continue to make nuisances of ourselves, because we have this quaint idea that creative talent should be rewarded fairly, and treated with respect.

What it all boils down to is the broadcasters take us all for granted. The creative talent, the writers, producers and directors who actually make television. They prefer to concentrate their cash, care, and chauffeur-driven cars on the front-of-camera talent, soap stars and celebrity chefs.

Meanwhile, both the BBC and ITV betray the behind-the-camera talent. At ITV they fail the talent creatively, because they want more of the same in drama, and dumber, cheaper, 'people shows', in place of scripted light entertainment and intelligent documentary.

MAURICE

A few successful writers and producers are courted and rewarded by ITV, as long as they more or less replicate their previous hits. Established talent finds it hard, and new talent finds it almost impossible, to foist an original idea on to ITV.

LAURENCE

The BBC believes *it* must maintain market share to justify the licence fee. This forces the BBC, more and more, to shadow ITV's programming, as it moves remorselessly towards the safe, the repetitive and the cloned.

This process is particularly noticeable in drama. If ITV has a vet, BBC wants a vet. If ITV has a moody cop, BBC wants a moodier one. This 'follow my leader' reflex is exacerbated by the chaos within the BBC drama department, which over the past few years has resembled a flock of headless chickens.

MAURICE

Access to ITV's Network Centre – theoretically open for all, just like a suite at the Savoy – is increasingly restricted to the big players, Carlton and Granada. They own ITV, they bankroll the Network Centre. If an indy wants to stay in the game, it usually has no choice but to go into partnership with the broadcaster, and give up a substantial slice of the rights.

We must take a moment here to mention Channel 4. Surely there we find an oasis for the poor indy wandering in the TV desert? Sorry, but no. Channel 4 may be a liberating network to deal with creatively, but they drive some of the hardest and cruellest bargains financially. Channel 4 seem rather hurt if you should try to make a healthy profit out of your show, rather than just have an artistically enjoyable experience.

We know whereof we speak. We're the writers and producers who this year were belatedly told we had to find £150,000 to insure our Channel 4 drama serial. Somehow we scraped the premium together, but the next time we shake hands on a deal with Channel 4, we'll count our fingers afterwards.

LAURENCE

Since neither ITV nor Channel 4 is likely to be the saviour of those independents who wish to build a real business, and as Channel 5 is still too young and poor, the BBC must remain the most important customer for talent.

MAURICE

Indeed, its success and its future are inextricably linked to its ability to find and foster talent, and, through talent, develop fresh ideas.

LAURENCE

A few tried and trusted contributors – like us – have access to the real decision-makers. We can even get our ideas accepted by lots of top men, and still not get the bloody thing made.

MAURICE

An example from the topsy-turvy world of BBC drama. A few years ago, we came up with an off-beat series. Just what the BBC were looking for. We pitched it to BBC1 Controller, Jonathan Powell, and his Head of Drama Series, Peter Cregeen. They both liked it. They both left the BBC.

So we pitched it to new Head of Drama Series, Michael Wearing, who said he loved it and wanted to make it.

LAURENCE
Then Charles Denton turned up as Michael's boss, so we pitched it to Charles. His response was a bit off hand. He was obviously distracted by the imminent release of *Harry*, a new drama Charles was sure had 'hit' written all over it. Mr Denton wanted to know why we'd bothered pitching it to him when Michael Wearing had already said yes. But then Michael moved on, so we pitched it to his replacement, Nick Elliott. Nick didn't much like it. Then we lied to him we could get David Jason, so then he did like it. But then Mr Elliott went to work for Mr Plantin.

MAURICE
We waited a while until the BBC appointed a new Head of [Drama] Series, Chris Parr. He adored our script, but said what Alan Yentob, Controller of BBC1, was really looking for was a half-hour drama, having suddenly been left with a hole in his schedules.

We reluctantly agreed our idea could work at thirty minutes, and we all trooped into Alan Yentob's room. There Alan told us he was crazy about our idea, and as soon as Director General, John Birt, gave him the extra eight million pounds he'd promised, we'd be in business. We left happily, our feet barely touching the sixth-floor carpet, only to be pursued down the corridor by Alan, reminding us that our conversation did not constitute a contract.

The trouble is that the creative leaders within the BBC have been marginalised. That is why the BBC now finds it so hard to recruit and retain good production talent. The power the creative staff once had has been usurped by legions of lawyers, accountants, business affairs executives and policy unit apparatchiks. They now are the gatekeepers of the BBC. Once there were dozens of executive producers at the BBC who could say 'yes'. Now even channel controllers only seem to have the power to say 'maybe'.

Most of these new gatekeepers have no particular interest in the programmes. They apply to the production of television the same discipline they would apply to the production of biscuits. Most of them have taken up their posts in the last decade. Like the Hitler Youth they know of no other system. One day they may have to be de-Birtified.

LAURENCE
Few of the gatekeepers are naturally sympathetic to the messy minds of the creative talent. They secretly think, what is talent, except a kind of

luck? Some people are good at writing plays or devising documentaries, others are better at making sure the production doesn't run over budget, or ensuring that no one forgets to hang onto the Australasian game-show rights.

MAURICE

If all else fails, the gatekeepers can always accuse the talent of being greedy. Television must change. Talent must be rewarded. Let us remind the lawyers, accountants, planners and consultants that they only have jobs courtesy of us, the creative community. We could lock all the planners in a dungeon for a month and they wouldn't come out with thirty seconds' worth of good ideas.

I think we've shown tonight, that for most of us here, British TV is a frustrating, and sometimes demeaning, system.

Independent producers, instead of being seen as representatives of a healthy pluralism, are often treated like the pushier sort of double glazing contractor, distrusted and derided even when they need what we're selling. Come up with a great idea, and get offered a fraction of the money you need to produce it. Scrape the money together somehow, and deliver a hit, and do you get rewarded with the chance to make another hit? Or are you treated as if you've fulfilled your quota, and told to get to the back of the line?

LAURENCE

How much longer do the BBC, ITV or Channel 4 expect to hold onto our talent when from all our perspectives it seems to be so under-valued? ITV has almost given up the business of directly employing and training staff. The BBC has continually betrayed its in-house talent through a remorseless process of casualisation. How many BBC people here are on a rolling six-month contract? You're lucky if it's rolling!

MAURICE

That's why the broadcasters have forfeited their moral right to own the fruits of your intellect and labour. Until we all get together and change things, it's difficult to see how to build a production business whilst working for the BBC. It's equally clear that the talent won't make a living out of channels three, four and five, plus a hotchpotch of cookery networks.

LAURENCE

How very different is the experience of the creative talent in American television. Recently the President of Time Warner, Gerald Levin, said, 'Without the talent, the writers and producers that serve this company,

Time Warner would be nothing.' Can we really imagine anyone in a position of real power in our industry saying that? Thus the American TV environment has long been one in which ambitious, talented, driven people try to come up with new ideas to titillate the networks. The waste is appalling, the behaviour disgusting, the ad breaks are maddening, but good and interesting work gets produced.

Successful or potentially successful writers and producers are courted, sought after, highly rewarded. Studio and network executives are judged mainly on their ability to attract and maintain talent.

MAURICE

When you watch the credits for *Friends*, or *NYPD Blue*, you may wonder why there are so many producers and apparently no writers. Some of you will know, but many of you won't, that in America all the writers on the staff of the show are also the producers of the show. They run the show, they even own a piece of the show, because the studios and networks know that without these people there would be no show.

The James MacTaggart Lecture 1998

Television versus the People

Peter Bazalgette*

Peter Bazalgette suggests that television is confronting a revolution in which power is shifting away from the 'sleek barons of British broadcasting' in favour of the viewer. But television is still plagued by regulators who apply ill-informed and outmoded criteria of 'quality' to programmes and content. They also fail to achieve healthy competition, which benefits the consumer: the key ambition for any regulatory regime. British television is 'mollycoddled by regulations, bloated on protected revenue and addicted to a system set up forty-five years ago'. Bazalgette argues that 'we need an end to the era of over-regulation'.

He offers a wide-ranging agenda for change. First, abolish the existing and 'absurd' regulators of television content. Second, remove the public-service remit from Channel 3 and Channel 5 and review Channel 4's remit for diversity. Third, phase out the ITV companies' payments for their licence to broadcast, along with their entire capacity for in-house production with the sole exception of local and regional news. Fourth, privatise BBC Worldwide and finally preserve and strengthen BBC's public-service role.

□

It's a truism to say we are staring a television revolution in the face. Up to now the government-appointed owners of the channels have held the

---

* Peter Bazalgette established the independent production company Bazal (now Endemol UK), which produced some of the most popular programming on television during the 1990s, including *Ready, Steady Cook*, *Ground Force*, *Changing Rooms* and *Big Brother*. In March 2003 he was awarded the Royal Television Society's Judges award for his outstanding contribution to UK television.

whip hand. But now we're seeing a fundamental shift in power in favour of the viewer. That is why I welcome the theme of this year's festival: Television versus the People. But our industry is rooted in the past. Will the sleek barons of British broadcasting change voluntarily? Will they hell. There are two things about change that are well acknowledged: first, that when an industry experiences revolutionary change it always comes from without (when did an *ancien régime* ever give up power voluntarily?); secondly, a key difference between healthy people or organisations and unhealthy ones is their ability to handle change. How healthy is our industry? I shall argue tonight that it's very unhealthy – the captains of our industry wouldn't accept the need for change if it bit them in the bottom . . . and it will.

The Best Television in the World?

To prove my case let's start by examining one of the great complacencies of our age: the way we still claim that our TV is the best in the world. What I want to know is, if we have the best TV in the world why doesn't more of the world want to buy it? We actually have a large imbalance of payments in TV shows. We buy in far more than we sell. While our new channels suck in imports we're not making comparable sales to the many new channels opening up abroad. Why are we missing this opportunity? Because while they'll buy our factual material (mating orang-utans, that sort of stuff) we've never left Base One when it comes to mass entertainment – drama or sitcoms. In multi-channel homes, moreover, cable and satellite now take a third of all viewers and getting on for half when it comes to children. And the new channels, of course, run a high proportion of foreign imports.

So the best TV in the world doesn't do quite so well with its own audience when faced with a bit of competition, does it? Then, when you add multi-entertainment houses with games consoles, the internet and so on, the picture becomes even more bleak. The Henley Centre[1] tells us that of those using the internet, half said that what they would have been doing otherwise was watching telly.

But still the Czars of pre-revolutionary TV land blunder on: 'The standard of broadcasting in this country is higher than anywhere else I've visited.' Lady Howe of the Broadcasting Standards Commission. (Where has she been?) The TV regulators obviously think they're doing rather a good job. Well they would, wouldn't they? The truth is they're living in a dream world. The air is thick with placemen trying to protect their jobs. But ours have failed us. Here's why.

From Regulation to Self-policing

How in touch with viewers are our regulators? Well, a reading of recent ITC annual reports reveals a catalogue of laughable verdicts that fly in the face of popular taste. Their verdicts are based on a dubious and undefined standard they call 'high quality'. They said the hugely successful *Police Camera Action* had little sign of 'high quality'. They attacked *Hollywood Women*, which then developed into a highly popular part of the ITV schedule. Meanwhile, a sitcom called *Outside Edge* didn't 'attract the audience its quality deserved'. Silly old viewers, eh? Fancy watching programmes the ITC disapproves of while not watching programmes the ITC likes. The fact is the ITC is rapidly disappearing up its own Quality Street: who cares? We'll choose our own programmes, thank you.

It isn't just the ITC that has this compulsion to impose its taste on the rest of us. Back to that biggest busy body of them all, Lady Howe, of the Broadcasting Standards Commission [BSC]. In their annual report this year we discovered they disapprove of Jerry Springer. Wowee. Diane Nelmes at the Network Centre must have felt her knees knocking in fright. Or not. Because Diane knows, like the rest of us, that this is no watchdog. It's a toothless poodle.

We need an end to the era of over-regulation. The absurd BSC should be swept away and its complaints function should be handed to the ITC. As for the ITC, its power as guardian of 'quality' (whatever it means) should be abolished.[2]

But now I come to the greatest irony of all. The most important thing a regulatory regime should be charged with – achieving healthy competition in every area of business to the benefit of the consumer – has been completely neglected in the TV industry.

The Campaign for Real Competition

What did Lord Thomson mean when he made his celebrated remark about the licence to print money? He could hardly believe his luck that winning an ITV franchise gave him the right to participate in a rigged market, not just as a broadcaster and earner of advertising revenue, not just as a producer of programmes, but as a distributor and seller of programmes too. The British regulators, while writing interminable essays about programme quality, allowed complete vertical integration in the UK broadcasting industry. Once you'd won your licence you joined the biggest closed shop of all.

In the US, they tackled the problem of a small number of over-dominant TV companies as far back as the early seventies. With the exception of news and sport the three networks were broadly not allowed to produce, own or distribute programmes. As a result America enjoys a competitive, pluralistic television economy in which programme funding can come from a number of sources – from the network, from a syndicator, from a studio or from sponsors/advertisers. And America's competitive producers now dominate the world's television economy. But, argue the spin doctors of the *ancien régime*, this shouldn't be about market economics – what about the viewer? Well, they lose that argument on two counts. First, because it is in the viewer's interests that creativity is rewarded and encouraged and, secondly, because recently the government has dramatically changed the agenda and put economics centre stage. Let's consider the point about creativity first.

If you watch our terrestrial channels reasonably often you'll be able to note that independent producers are responsible for a disproportionate number of the new ideas on the screen. Why then, at the end of two decades of independent production, are the creators of these programmes running such small, weak companies? The feather-bedded broadcasters employ a range of restrictive practices from dictating prices, to controlling distribution, to denying programme sales to secondary channels. All of these prevent the creators of shows deriving the full economic benefit of their product. We producers could be much more productive. The way a healthy market works is that creators of new ideas are rewarded as directly as possible by consumer approval. The current system doesn't do this and it's to the detriment of viewers.

In twenty years time this will have happened anyway. Your EPG[3] will select the shows you want to watch from a variety of channels. So why worry? If all this change is inevitable, why get agitated? The Minister for Culture has the answer. In his book – *Creative Britain* – Chris Smith writes: 'The industries that depend on creative skill and intellectual property for their added value – media, design, film, fashion, music, publishing and cultural endeavour – are the ones that will deliver the growth, the jobs and the international success of the future. And television is at the forefront of that movement.' With that statement he has dramatically altered the political agenda for television: be creative, export, add to the wealth of the nation. But is that going to happen with our over-regulated market dominated by just a few companies – the old lags of the *ancien régime*? Indeed, will it happen with our current independent producers? Some seem actually to enjoy being tied to the apron strings of the broadcasters.

Health, Wealth and Happiness

New Labour need to take decisions now: if they don't the economic benefits we could earn from a dynamic, international television business will never materialise. The Yanks will clean up again – it'll be their health, wealth and happiness, not ours. Our TV industry is mollycoddled by regulations, bloated on protected revenue and addicted to a system set up forty-five years ago. Don't look to the *ancien régime* for ideas.

First, the government should put the ITV network and its companies into rehab. to wean it off protection and prepare it for survival in the future. To that end its public-service remit should be abolished. It won't have to pretend that crime shows are so many hours of adult education any more. It will never again hear the middle-class voices of those regulators spluttering about quality. But what about the regional programmes they have to make, the cornerstone of the ITV system? Well, if there's demand for regional shows, they'll continue to make them. Let the people decide. And let's set ITV free.

But (and you feared there was a 'but' coming, didn't you?) there's a quid pro quo here. ITV companies must cease in-house production of everything but news. (Regional news is part of the companies' identity and there's nothing wrong with their owning a national news provider. But I'm only talking news and news features such as GMTV provide. Not current affairs.) So here's the deal for Messrs Green, Hollick and Robinson. No public-service remit, no licence-bid payments but, in return, no vertical integration either.

Telling the ITV companies to divest themselves of their production arms is not such a radical idea. It happened in the US twenty-five years ago and the plural TV economy I described earlier emerged. It's how the ITV's Network Centre already operates. Why not liberate the excellent new team there so that they can genuinely pick the best shows? And that includes commissioning *Coronation Street* and the like from some of the very good production departments that would be floated off from Granada, Carlton, United and Scottish. There are plenty of good shows on ITV – there's no need to lose them. But what about the BBC – why haven't I talked about them? Have patience – I'm working up to it.

There's an unavoidable logic developing here. And it is that we have to decide whether we want public-service broadcasting. If we do (as I do) then clearly delineate it and – certainly – give it regulated responsibilities. Let everyone else in broadcasting get on with serving the audience, according to the audience's demands and tastes. So remove any public-service requirements from Channel 5 and decide, publicly, whether we still need a diversity remit for Channel 4. Personally I'm in favour of it.

Now: the BBC. Clearly the BBC has a massive public-service remit. I personally think it should be strengthened and more clearly defined, if for no other reason than it keeps everyone else honest, as Michael Grade put it. And for those of us – as viewers – who value the BBC's massive contribution to our culture there are some important issues to be faced. How can we preserve the BBC we value in the multi-channel market of the next century?

One of the major issues is the BBC's in-house production. Great brands like St. Michael or Benetton are about great selling and marketing. They don't have to manufacture – that's often contracted out. It may be that there are good arguments for our main public-service broadcaster having in-house production. Maybe it should even get 60 per cent of its programmes to make. But that's for us all to decide, not for it to announce.

Intangible Value – Brands for the Next Century

Traditional ways of valuing companies (with capital assets and so on) are rapidly becoming history. Brand value is what matters. Television brands which earn the loyalty and emotional adherence of consumers will stand out amidst the multi-channel noise. They might be channel brands but they're more likely to be programme brands. If Chris Smith's wish is to be realised and we really do turn our slumbering TV industry into a vehicle of economic growth, we're going to have to create a helluva lot of brands. And we'll need to learn how to exploit the brands in a way we never have – that's where the economic value is.

Another problem in the UK is that we don't encourage brand exploitation. In fact, we go out of our way to prohibit it. Unbelievable. The ITC has all sorts of silly rules preventing viewers from doing what they want to do – buy into brands by purchasing merchandise off screen. What on earth's wrong with that?

The situation with the BBC is even more bizarre. It's a nonsense to believe that the BBC can be both commercial and non-commercial at the same time. And as we begin to define what sort of public service the BBC should offer, there is an obvious first move. BBC Worldwide[4] should be privatised. I'll leave the City wallahs to work out how. But the massive proceeds, possibly around two billion pounds, could certainly deliver the BBC the increase it wants in the licence fee, via the interest alone. We really could liberalise the television market: with a more transparent BBC, with deregulated commercial networks and with a revitalised independent production sector incentivised to create the brands of the future.

What Do Viewers Want?

Who are these people we want to attract to our programmes? As consumers they're now much more aggressive and much more individual. They have less free time and their leisure time is not a treat. It's a fundamental right. So they're going to take their happiness seriously. At the same time they're uninterested in politics and less motivated by religion. It doesn't mean they're any less intelligent. But, as programme-makers, we have to understand: consumerism is their religion. We have to search for the trigger points for all these people, things that can still unify significant segments of them when it comes to watching the box. Research will help that process, as all advertising agencies know. There's much we can learn from them.

In the world of advertising it's axiomatic that creativity happens – on cue – in response to a brief. In the softer climate of British television we've never had the same disciplines. We teach people to edit videotape but we don't teach them how to answer a specific brief with a creative scheduling solution addressing the intended audience. We hope to have the ideas by accident. We're going to have change. That's why, in my company from September, we're going to borrow some of the clothes of an advertising agency. We're going to appoint a Creative Director and we're going to recruit young 'creatives', perhaps from advertising, who demonstrate an aptitude for inventing new TV shows. Will there be some differences between our group and an ad agency? Of course. Our programmes will be longer than thirty seconds and we plan to consume rather less cocaine.

Advertising not only provides a creative model for television production. More and more, advertisers will provide direct funding for programmes. Remember, even documentaries are sponsored on PBS in the States. That's why our group now has links with all the major ad agencies. It's quite a change for someone like me who's spent so many years making consumer programmes.

The People's Television – Some Modest Proposals

Let me repeat some of the modest proposals I have suggested to further the process. First: abolish the Broadcasting Standards Commission and curtail the ITC's responsibility for content. Second: remove the public-service remit of most of the commercial terrestrial channels. Third: phase out ITV companies' licence-bid payments and divest the ITV licensees of their production arms (with the exception of news). Fourth: create a real market in distribution by giving creators control over their product. Fifth: define the BBC's public-service role. Establish a long-term policy to preserve and strengthen it. Sixth: privatise BBC Worldwide.

But what chance is there of any of this happening? A fat chance, do I hear you say? Well, the thing is all of this will happen in the next twenty years simply because of the force of change in our industry. In fact, probably in the next ten. But will it happen sooner so that we become masters and not victims of the market? Not if we always keep a hold of nurse for fear of finding something worse. But we have a great opportunity to get it right. Instead of talking about Television versus the People, as we are this year, we could return to Edinburgh another year to talk about Television and the People.

Notes

1. The Henley Centre conducts and publishes research on all aspects of media but with a particular focus on audiences.
2. The Broadcasting Standards Commission and the Independent Television Commission have both been superseded by Ofcom since December 2003.
3. Electronic Programme Guide.
4. BBC Worldwide was established by Director General John Birt in 1996 to be responsible for the marketing, sales and distribution of BBC output.

The James MacTaggart Lecture 1999

Public-Interest Broadcasting: A New Approach

Richard Eyre*

Richard Eyre's 1999 MacTaggart Lecture announced the imminent demise of public-service television: 'It's a gonner' – and for three reasons. First, public-service broadcasting relies on regulators who are increasingly overwhelmed by the expansive sources of broadcast information: this will result in inequities. Second, it relies on an active broadcaster and a passive viewer, but 'at the end of a tiring day viewers don't always choose what's good for them'. Third, public-service broadcasting lacks any agreed definition. Modifying Oscar Wilde's judgement of fox hunting, Eyre declares public-service broadcasting to be 'The unsustainable in pursuit of the undefinable.' Public-service broadcasting must give way to public-interest broadcasting, which will provide salvation for the BBC because it will oblige the Corporation to engage with viewers 'more wholeheartedly'. The key difference is that while 'service is what you do for people . . . interest is what they give you and what you elicit from them'. It implies a contract and consensus between broadcasters and audience.

This shift does not imply the end of quality television. Broadcasters cannot merely pursue the lowest common denominators, because it is not in their interest to do so. ITV must be a public-interest broadcaster if it is 'to draw large audiences. So must the BBC, S4C and Channel 4. And Channel 5.' The difference between public-interest broadcasting at the BBC and ITV is that the former must try to achieve maximum weekly reach while commercial common sense will sustain an ITV that is unequivocally

* In 1999, Richard Eyre was Chief Executive at ITV. He resigned shortly after the MacTaggart Lecture, moving to the post of Chief Executive of Pearson plc.

in the public interest by generating diverse and high-quality programming: to do otherwise risks forfeiting market position.

Eyre concludes by asking, who will regulate television in the age of public-interest broadcasting? 'Who is going to take responsibility?' Eyre's answer: 'You and me . . . and the viewers.' He acknowledges that it 'doesn't sound like a very big finish' but argues that 'there is no other grand design, no great construct that will swing into play to relieve us individually of such burdens'.

It is a great privilege and a fearsome responsibility to be giving the final James MacTaggart Memorial Lecture of the millennium. The more so since my subject is the future of public-service broadcasting and the lecture is named for a man whose life's work was devoted to crafting some of the finest examples of public-service broadcasting we have seen.

I'm billed as posing the question: is there a post-Reithian model of public-service broadcasting that can thrive in the communicopia of the future? I hope I can make a contribution to what will be a continuing discussion of this. But I also want to use this unique opportunity to talk about our responsibilities as the people who shape British television, in a future in which I believe it will not be realistic, for the state and its trustees to determine what we do. So then, to the future. Here is my answer to the question: public-service broadcasting will soon be dead.

It will soon be dead because it relies on an active broadcaster and a passive viewer. Once upon a time, viewers (and listeners) could reasonably be expected to eat what they were given, because we, the broadcasters, knew it was good for them. As a model it's been the defining structure of the last seventy-five years, but as we reach the turn of the century, it's a gonner. It's a gonner because given the choice, at the end of a tiring day viewers don't always choose what's good for them. Many will always pass on the wholesome, healthy and carefully crafted in favour of the easily digestible, prepackaged and the undemanding. They devour the entertainment, play with the information and leave the education on the side of their plates, thank you very much.

Public-service broadcasting will soon be dead because it relies on regulators who will, in time, no longer be able to do a comprehensive job, because the vast number of sources of broadcast information will be impossible to monitor. And because it will become unfair to apply constraints to some and not all market participants.

Public-service broadcasting will soon be dead – for lack of definition – or at least a definition that will endure for the next seventy-five years. The ITC haven't got it taped. As one learned member said to me, 'we keep trying to get our heads around it, but we don't get very far'. The unsustainable in pursuit of the indefinable.

So in this lecture I'd like to tackle an agenda with three items: public-service broadcasting, the role of television in our culture and our role in television.

Ripple dissolve to John Reith in discussion with his colleagues on the role of broadcasting. It's 1923, an era of renewal. Interestingly, the public-service broadcasting of John Reith was designed for radio. He hated television and saw it not just as an unsuitable vehicle for the high public purposes he had fashioned for radio, but as a pernicious corrupter of man and morals, of the same ilk as jazz music and Noel Coward musicals which he dismissed as 'filth'. He was a man of high principle. A man who was suspicious of governments and politicians but who believed strongly in the role of the state to do good things for the people. And within that, that broadcasting could be a powerful force for good, for the improvement of humanity. Social improvement was his goal. Giving the public what it wants was therefore regarded as morally and socially irresponsible. Giving the public what it ought to have was proper.

That is why in the first forty years of the BBC, the anima is one of improvement. The high water mark was in 1962 when the Pilkington Report asserted that the duty for public-service broadcasters was to 'help towards a broadening and deepening of public taste'. Aim above their heads so they have to grow a bit. Enlighten their minds and elevate their tastes.

But in the 1980s, aided and abetted by economic empowerment on an unprecedented scale, the dawn of real television choice brought broadcasting tumbling into line with a social mood of more choice, more individualism, what the Americans called 'de-massification'. The notion of citizen as 'material to be improved' caved in to citizen as customer. So giving them what we think is good for them, the driving force of the first phase of British broadcasting, has had it as a rationale for television content.

Every component of that phrase 'public-service broadcasting' has changed; broadcasting is clearly different on a scale that Reith would not have envisaged. Our ideas of public service have moved on from the patrician ideals of Reith and his chums. This means the market has control, doesn't it? The Castor and Pollux of change, consumer choice and technology, are driving 'individualisation' with hurricane force. The opportunity to 'serve' a public by slipping in a little of what's good for them is diminishing as spectrum limits vanish and the breadth of choice grows. Free school milk doesn't work when the kids go and buy Coca-Cola because it's available and they prefer it and they can afford it. Yet this is the foundation of public-service broadcasting.

So public-service broadcasting will soon be dead. What will replace it? Have we reached that point, urgently sought by some of my commercial colleagues, when we're ready to let the market decide – or rather when we're obliged to let the market decide? And does that mean it's all over for quality television?

Well, no. Because whilst the elegant notion of public service through broadcasting is unsustainable, it is not true to say that broadcasters can thrive without reference to the public interest. Service is what you do for people. Interest is what they give to you and what you elicit from them. The initiative flows in the other direction. Interest involves a signing up, taking part; it implies consensus. It is not imposed. It isn't done to you. There is a subtle but substantial evolution here that has to shrug off the indefinables and unregulatables of public-service broadcasting. Not into a lowest common denominator for all, because that's not where I think it inexorably leads, but into a notion of broadcasting as a part of the culture that's bigger than the mere satisfaction of public taste. And one that is sustainable without minute by minute content regulation.

Because though we are right now blessed with plenty of regulators to help us get it right; their job in the next ten to fifteen years will become impossible. Effective regulation needs teeth and an ultimate sanction. But if you don't have a licence from the regulator, there is no ultimate sanction. And many of the suppliers of television services to the UK will possess no licence. In fact a gathering number already do not. Slip to the websites of any major overseas broadcaster and you can enjoy their programming. The launch of television hard disk recorders will add a new dimension still. We are in a period of transition. The unregulatable future that Peter Bazalgette so compellingly set out for this lecture last year is not yet with us. But it's coming. The kind of regulation that is there to underpin public-service broadcasting, however we're defining it, can't last.

So if content regulation will no longer be realistic, because there will no longer be an easy turnstile between broadcaster and viewer for the man in a cap to keep watch over, does this mean an end to quality television? Because no one went broke underestimating the taste of the public, are we inevitably in for 'lowest common denominator' broadcasting?

Well, yes, we are. There's going to be plenty of stuff that's going to upset people. But in my view that will not be an accurate description of the whole range of British broadcasting. But it's a fact of life that future broadcasters will push the boundaries of taste and decency and some people will be very uncomfortable. Will ITV go that route? Absolutely not. With or without me involved in the decision, a broadcaster like ITV cannot countenance such pursuit of lowest common denominators, because quite simply it is not in its commercial interest to do so. ITV must be a public-interest broadcaster if it is to continue to draw large audiences. So must the BBC, S4C and Channel 4. And Channel 5.

If public-interest broadcasting doesn't need a regulator to sustain it, 'Can it be worth having?' Well, yes, I think it can. Let's look at how the principle of public-interest broadcasting works through the BBC and ITV.

Public-interest broadcasting, not public service, will be the salvation of the BBC, because it will force the Corporation to engage with viewers and listeners more wholeheartedly. To do this it really must forget about chasing audience share and lead a path by caring passionately about the provision of something spectacularly good, regularly and for all of its licence payers – its customers and shareholders if you like. It won't be enough to produce a portfolio of undeniably brilliant programmes to wrap around the Corporation at times of creative challenge or government inquiry.

Share is a snare. What's it to do with the BBC's *raison d'être*? 'Because the rationale for the licence fee will be hard to maintain if BBC1 falls below 30 per cent.' Why? Why 30 per cent or 35 per cent or 25 per cent? The case for the licence fee becomes impossible to make, not when its share passes some random threshold, but when the British public thinks it isn't value for money anymore. And they will think that all the sooner if they sense that the BBC has lost the ambition to be the greatest broadcaster in the world.

How then do we describe the difference between BBC public-interest broadcasting and ITV public-interest broadcasting? It's terribly difficult if you've got to try and do it in terms of a differing scale of creative ambition. But I think it's simpler than that.

The appropriate mix of programmes will flow from the BBC if it is tasked quite simply to achieve the maximum possible weekly reach. This will mean that the BBC must engage in the full breadth of viewers' interests, even those which are not most sought out by commercial broadcasters. It means it will have to engage in the massively creatively ambitious risk-taking, very large-scale programme enterprises like *Life of Birds* that only it will do. Very high weekly reaches cannot, of course, be achieved solely by programmes of this sort. So at the same time, this mechanism dismisses the self-serving notion, put about by some of the BBC's rivals, that the BBC should be reserved to tackle only what the commercial sector will not. That would certainly spell the end of the licence fee, because the BBC's reach would never achieve the 90 per cent plus figure week after week that is the sure sign that it is engaging the full range of interests of the whole population. So you have to have *EastEnders* and *Casualty* and you have to have big sport as part of a mix that creates something for everyone.

The beauty of this simple mechanism is that it can't be sidestepped by well-worded statements of intent. It isn't subjective − it's an accountable measure that will underwrite a highly desirable but esoteric and indefinable ambition. This, I think, moves the debate about the scope of the BBC on. I offer it as the most important single regulatory criterion for the BBC, obviously upheld by an independent Board of Governors.

To justify special funding, you have to be special. To avoid having to earn your revenue in the market, you've got to be so distinct from the market that your shareholders and your rivals are happy with the deal.

Like any player in any market, the BBC must secure, bank and develop the unique and uncopiable aspects of its output − ring-fence a persona which belongs to it uniquely. As the only player in UK broadcasting pursuing a weekly reach objective, it will look and feel different from the others in a way which is sustainable for the very long term.

Above all, the licence fee needs consensus. That is my biggest worry about the BBC, the slipping-away of public consensus.

So, what about ITV?

ITV is designated a public-service broadcaster. In its origins it was modelled on the BBC. That was over forty years ago, but the notion has stuck that ITV is somehow a junior version of the BBC. We too have worn a public-service mantle sometimes uneasily, sometimes with great pride and distinction. But if it is to continue to thrive in the new market competition, it cannot be regulated with reference to the BBC while forging its way against legions of other channels that are not similarly bound.

You may have read in the papers that this lecture was to be a wild swing at the Corporation. No. I think it *is* a superb creation. This is not the cynical whingeing of an advertising-funded rival worried about the death of the licence fee. That would indeed have a devastating effect on the commercial sector and the public would unequivocally be worse off. But I worry because I believe our culture would be desperately impoverished without a vibrant BBC confidently wearing its mantle of benchmark broadcaster.

What about quality and diversity? Well, in the advertising market place, ITV has a unique offering. No other seller of media services can offer the proven advertising effectiveness of ITV. No other advertising medium in the country can offer a sheer weight of advertising pressure that is anything like it. To sustain that, we have to continue to attract very large numbers of viewers who are ever more media literate, who recognise cynical commissions when they see them, and who expect the highest quality of production techniques.

Meanwhile, the advertising community wants not more viewers of any old sort, but more lighter viewers of television. More of the younger, more upmarket people who are more selective about their use of television. So once again, we are withheld from the lowest common denominator broadcasting, not by the diligence of regulators, but by the simple fact that if we cease to be public-interest broadcasters, we will forfeit our market position.

But the market common sense is that our most unique selling proposition to advertisers is the sheer scale of ITV's audiences. How then does that market imperative to retain high reach affect ITV? Quality and diversity of output. The highest levels of domestic production. News, drama, sport, current affairs, comedy, documentary, arts, entertainment, children's programmes, movies, a selection of the best acquired programmes, regional services, deals with the very biggest talent names. There may be some marginal differences in provision, but commercial common sense will sustain an ITV that is unequivocally in the public interest. Because public-interest broadcasting is the economic mainstay of mass television.

So I offer you a vision of an unregulated ITV, that on all the major dimensions looks a lot like . . . ITV. It is not ITV of the 1970s, because ITV for the 1970s would die in the nineties. But it is high-quality, regional, diverse popular television.

The inter-relationship of a BBC pursuing weekly reach and the ITV that I have described sustains them both. In this model, the BBC is the benchmark. If it stops being a benchmark and tries to become just another of the players it will destabilise that inter-relationship that works so strongly in the public interest because a BBC and an ITV slugging it out for share points will produce programme decisions that will devalue the deal for the public. We've seen a bit of that break out from time to time. If that happens the BBC will inexorably become more and more like a commercially funded broadcaster. And at that point there will be no argument to prevent the Incorporated Society of British Advertisers from winning their relentless case – driven by American companies – that the BBC should carry advertising.

So the evolution of the system needs careful husbandry, but even after the death of public-service broadcasting I'm optimistic about the potential shape of broadcasting in the UK. I do though believe that much of the debate about the future has been inadequate. In particular the debate about the future shape, scope and cost of the BBC hasn't really happened. Shouldn't the public be involved – or do we think they wouldn't understand?

The death of public-service broadcasting isn't going to leave us as bereft as we thought. And a changed and reduced role for the regulator in the future won't necessarily mean wholesale change in the standards and the range of provision we've got used to. I don't foresee a wholesale lapse into the murk; but there are aspects that concern me.

So my question is this: who is going to take responsibility? Are we just players in an ungovernable market, incapable of taking an interest in the effect television is having on our society because there's nothing we can do about it? Of all the tasks we could have tackled in our society, being a broadcaster, a producer, a participant in the great television adventure, in front of or behind camera, is a privilege. But on the principle that you get nothing for nothing, it's a privilege that confers on us a responsibility, maybe even one that will carry some hardship.

One of our principal problems is that, because we've always been very heavily regulated, the public has been conditioned to believe we won't behave responsibly without it. We've never been fully put to the test, but we're about to be. So I believe that together we now have a job to do on the reputation of television. My experience of television is that we are not cynical. That the mood of our industry is not one of trying to get away with stuff we'd be embarrassed to show to our mothers in the hope that it might grab a few ratings. But that's what a lot of people think of us.

The way I see it is that those of us who are in broadcasting are all responsible for the direction of our craft. If one shines, the gleam reflects off all of us; if one sinks, in some way it drags us all down.

Our consciences are going to be vital organs if we are to grasp the immeasurable potential of the new broadcasting world in the public interest. In the long run, regulation as a sort of conscience by rulebook won't exist. What will replace it? You and me . . . and the viewers. Doesn't sound like a very big finish, does it? But there is no other grand design, no great construct that will swing into play to relieve us individually of such burdens.

If we pass on the responsibility because we somehow feel that there's a corporate or an industry agenda that is bigger than us, and unstoppable in its momentum, or that it's someone else's lookout, then not broadcasting, but our society will be impoverished.

But if together we pick up that responsibility because we recognise the incredible power of the medium to work in the public interest, and because we acknowledge that we hold the reins to the potential of television to enthral and enlighten, but also to influence and inspire, then we too can have a share in greatness.

The James MacTaggart Lecture 2000

A Time for Change

Greg Dyke*

Greg Dyke's second MacTaggart Lecture states his vision for a new BBC, which involves melding the public-service tradition with the realities of the digital television market in order to forestall the emergence of a 'digital underclass'.

Dyke's vision embraces a number of concrete programming proposals, including shifting the BBC's nine o'clock news bulletin to the 10 p.m. slot and the creation of two new children's channels. BBC1 will remain the 'gold standard of mainstream television' but will become more focused on entertainment, drama and factual programmes. Some programmes currently at the margins of BBC1's schedule will be given a higher profile slot on BBC2, which will broadcast more specialised 'highbrow' programmes. BBC3 will target a youth audience and while BBC4 will be 'unashamedly intellectual' and offer a televised amalgam of Radio 3 and Radio 4 with an emphasis on culture, music and arts. BBC News 24 will comprise the seventh BBC television channel. Dyke acknowledges that his vision will require the agreement of the BBC Governors and the Culture Secretary before it can be implemented.

□

Tonight I don't plan to talk about change and why it is difficult to bring about in an organisation like the BBC. The myth of the BBC is that there

---

* Greg Dyke has been Director of Programmes (1987), Managing Director (1990) and Group Chief Executive (1991) of London Weekend Television (LWT). In 1994 he joined Pearson Television and chaired the consortium which bid successfully for Channel 5. In 1999 he joined the BBC as Deputy Director General and became Director General in January 2000. He resigned on 28 January 2004 following the Hutton inquiry.

is a single flame, a single idea handed seamlessly from generation to generation. The flame is public-service broadcasting and each generation understands its inheritance and fights not to change it but to defend it to the death.

The truth, of course, is very different. John Reith ended up disliking Carleton Greene[1] with an intense passion. Reith's view was that Greene had trivialised his great institution; that Greene had – dare I use the words – 'dumbed down' the BBC. As Reith put it when talking about Carleton Greene, 'I lead, he follows the crowd in all the disgusting manifestations of the age . . . Without any reservation he gives the public what it wants; I would not, did not and said I wouldn't. I am very annoyed that I even got on to terms with him.'

Outrage from journalists, politicians, the great and the good and even some of the BBC's own staff at any mooted change in BBC radio or television is a pattern you can find throughout the history of the BBC. Remember the fuss when the BBC created Radio Five Live with the idea of starting a radio station aimed at a younger audience and based around news and sport? Today Five Live is supreme in its field and its audience is still growing rapidly year by year. Remember when John Birt set up BBC Online? He was widely accused of wasting licence payers' money and yet now it is the most visited content site in Europe and widely loved by some of the very people who accused him of wasting money at the time.

None of this is new. As the BBC's Chief Archivist described it to me: 'The BBC has been accused of dumbing down from the day Reith invented it.' Propose any significant change and the BBC is accused of betraying its heritage. The real genius of the BBC is that it has adapted and changed over the years. Successive generations of leaders have not simply taken the flame of public-service broadcasting as a whole and passed it on unchanged. At crucial times in the BBC's history they have recognised that change was essential and have taken the bold decision to introduce it despite loud protests from all around them.

So given this history, why try to change the BBC? The answer, of course, is we have no option. I believe the stark choice facing the BBC today is that we either change or we simply manage decline gracefully and none of us joined the BBC to do that. The changes happening in technology, in the wider society and in our competitive environment are what make this one of those times in history when change at the BBC is essential.

Let's take technology first. Digital television, and with it as many as 160 channels in digital satellite homes, has arrived at a pace faster than any could have imagined. But we are only just beginning to see what digital television can really bring. Electronic programme guides are already changing viewing habits in digital homes dramatically, but the real revolution will come with the arrival of the TiVo box[2] and similar in-home, hard disk recording technologies which will give the consumer complete freedom to watch what they want, when they want it.

Secondly, society is changing. Huge gulfs have opened up in the attitudes and values of different generations in a way not seen before. In recent research people from different age groups were asked if they agreed or disagreed with the following statement, 'There is too much sex, bad language and violence on TV and in cinema today.' Amongst the over forty-fives 72 per cent said they agreed. Amongst the 25- to 34-year-olds 79 per cent disagreed. If the BBC is to stay relevant over this decade we have to understand this generation and meet their needs, not only because they matter, but because we are all being influenced by them. In the old days kids wanted to be like their parents. These days parents, terrified of growing old, want to be more like their kids. As Bob Dylan wrote: 'I was so much older then I'm younger than that now.'

The third reason the BBC has to change is that the BBC's competitive environment has changed and will be transformed beyond recognition in the next decade. Consolidation and merger are the order of the day amongst media companies. Our competitors today are bigger, richer and more ruthless than at any time in the BBC's history. They are increasingly part of a global media industry which has access to vast capital funds. This is competition on a scale the BBC has never seen before.

It's this combination of factors which mean that this is one of those periods when the BBC, and BBC television in particular, has to go through fundamental change. In the words of Margaret Thatcher 'there is no alternative'.

Let me explain our plans in three parts. First of all I want to talk about money and what the BBC can and cannot afford to do. Secondly, I'd like to talk about our proposals for a portfolio of BBC public-service channels, which will eventually be available in every home in Britain. And finally I want to talk about the purpose of the BBC and public-service broadcasting in the digital age.

Starting with the money then. One thing I have learned in my years in the television industry is that money matters when you're trying to make outstanding programmes. It's not enough on its own, but trying to make fantastic programmes without the right budget is incredibly difficult. In fact I believe one of the problems of BBC television today is that too many of our services have been underfunded, but if we want to spend more money on our traditional services, there are certain consequences. Firstly, we have to find the money and, secondly, we have to limit our plans for new services to what we can afford.

This year's licence fee settlement, which gave us an increase of inflation plus 1.5 per cent every year for seven years was a fair, even generous, award. But if we want to shine in the new competitive digital age, we need to spend more money now, which is why I've spent so much time in my first six months as Director General looking for ways to save money right across the BBC.

I have to say I believe the potential for savings is significant. The BBC currently spends 24 per cent of its income on running the institution of the BBC. Our target is to reduce that figure to 15 per cent over the next three years which will give us an extra £200 million a year to spend on programmes and services. I also believe we can increase our commercial income from BBC Worldwide and BBC Resources Ltd – and we've established BBC Technology Ltd with the aim of bringing additional revenue into the BBC.

The second thing we have to do, if we want better-funded services, is to limit our ambitions for expansion. A criticism of the BBC over the years has been that it has tried to do everything the commercial sector has done. We cannot possibly afford to have a tank on every lawn, or compete in every area of the market place.

The combination then of the licence-fee increases, the major savings we're making inside the organisation and our growing commercial revenues means we can afford a significant increase in our spending.

In this financial year we will be spending £100 million more on programmes than last year. Next year we plan to increase that by a further £250 million above inflation and the year after by another £130 million. That means in the year 2002/3 we will be spending £480 million a year more on our programmes and services than we spent last year – a 30 per cent real increase in programme spend over just three years. This amounts to the biggest increase in programme expenditure in BBC history.

So what are we planning to do with the money? We believe that in the age of digital television it will not be sufficient for the BBC to offer only two mixed genre channels which are somehow supposed to meet the needs of everyone. That is not how audiences will want to receive television in the future. We need a more coherent portfolio of channels.

However, as I've already said, people have an expectation of BBC channels in terms of quality which we have to meet. As we are inevitably constrained by money, this means we must limit the size of this portfolio. But there is another more important reason for limiting the number of channels: the principle of universality. What universality means is making all our publicly funded services available in all homes.

Universality has been one of the core principles of public-service broadcasting and should remain so in the digital age. It means that everyone regardless of race, creed or bank balance will have access to the BBC's services. We must avoid the emergence of a digital underclass, a world where some are information rich while others are information poor. The BBC should be an essential part of the glue which binds this society together in the digital age.

In order to achieve this principle of universality we believe we should offer a portfolio of seven services across five channels. So what are these seven services? Well, two of them are pretty obvious. BBC1 and BBC2 will continue as the mainstays of BBC television for the foreseeable future.

BBC1 needs to have a greater impact on people's lives. It needs to be more modern, more in touch, more contemporary. It needs more programming that you simply cannot miss. While this may mean that some old faithfuls disappear and others move from the fringe of BBC1 to peak time on BBC2, it does not mean we are banishing all current affairs, documentaries, religion and arts to other channels. Far from it. But programming in these genres, just as in drama and entertainment, needs to be more engaging, more exciting, more gripping if it is to be on BBC1. Our aim is to make BBC1 the gold standard of mainstream television.

Now all this is going to cost and we plan a major injection of cash. More than half of the extra money to be spent will go on improving and modernising BBC1 and 2, with most going onto BBC1. Next year alone BBC1's budget will be increased by £95 million.

Let me move onto news. News is the cornerstone of public-service broadcasting on the BBC and I think I can say with some confidence that the BBC is now Britain's pre-eminent news supplier. Currently we have a 66 per cent share of all network television news consumed in Britain. After a great deal of thought we have decided that we will move the BBC's nine o'clock news to ten o'clock next year. Editorially we believe it is a better slot, after the US markets close and in time to report on Commons divisions, but the main reason for the move is that we believe that more people will watch it; it's as simple as that. The move to ten o'clock also gives us the opportunity to expand in an area which is increasingly under threat on ITV – regional news and regional programming. So with the move of the nine o'clock news to ten we plan to double the length of our late regional news bulletins and improve their quality. For viewers of news and current affairs this all means that there will be a full hour and a quarter available on BBC television after ten o'clock, starting with UK and local news on BBC1 followed immediately by *Newsnight* on BBC2.

Let me move onto BBC2. In the long term we plan that BBC2 will increasingly focus on intelligent specialist factual programmes, our key leisure and lifestyle programmes, thoughtful analysis, creatively ambitious drama and comedy, and specialist sports. That won't be for some years, maybe not until analogue switch off. It will retain, of course, its wide-ranging commitment to serious programmes of all kinds. It will also provide a peak-time home for some of the programming which is currently shown late night on BBC1.

Now for the new channels. Imaginatively, we've given them the working titles of BBC3 and BBC4. Given what I said earlier about the importance of reaching younger audiences it will come as no surprise to learn that we propose to use the evenings on one of our digital channels for programming aimed at this age group. BBC3 will offer original British comedy, drama and music as well as providing arts, education and social action programming delivered in a way likely to be attractive to a young audience. We've also been piloting a very different sort of news bulletin that breaks many of the conventions of traditional news services. I suspect in developing BBC3 we will need to break a lot more rules before we're through. BBC3 will emerge out of BBC Choice but will have a significantly higher budget.

BBC4 will be very different. It will be unashamedly intellectual, a mixture of Radios 3 and 4 on television. It will be based around arts, challenging music, ideas and indepth discussion. It will be serious in intent but unstuffy and contemporary. It will be a style of television which you can't find anywhere else. We know there's a potential audience, the challenge is to attract it to the channel. BBC4 will be developed out of BBC Knowledge. But again it will have a significantly higher budget. In all we plan to spend £130 million a year on BBCs 3 and 4.

Our fifth channel will be News 24. While not a favourite of Rupert Murdoch or Gerald Kaufman, I happen to like it and believe in its future. It seems obvious to me that the world's biggest news gatherer, the BBC, needs a 24-hour news service as part of its channel mix. Increasingly this is how the viewer will watch news and I believe it's the BBC's responsibility to provide news in the way people will want to receive it.

Finally we plan two new children's services to be played in the daytime on the channels occupied by BBC3 and BBC4 in the evenings. One will be for pre-school children and the second for children aged between six and thirteen. These will have separate identities from BBC3 and BBC4, if only to enable them to be easily found in the children's section of the electronic programme guide.

Nearly half of all children live in multi-channel households where for much of the time they are watching predominantly American-owned channels, largely showing American programmes. Shouldn't they, and their parents, at least have the option of choosing British children's programming on channels free from advertising?

Finally we do plan to continue with BBC Parliament on the same basis as now, which means it will be fully available on digital satellite and cable but digital terrestrial homes will only receive an audio signal.

This, then, is our proposed channel portfolio. Together the channels will deliver the BBC's core aims. All will carry predominantly British original productions. All will make a contribution towards achieving our educational goals which I regard as one of the principal aims of my period as Director General. All will include a broad news and current affairs agenda, and all will carry challenging factual programmes. However, over time each channel will develop its own personality and will increasingly be aimed at particular target audiences.

So is all this public-service broadcasting? I believe it is. The BBC's role in our society will always be complex – we're the guardian of impartiality and political independence, we're arguably the country's most important cultural organisation, we're a major player in the world of education, and increasingly we're Britain's leading global media player. But in the digital era I believe the BBC's single most important role will be to make possible the production of great British programmes.

Our channel strategy is a means of achieving this – a way of commissioning, producing and broadcasting original British programmes of all kinds on a mix of channels which will make sense to audiences in the digital age. Over time the channels will inevitably change but the commitment to creating exciting British programmes will not.

We've started our digital journey. We've changed the structure inside the BBC, we're making considerably more money available for programming and we've got a coherent plan for our channels. But this alone is not enough. Making television is a creative process and if we really aspire to be the engine of a new era of great British production in all genres of programming we have to be able to attract the best talent to work with us, both inside and alongside the BBC. In every area of programming we need people who are passionate about their subject, be it opera, science, comedy or any one of a dozen others. This means creating inside the BBC an environment in which talented people can flourish. I do understand why people look back to some earlier periods at the BBC as a golden age for programme-makers. They were. But the world has changed and changed dramatically and going back is not the answer, even if it was possible. It never is.

Notes

1. Hugh Carleton Greene, brother of the novelist Graham Greene, a former *Daily Telegraph* journalist and a BBC Director of News and Current Affairs, was appointed Director General of the BBC in 1959.
2. The TiVo box is an advanced digital, computerised recording system which allows viewers to record many hundreds of hours of their favourite television programming. Replay facilities allow audiences to delay or skip advertising breaks in programming.

The James MacTaggart Lecture 2001

The Soul of British Television

David Liddiment*

The key theme in David Liddiment's MacTaggart Lecture is that the soul of British television is in danger as a result of a battle for ratings in which 'we're losing sight of the innate value of programmes'. But television is about more than 'just putting bums on seats' and broadcasters must seek to make television interesting, ambitious and diverse as well as popular. Liddiment argues that broadcasters 'have to take risks'.

The BBC is the most powerful and dominant force in British broadcasting: £2.4 billion a year of public money and 43 per cent of all viewing and listening in UK homes. Its role in providing creative leadership is crucial: 'this beast is the keeper of the soul of British television. No one else can do this job.' But Liddiment is concerned that the BBC is losing sight of its cultural responsibilities in its 'rush to beat the commercial competition at its own game'. This failure in turn reflects a failure in corporate governance. The 'committee of part-timers' known as the Governors must decide whether they are regulators or management: 'they cannot be both'. There is a need for 'a new way of governing the BBC that puts creative leadership back at the centre of its public purposes'.

As the flagship of public-service broadcasting, the BBC 'is looking leaky', deluding itself, and doing a grave disservice to its viewers, its programme-makers and its public-service competitors, by taking 'its core values from the market place'.

---

* In 2001, David Liddiment was Director of Channels at ITV.

This is the MacTaggart Lecture, so I want to concentrate on the thing that I'm most concerned about. How can we guarantee the future supply of great programmes from creative people when there are so many fatal attractions and distractions around us?

In the beginning, television had soul. It was about individual acts of creation and communication: ideas, scenes and spectacle shared with an entranced and receptive nation. The business of broadcasting embodied values beyond and separate from monetary reward or public duty – though both came into it.

Despite the inherent conservatism of the early years of BBC television and ITV's profit motive, there were forces at work that ensured that for the first thirty years or so originality, bravery, innovation and excellence for its own sake were valued and promoted. During these years public taste for quality drama and factual programmes developed and public expectations grew. People embraced television because it met their expectations but sometimes shocked, surprised and stimulated them. And it had relevance to every aspect of their lives, public and private. There was no question that it had become embedded at the centre of national cultural life.

We know why this came about: the relatively late arrival of commercial television; a strong tradition of editorial freedom; blissfully secure funding; and strictly limited competition. Creative endeavour and risk-taking were encouraged by the leadership of those who ran television. Creativity was given special licence and structures were broadly sympathetic to its needs. It may at times have been undisciplined, indulgent and badly managed, but it created a strong production sector of people who knew their own worth. And it created a television ecology in which each broadcaster had a clear and distinctive programme offer.

I've airbrushed out the well-known downsides to this cosy idyll, but you'll get the point that our collective history has given us – as workers in and consumers of television – an expectation that programmes and the people who make them should be at the heart of broadcasting. And that its soul depends on the courage of those in charge to put programmes and the creative process first. Neither that expectation nor our ability to fulfil it has yet expired. But the soul of British television is in danger.

This may be part of a wider crisis of confidence about what culture and cultural institutions are *for* in a consumerist society. Culture is now an *industry*; it supports an industrial-scale workforce of 1.3 million people, and it's bigger than our traditional manufacturing sectors. This confusion of weighty economic and social objectives means cultural institutions and their public risk losing sight of their essential function – that of supporting and showing creative work.

Numbers now seem to be the only universal measure for excellence we have: how many, how much, how often. We're losing sight of the innate value of programmes in our fixation on the success that everyone can understand, the success that can be measured by profit, profile or performance. Whether we're operating in the public or the private sector, we're all commercial now.

The commercialisation of public-service broadcasting has eroded that diversity of voices and influences that once distinguished and defined BBC and ITV as different but complementary mainstream mass broadcasters. The diversity that allowed room for creative ambition and risk-taking, and accommodated failure as well as success.

The relentless quest to find out what viewers want and then to give it to them has made for sameness as we all seek to engineer the most effective schedule. It's a big part of what ITV does, I don't knock it. But it is *pure* commercial television. At worst, it can encourage the replication and regurgitation of ideas and so squeeze the time and money available for originality. It can churn out job lots of subject, genre and talent clones and atrophy a schedule into dull predictability: the back to back crime dramas, the Top 100's of everything and the acres of garden makeover shows.

Really great television has to do more than just give people want they want. More than just bring in the numbers. Satisfying viewer tastes is what we all strive to do, and it's the essence of commercial broadcasting, but it's not enough if you call yourself 'public service'. There has to be a margin for the unexpected, serendipity, a margin for programmes that the public has no idea it wants until it sees them, a margin for backing your own judgement and taking a punt on talent. We must lead audiences as well as be led by them. We must sometimes choose the creative over the obvious, the risky rather than the safety-first option.

This is rich coming from him, you're thinking. What risks does ITV take? Those *Frosts* and *Heartbeats* and *Peak Practices*. Or what the ITC calls our 'preoccupation with crime and medicine'. I don't apologise for those things. They will always play a part in a mass broadcaster's schedule. Since *Softly, Softly* and *Emergency Ward 10* they have been the fixtures and fittings of popular television. But if we believe television has a wider cultural role than just putting bums on seats, we must look beyond the focus groups and what we can copy from the competition, to how we can make popular television as interesting, ambitious and diverse as it can be. To do this we have to take risks.

This is scary, exhilarating, perhaps even rather *creative*. Risks are expensive for any channel, but on ITV1 if a risk doesn't pay off, the penalties are very severe. It's a mass channel or it's dead. To survive as a mass channel, ITV must have many different manifestations to meet segmenting tastes and interests. With a few obvious and honourable exceptions, one size no longer fits all. So the element of excitement and surprise is essential if we're to draw a thousand niche groups into a mass audience.

So, how can we make sure television stays an exciting place for viewers and gives them more than just what they think they want? How can we make sure it still has cultural as well as commercial value? I believe some of the answers lie in restoring balance to the producer–broadcaster relationship and in strengthening the hand of the production and creative community. I have some ideas about that. The other thing that will determine what kind of television we have in future is the role the public-service broadcasters – especially the BBC – choose to play in creative leadership. I have some ideas about that too.

We talk a lot about the diminishing power of broadcasters, but it's only relatively recently – within the last decade – that something called 'broadcasting' rose to ascendancy at the expense of programmes. Before that, broadcasting was just the means by which programmes got on the air. But once the old vertically integrated broadcasters broke down into their constituent parts and became two businesses, the balance of power changed decisively. The money went to broadcasting, and programme-makers found themselves cap-in-hand. They had to learn to pitch to a brief, deliver a demographic, fill a slot or suit a star name. This isn't good for programme-makers and I don't think in the long term it's good for broadcasters either. Here are a few ideas for restoring equilibrium to this relationship.

First, let's look at the structures and bureaucracies we're making for our own creative teams.

Good programme-making is a human business: it takes place in small teams, not big, efficient units of production. Some of the best people are also the most difficult to manage. Maverick talent should not only be tolerated, it should be given room to breathe.

Next, programme-makers shouldn't have to be salespeople.

Some programme-makers are judged to be so good, they're distanced from the creative process and made into managers and salespeople: a kind of death-by-promotion. We need to find a way of rewarding our talent without removing it from the main theatre of creative action.

Third, creeping centralisation is a threat.

Metro-centrism may be cost-efficient but it's a throttle on creativity. Regional production centres can grow talent, provide a drip-feed of new projects, and inject vitality and diversity into network programmes. Continued investment in the regions is vital to the creative health of ITV as a whole.

Fourth, broadcasters – and particularly publicly funded broadcasters – should not be in the rights business.

Hoovering up all non-broadcast rights as a kind of *droit de seigneur* is an abuse of broadcaster power and a real disincentive to building creative businesses. Broadcasters should not exploit their market power to exhaust the commercial capital of those who've created the ideas. It's not fair, and it's dangerous short-term-ism.

This brings me to my final suggestion and to the BBC's own production function. *The most effective boost* we *can give the creative community is to open up the UK's biggest producer to the market.*

Is there any compelling public service or creative justification for keeping BBC production tied up as an expensive publicly funded in-house operation?

A true market in creativity would deliver two significant benefits: it would unlock the good ideas that just wither away now if they are not taken up by the BBC; and conversely, the BBC itself would have to open up fully to other suppliers in a properly level playing field. If BBC production is competing in the market, it can't also have guaranteed access to what is effectively 75 per cent of the BBC's output. There has to be genuine competition to make what the BBC shows.

This has important implications for its future role. *If,* as I believe, the BBC's principal function should be to deliver excellent, distinctive and creative programme services to the public, then this – and no other – is the role it should be publicly funded for. In this scenario, it shouldn't matter where programmes come from and who produces them, only how good they are.

So, here are some of the remedies if the broadcasters are prepared to take the medicine:

- Open doors for creative talent.
- Don't turn your best creatives into salespeople.
- Maintain and invest in regional production.
- Don't hog programme rights.
- And open BBC production to the market.

I believe this modest handful of suggestions for improving the programme-maker's lot would help put creativity back nearer the centre of what we do. But there's something else that matters far more. All these changes would count for nothing unless the organisation that describes itself as 'the leading showcase for British creativity and talent' is prepared to give creative leadership. I'm referring, of course, to the BBC.

The BBC is the most powerful and dominant force in British broadcasting and production. We hear the figures often enough, yet we're still amazed by their scale: £2.4 billion a year of public money; 24,000 employees; and here's the real mind boggier: it has 43 per cent of all viewing and listening in UK homes. It dwarfs everyone and everything.

We're content to keep feeding this beast only for as long as we believe it gives us something valuable the market can't. As far as I'm concerned, that 'something' is the freedom from commercial constraints to lead, dare, risk and sometimes fail in creative terms. It may be big and have some pretty unattractive features, but this beast is the keeper of the soul of British television. No one else can do this job. The BBC's creative leadership role is *the* key. I believe in it, I support it, I use it. But I worry that it is losing sight of its cultural responsibilities in its rush to beat the commercial competition at its own game. In its confusion about equating the value licence-payers place on its services with the how many, how much and how often of the ratings race, it is failing in its most important role.

In my view, this failure is a direct result of a failure in corporate governance, who's in charge? Who's making the decisions about the direction the Corporation takes and the priority it gives to creative leadership? It's the Governors, stupid. Three captains of industry, two economists, two academics, two career civil servants, a man from the unions and a man of the theatre. All excellent people without doubt. But am I the only one who is disturbed by the idea that the creative heart and soul of the industry is in the hands of a small group of people who appear to be accountable to no one?

But it's the Governors who determine the BBC's overall strategic direction. They alone have the power to halt the slow slide into commercialism and pull this leviathan round from its plotted, but I believe disastrous, course. Do I trust them to do the job? No. Nothing personal, but this is not the way to run a twenty-first-century public body with huge cultural obligations as well as significant commercial interests. *They are either regulator or management. They cannot be both.*

I'm quoting here from Greg Dyke's last-but-one MacTaggart. Different times of course, but it's still true. The BBC's failure in creative leadership is compounded – and to a large extent explained – by its failure of corporate leadership. It is too rich, too powerful and too valuable an organisation to be governed by a committee of part-timers who shouldn't be asked to adjudicate the results of the strategies they've had a hand in creating. We need a new way of governing the BBC that is informed, professional and genuinely accountable but above all, a form of governance that puts creative leadership back at the centre of its public purposes.

I hear the stirrings of the BBC's corporate legions, ready to spring to its defence . . . Let me save them the bother. I know what they'll say:

> It's not just about reach or share, it's about ambition and range.
> We don't judge success or failure by pure numbers.
> What matters most is creativity.
> Innovation is the key word.

These are all quotes about BBC1, by the way. Splendid stuff.

And here are the titles to prove it: *Walking with Dinosaurs, Warriors, The League of Gentlemen, Cops, The Royle Family* . . . and so on. There's no doubt that excellent stuff is still being produced. This is not the point. Look at the more significant programme developments that are changing the character and purpose of our quote 'flagship public service network'. There's still the sprinkling of ambitious landmark programmes, but so many other less reassuring signals that these begin to look like fig leaves preserving the decency of a nakedly commercial beast.

Mid-peak news sacrificed for more competitive programmes. BBC news viewing hasn't grown year-on-year, whilst viewer choice has narrowed. Pushing PSB programmes further to the margins: *Panorama* to its Sunday night retirement home and for only thirty weeks of the year – couldn't that extra £95 million a year stretch to a year-round current affairs series for the main channel? The shunting of *Omnibus* to BBC2, with no regular arts strand to take its place. *Inside Story* phased out, and the threat of a fine documentary unit scattered to the four winds. That's what's gone. What we've got instead is year-round *Holby City,* year-round *Casualty,* a fourth and probably soon a fifth *EastEnders,* and more crime dramas than Jack Frost has had canteen dinners.

Yes, these are all valid parts of the schedule. Yes, viewers like them. Yes, they are well made. But shovelling on more of the same eats up the available hours and makes the BBC's claim to value ambition and range over ratings look deceitful.

Come clean, BBC, about your ambitions for your main service. Cut the corporate hyperbole and the public-service justifications and just be honest. We've been around a bit. We can take it. If you no longer see a role as creative leader on your flagship service, if you're shaping BBC1 for commercial not creative success because you believe that's the only way the Corporation can survive, shouldn't we all at least talk about it?

The flagship is looking leaky. The public utterances just don't match reality. A flagship public-service channel that takes it core values from the market place is deluding itself, and doing a grave disservice to its viewers, its programme-makers, and its public-service competitors. A more commercially focused BBC reduces the scope for range and creative ambition by ITV, Channel 4 and Channel 5.

The end result is more formula product and a reduction in creative opportunity all round. And it means the eventual squeezing out of less mainstream programming – arts, science, religion – to minority and subscription channels. People shouldn't have to go to Artsworld or the History Channel for something they used to get for free as part of a mixed mainstream public-service channel.

I don't want this to happen. I expect ratings competition with the BBC but I'm looking for creative competition too. This means accessible new work, genuine programme range, challenging subjects and treatments, as well as the reliable audience bankers. More *Clocking Off*, less *Mersey Beat*.

I've tried to show that the BBC has a very special obligation to sustain creativity in these competitive times, but I don't shrink from my own role in this endeavour. Saving the soul of television isn't just a job for one broadcaster, commissioner or producer; it's a job for us all.

The James MacTaggart Lecture 2002

Television's Creative Deficit

Mark Thompson*

Mark Thompson's MacTaggart Lecture identifies a 'creative deficit' in British television resulting in many programmes appearing 'dull and mechanical and samey'. The culprit is not competition (identified by David Liddiment in the 2001 MacTaggart Lecture), which can have positive effects, but a twofold conservatism: the 'risk-aversion of the schedule' in tandem with 'an older cultural conformism'. Even Channel 4, which was initially inspired by a commitment to risk, diversity, originality and a schedule in which 'everything was an experiment', has become 'distracted by its ambitious digital plans' and allowed its 'creative decision-making to become too centralised and risk-averse'.

Thompson argues that Channel 4 must be revitalised to resume its place as 'the creative space in the centre of British television' where it must offer a distinctive kind of public-service programming to the BBC: 'an improvised rhythm of experimentation and alternative ideas against the steady drum-beat of information, education and entertainment'. To achieve this, Thompson promises a fundamental review and restructuring of the schedule at Channel 4. But creative thinking alone will not suffice: the channel faces financial and other difficulties. Thompson rejects privatisation since 'independence is a vital part of Channel 4's DNA', but hints at the need for public support in the deregulated television market place. Government legislation, moreover, promises to liberalise media ownership in the commercial sector – creating the prospect of a single owner for Channel 3 –

* In 2002 Mark Thompson was the newly appointed Chief Executive of Channel 4 having previously been Director of Television at the BBC. In June 2004 Thompson became the new Director General of the BBC.

with evident and deleterious implications for the public sector of broadcasting, including Channel 4.

□

Greg Dyke is a very nice man. So nice in fact that earlier this year, while I was still working at the BBC, he actually paid me to sit at home for a few months just to watch television. I wish someone had warned me. After a bit, I began to wonder if Greg was paying me enough. It's not that today's TV is bad exactly. In many ways production quality and professionalism are higher than they've ever been. And it's not, as it's often claimed, that modern British television is stupid. The problem is that so much of it just feels so dull and mechanical and samey. It's odd how often when you're looking for ambitious, complex and above all modern TV, you find yourself watching not British, but American pieces: *Six Feet Under*, say, or *24*. Now of course there are exceptions. I fell in love with Annie Griffin's *The Book Group*. And when I summoned up the supreme effort to actually change channels, I enjoyed *Cutting It* and *Conspiracy*, that pitch-black snapshot of the origins of the Holocaust. But the idea that, taken as a whole, British television is teeming with that kind of creative risk is a joke.

A creative deficit has opened up in British TV and it affects every channel – including Channel 4. This evening I want to explore how we got into it and how we could get out of it again. I don't think it's all the fault of competition. I lay most of the blame on two kinds of conservatism: the modern, technocratic risk-aversion of the schedule; and, lurking in the shadows, an older cultural conformism. We have to overcome them both. You'll also hear why I'm confident about the future. I'm certain we can build a Channel 4 that is stronger and braver than ever. And we have to do that, because in the end I believe it's only Channel 4 – together with a strong independent sector – that can blaze a trail back to creativity.

The Early Channel 4: The Risk that Paid off

But I want to begin with that rather tricksy word 'risk'. I don't know what your attitude to risk-taking is, but at my end of British telly we can't get enough of it. When Channel 5 was first starting, Dawn Airey told the press: 'the future of television is routine, routine, routine'. Now Dawn, as usual, was on to something – all modern schedules need familiar shapes and patterns – but Channel 4 began twenty years ago with exactly the opposite philosophy. Nothing was routine: everything was an experiment. And that was the intention.

In 1979, the year I entered television, the IBA published their blueprint for the fourth channel: 'Our wish,' they said, 'is that enterprise and experiments will flourish. It must provide opportunities for talents which have not been fully used, for needs to be served which have not been fully defined and for the evolution of ideas which . . . have yet to be revealed.' The early Channel 4 put that philosophy into practice.

Its soap, *Brookside*, was the first to be set not in some imaginary television world of stereotypes and stock situations, but in the real Britain of dizzying social and political and sexual change. The channel re-invented talk on television with programmes like *After Dark*. Before Channel 4, multiculturalism usually meant current affairs and documentary and it always meant gloom. At Channel 4, it could and did mean drama, music and comedy. Innovation at this point in the channel's development wasn't a piece of empty television rhetoric. It was a practical programme strategy.

These were the values which won me over as a viewer and which I envied so much sitting inside the citadel of the BBC. They're what make Channel 4 so exciting and liberating for me.

Taking Channel 4 for Granted?

By the end of the nineties, Channel 4 Television Corporation was in danger of taking Channel 4 itself for granted. There were still many people who were totally committed to the main channel. But the Corporation began to become distracted by its ambitious digital plans and to allow its creative decision-making to become too centralised and risk-averse. It wasn't alone of course, or even the worst offender. But it was a Channel 4 executive who told me that innovation within individual programmes wasn't where the action was anymore. To get noticed, you had to create entire new services. E4[1] would be the test-bed for new programmes and new talent; Channel 4, the exploiter of known success, the cash cow.

The model felt intuitively right: digital new, analogue old, digital innovative, analogue conservative. And, again, it wasn't just Channel 4 who believed it. It was part of my thinking at the BBC about the proposed BBC3 and the role it could take over from BBC2 and BBC1. ITV was concentrating much of its investment and management time on its new digital platform. And around the world, from AOL-Time Warner to FT.com, other media players were doing the same. Well, perhaps it's easy to say in hindsight, but it's clear today that much of this thinking was just wrong.

First, it's nonsense that innovation within individual programmes doesn't count anymore. This is the age of the blockbuster, when a single breakthrough hit can transform the performance of even the largest network. In the digital environment, the big brands – the *EastEnders*, the Ali Gs – stand out more than they ever did in analogue. They're also the most immune to multi-channel fragmentation. And it's only the terrestrial channels that can launch them.

Secondly, the hold that established channels and media brands have on consumers is impossible to reproduce quickly with new digital services. Nowhere is this more true than if you're trying to innovate. It's desperately difficult for digital channels to launch new shows or new talent on their own. Most just disappear down a deep, dark, digital hole.

We shouldn't over-react. The future will be broadly based across platforms and media. Channel 4 should exploit its lead in creating rich cross-platform offerings from *Big Brother* to *Grid Club*. E4 is already performing brilliantly, far ahead of its audience targets and our film channels also show real promise. But the centre of creativity and originality will not be E4 or any other of the new businesses. It will be Channel 4 itself.

Corporate versus Creative?

By the end of the 1990s British television was changing in other ways and Channel 4 was changing with it. It had become more corporate in tone. Staff numbers had grown from a few hundred to well over a thousand and they were now housed in a brilliant and imposing new building in Horseferry Road. Indies still clearly felt a strong affinity and sense of loyalty to the channel but they'd begun to question whether it still meant what it said about creative risk. They also found that the process by which programmes were developed and selected was becoming more schedule-driven and centralised.

Professionalism in the scheduling and marketing of programmes has probably never been higher. Think of the launch of *Millionaire* or moving the *Nine O'Clock News* in two and a half weeks. But the risks you take in the name of the schedule tend to be strategic and structural rather than creative, and the highly sophisticated, analytical atmosphere we've created can militate against purely creative courage. In my view, this is one of the main reasons why a creative deficit has opened up.

The Scourge of Competition?

Many people in our industry accept that we face a creative problem. But we're all a bit prone to the ITV defence: it must be someone else's fault. It's the BBC. It's Sky. It's the government. It can't be us. The most popular culprit is competition. David Liddiment put the case against competition from this platform last year: 'commercial pressures on all of us', he said, 'risk making television a more homogenous, more driven, less interesting place'. Plenty of people think David is right, but I'm not so sure.

Competition can have positive effects; far from destroying creativity it can encourage it. The arrival of Channel 4 forced BBC2 to get its creative act together, just as the growth of Channel 5 is challenging the rest of us right now. Consider America, where competition and fragmentation are even more intense. When MTV was in danger of being swamped by imitators, they didn't wring their hands or fret about the 'soul of television'. They turned to a series of bold, genre-busting commissions: *Celebrity Deathmatch*, *Jackass* and, of course, *The Osbournes*, coming to Channel 4 this autumn. This is creativity as a practical survival plan. The main thing I take from the experience of our colleagues at MTV is the spirit with which we should approach competition. We shouldn't just moan about it. We should engage with it, get inspired by it.

Competition has raised the stakes. It's made risk-taking more frightening for commissioners. It's also clearly put pressure on some of the less popular genres, which public-service broadcasters like Channel 4 have to protect. But anyone who thinks that we can react to competition simply by playing safe should think again. Audiences are showing signs of getting bored with safe television.

As Controller of BBC2 I made my share of 'safe' or cynical choices, nearly all of which ended up being disappointing, not just in critical but in audience terms. But it's the mad choices, the choices you don't really understand, it's *The Royle Family*, *The League of Gentlemen*, *The Cops*, which not only strike a chord with the critics but often go on to get good or even great audiences. A policy of taking bigger risks, then, isn't a simple recipe for commercial suicide. Sometimes that mad, brave choice will more than pay for itself.

A Conservative Culture

So let's not get too hung up on the horrors of competition. No, if you're looking for a root cause of the current creative deficit, I'd point to the

deep wells of conservatism in our television culture: the urge to pas-
tiche and re-make rather than to invent. The urge to look backwards.
When you add this older conservatism to the modern risk-aversion
I've already talked about, you have a cocktail which is almost lethal
for creativity. British television used to be famous for its risk-taking.
Now we're clearly trailing, not just behind America, but our own
viewers.

A Different Kind of Public Service

So what should we do? I believe that the purpose of Channel 4 is to be
the creative space in the centre of British television where new ideas,
new genres, new kinds of programmes can be invented; to be the place
where new talent and new opinions can find their voice; to be on the
side of the iconoclasts, the awkward squad, the rule-breakers. For all
the reasons I've set out tonight, the need for a Channel 4 like that is far,
far greater than it was twenty years ago.

It's a different kind of public service to that provided by the BBC, an
improvised rhythm of experimentation and alternative ideas against
the steady drum-beat of information, education and entertainment.
That's why, although the BBC does wonderful work, public service
would be impoverished without Channel 4.

A More Creative Channel 4 . . .

But from now on we must put creativity first. That means change. Right
now we're trying to approach the Channel 4 schedule not as a legacy of
the past two decades but as if we were launching an entirely new
channel. We need to look hard at the current line-up of programmes.
The public don't want tired programmes from Britain's most innovative
broadcaster. And we have to create space for the new.

We want a schedule which is full of fresh ideas, with more creative
energy, with more live programming where neither we nor the viewers
know quite what to expect. We want more drama – subversive, full of
attitude and fun and backed by a real diversity of talent and voices.
That's not a commercial decision – it's unlikely that these pieces will
cover their costs in advertising revenue – but a creative one.

And we must be braver in the way we schedule, placing new programmes we believe in in prime slots and standing by them. Placing
great programmes in the wee small hours sends a signal to talent and
viewer alike that you don't mean what you say about risk.

Now you can dismiss all this as just words but it's my recent experience at the BBC that you really can move to a practical strategy of greater risk-taking. And that's what we're going to do. Last month we drastically reduced the number of commissioning departments at Channel 4 and clarified their roles. That will enable us to pass much of the decision-making back to individual commissioners. We want to back their instincts and recognise that sometimes they'll make mistakes. We want a new, closer relationship with our indies, one that is strategic and based on trust. That means quicker decisions and less interference from us, a total commitment to originality and quality from them.

We should be less frightened of cock-ups and failure. Every original piece of work I've ever commissioned has given me at least one complete dark night of the soul. But so what? Misfires and even truly dreadful television are usually more interesting than the merely bland. And if we don't expose ourselves to the risk of real failure, we won't find the breakthroughs either.

A Climate under Threat

But nothing I've talked about tonight will be possible if we don't have a climate in broadcasting in this country which will support creativity and risk-taking in the long term. And that climate is under threat.

Earlier this year the government published their Draft Communications Bill.[2] It's a realistic picture of how our industry might develop over the next decade and it offers an ambitious vision for public-service broadcasting – including the unique contribution that Channel 4 makes – as an essential part of the future.

Unfortunately that ambition is not underpinned by any specific measures to strengthen Channel 4's position: the Bill wills the ends without enacting the means. The government a few years ago took the step of securing one part of public-service broadcasting by substantially increasing the BBC's licence fee. But there's nothing equivalent inside or outside of this Bill to secure an independent Channel 4. And very little to support and strengthen an independent production sector either.

The government believes that you can change great swathes of the commercial production and broadcast sectors in this country without that impacting on that part of public-service broadcasting which is also funded commercially. I think they're wrong. Sooner or later some of the consolidation that the Bill allows – for instance between the ITV companies or perhaps between Channel 5 and Sky – will take place. The Secretaries of State say they hope the result will be new investment, new creative opportunities and new jobs. But this isn't the car industry. Consolidation in British television industry has always tended to focus on cost-cutting and it's always led to job losses. Nor is it likely that inward investment will lead to lots of new programme factories across the land.

All of this could impact on Channel 4. So far the original Channel 4 financial model has stood up remarkably well, but we're heading into uncharted waters now. The danger is not that the channel will go bust – we can and will return to profitability – but rather that our ability to take the kind of creative chances that I've discussed will eventually be curtailed. A richer programme mix with more risk-taking in some of the most expensive genres can't be achieved within a falling programme budget.

Some people might argue that the solution would be for Channel 4 to move entirely into the private sector. That might indeed provide some of the investment the channel will need and give it the protection of being part of a larger media group. But, unless the public model for Channel 4 fails utterly, I don't believe that privatisation is the right answer. Independence is a vital part of Channel 4's DNA, the basis for its diversity and its editorial courage, and that would be lost if the channel was privatised. I also believe that the fact that the channel is there for viewers rather than for shareholders is a critical part of our culture.

I believe that an independent and publicly owned Channel 4 remains the best option for the future. We intend to secure it by making the channel as competitive as possible. Looking ahead, however, it's possible that the changes in the market which the Communications Bill foresees, combined with the impact of digital conversion, could reduce the channel's income to a point where its ability to deliver its unique brand of public service is compromised.

That's why over the coming months we want to look with the government at ways of underpinning and guaranteeing Channel 4's core programme budget in the long-term. We don't expect to call on public support over the next few years. Indeed we may never do so. Channel 4 should always aim to pay its own way. But if changes in the broadcasting landscape mean we have to choose between financial survival and our public-service remit, then the case for public support will be overwhelming. I'm confident that we can win that argument because I'm confident we can deliver on the promise of creativity.

Words are slippery things in television. I've used quite a few tonight: risk, creativity, even that dreaded phrase 'public-service broadcasting'. I believe we can make them mean something again. But I also recognise that we won't be judged by our words, but by what we do.

Notes

1. E4 was a new service provided by Channel 4 which came on air in January 2001.
2. This was eventually enacted as the Communications Act 2003.

The James MacTaggart Lecture 2003

Freedom of Choice: Public-Service Broadcasting and the BBC

Tony Ball*

Tony Ball, then Chief Executive of BSkyB, announced in the MacTaggart Lecture that an unprecedented majority (51 per cent) of the public, responding to a National Opinion Poll survey, believes that the BBC licence fee no longer represents good value for money. Worse, the poorest people feel most aggrieved with 60 per cent reporting their dissatisfaction with the value offered by the licence fee. With BSkyB now reaching 7 million homes offering viewers an 'explosion of choice', Ball argues it is time to reassess the relationship between broadcasters and government, as well as the character of public-service broadcasting. It is time to raise a 'red flag' to halt the BBC's 'expansionary ambitions'.

Ball underpins his argument by offering three 'cardinal points' about government and broadcasting. First public funding offers no 'sure-fire guarantee of quality'. Second, the greater the degree of public funding and government control, the greater the 'scope for abuses'. Finally, in an age of spectrum abundance, publicly funded television must work harder than ever to justify its subsidy. Funding for the BBC is 'money coerced from people under legal sanction, ultimately under the threat of jail' and consequently there is a need for programme-makers to be accountable.

Balls offers three specific proposals to enable the BBC 'to flourish' while also setting 'clear limits to its role'. First, every BBC network should be allocated a specific remit alongside a set of 'measurable criteria against which to judge it on a regular basis'.

* Tony Ball was the Chief Executive of BSkyB when he delivered the MacTaggart Lecture but on 23 September 2003 he resigned to take up a consultancy role with News International.

Second, a limit should be imposed on programmes which 'clearly fall outside any reasonable remit for a publicly-funded broadcaster': for example, bought-in American programming. Third, Ball proposes a system of 'programme syndication' in which commercial broadcasters would be given an opportunity annually to bid in a competitive auction for the programme rights to 'half a dozen or so' established BBC programmes. This would effect a 'recasting of the relationship between the BBC and the commercial sector'.

□

Dennis Potter, in by far the most brilliantly crafted and funny MacTaggart, thought that Sky's introduction of choice into television was verging on the criminal, calling for Rupert Murdoch to be given a show trial complete with gallows, and attacking his 'team of wild-eyed horses'. Still I suppose it could have been worse; in fact, compared to John Birt we got off rather lightly. The serious point is that there have always been people in our industry who have been deeply sceptical both about the value of choice and the appetite for it.

About 30 per cent of all homes in the UK now receive their television via digital satellite. And a further 20 per cent receive Sky channels through cable and Freeview. Our progress has meant an explosion of choice for viewers. By investing over £2 billion in digital services and infrastructure, and persuading 7 million homes to take boxes, we've paved the way for other organisations to become national broadcasters at a fraction of the cost.

All of this has happened, in the end, because the British people wanted it to happen. Though they have to pay their BBC licence fee and have their programming interrupted by the commercials that fund ITV, they don't have to subscribe to Sky. They are free to choose. That's the true revolution – a revolution of choice for viewers. Today television is much, much more democratic. Once the sole preserve of states and the largest corporations, now, for the price of a Georgian town-house in Edinburgh, anyone can launch a television channel.

Like democracy itself, the results are not always pretty – for every uplifting History Channel, Artsworld or National Geographic there's a tacky, downmarket, ratings chaser – and I'm not just talking about BBC3. But I hope this will never be an industry that despises its viewers. An industry that isn't confident enough to trust the choices of its consumers and direct its resources accordingly is not one that is positioned for long-term success, or one in which Britain can aspire to world leadership. The indispensable condition for that success is to satisfy the consumer.

It often happens, though, that old attitudes persist long after the conditions that gave rise to them have vanished. So, in case they do, let me re-state three cardinal points about government and broadcasting – ones, incidentally, on which we should all now be able to agree.

First, public funding is no more a sure-fire guarantee of quality in the making of programmes than it is in the making of anything else. It's often suggested that creativity and the market don't mix. There may be something in this. But we shouldn't suspend the healthy scepticism that comes from years of observing this argument applied in other contexts. Who now mourns the creative risks which state funding allowed British Leyland to indulge in? The public sector backs losers as well as winners.

My second point is that the more state subsidy and government control you have in broadcasting, the greater the scope for abuses will be. And I mean serious abuses. Of course measures are in place to protect publicly funded broadcasters from political diktat, but as with any publicly funded body, ultimately the government of the day holds most of the cards.

It's a funny thing, isn't it? Some people get very excited about the dangers of concentrating ownership and power in the highly fragmented commercial sector. Yet they hardly seem worried at all about having a much greater concentration in the public sector. And there, indeed, we have just one proprietor with its own large vested interests enjoying a far, far greater audience share. Inconsistencies like that eventually lead to trouble. We should reflect on them.

The third point follows from these other two. It is that publicly funded broadcasting in an age of spectrum abundance has to work harder than ever to justify itself to the taxpayer. Money spent by the BBC is money coerced from people under legal sanction, ultimately under the threat of jail. Such coercion is clearly not ideal in a free society where consumers have great choice. So it is certainly incumbent upon those who receive the funding to be accountable, and it is where that breaks down that problems arise.

So what are the arguments in favour of public-service broadcasting in an age of spectrum abundance – and how strong are they?

Gavyn Davies'[1] report, four years ago, was impressive: it justifies public funding of broadcasting by reference to market failure. It states that 'It is impossible to argue for a public service broadcaster unless market failure can be shown' but then argues that a fully commercial environment wouldn't produce outcomes that were economically efficient or socially desirable for three central reasons.

First, public-service broadcasting is what economists call a public good. Like a lighthouse or national defence, the consumption of it by one person doesn't affect consumption of it by someone else, and nobody can be excluded from enjoying its benefits. As a result, it shouldn't just be left to markets to provide. Second, he argues that public-service broadcasting is a merit good. Like education, it is worth more to society than people would pay for it. Third, the end of the spectrum scarcity which created it should not in itself spell the end of public-service broadcasting. Fragmenting audiences in digital homes, he says, will mean that the commercial sector won't have the money to produce the quality programmes that society collectively wants. So neither advertising-funded nor Pay-TV channels would fully serve the consumer's need.

And my view of these arguments put forward by Gavyn Davies? Well, basically, I agree with them all. Yes: free-to-air broadcasting can be a public good, and there should be some public provision. The best broadcasting is also a merit good – and please note that little word 'best' – because it provides more value to a society than viewers would pay for when they sat down to watch. And advertising and subscription TV will not produce all the quality television we need. So, there is still a case for public-service television in my view. Too much time has probably been spent denying the benefits of it. A truce should be called. The debate between those who say that public-service broadcasting has no place in our society any more and those who argue that it should have an ever expanding role isn't really worth continuing. But how much public-service broadcasting is needed? How much market failure is there? That's the two and a half billion pound question.

Charter review allows us to start from first principles. So let's start, as in Hobbes' *Leviathan*, with the State of Nature. Imagine we live in a digital TV State of Nature where there is no BBC, no public-service broadcasting, no government and where life is – according to Hobbes – 'solitary, poor, nasty, brutish and short'. In that frightening world, the only funding would be from advertising and subscription. Let's, then, think of state intervention in £100 million blocks. The first block added to this world might actually be a waste of time – it could sink without trace, and produce little benefit. But as we add further blocks of £100 million, the benefits of addressing market failure kick in. The state-funded broadcaster can spend money on programming that others wouldn't find commercially attractive. It can take greater creative risks, because there is no need to chase ratings or subscribers. There could be other benefits too, as commercial broadcasters were forced to raise their game in offering quality programmes.

Yet, at some point, this virtuous circle turns vicious. We encounter, as every economist would recognise, the law of diminishing returns. Each new addition brings somewhat less benefit. There's a crowding-out of private investment. In other words, as more and more viewing goes to the state broadcaster, the opportunity for other broadcasters to generate advertising and subscription revenues to fund their investment in programming declines.

Of course we all have different views of where we are in that process. My view is that it's already gone much too far. The BBC's massive funding boost some three years ago was secured in the heady days of the technology boom when capital was nearly free and when dotcom seemed to spell destiny. The government bought into the BBC's ambitious plans at what turned out to be the very top of the market.

But what matters, in the end, is not my view, or the views of others in the industry. What matter are the views of the people who pay the licence fee. So we asked them. We commissioned an NOP survey and asked some of the key questions asked by the Davies Committee in 1999, to assess how opinion has changed on the BBC's value for money in the intervening years. The results are published today.

They show a sharp increase in the number of those who think the BBC licence fee isn't good value. In fact, for the first time ever, a narrow majority of those asked – 51 per cent – don't agree with the proposition that the licence fee provides good value for money – that's up from an already high 42 per cent four years ago, before the BBC embarked on its massive digital expansion. And the number that strongly disagree that the BBC is good value has leapt from 19 per cent in 1999 to 27 per cent today.

Perhaps most worryingly of all for the BBC, and the government, is that it is the poorest who feel most aggrieved. What the jargon calls the 'C2DE's' are especially dissatisfied – a full 60 per cent of them don't think the BBC licence fee is good value. The recent sharp hikes, to fund digital channels that are disproportionately viewed by the rich, have impacted severely on the poorest in society.

There is a very special reason why this public discontent must be taken into account. The licence fee is a regressive, hypothecated tax. Such taxes can only ever be justified if they are set at a reasonable level, and if the services they fund are highly appreciated by the people who pay for them. It is clear that those who ultimately own the BBC – the British people – are becoming less and less convinced.

So what should we do? Well, one proposal is that we follow the advice of the person who gave the MacTaggart Lecture nine years ago. He was unemployed at the time, and so the only lecturer with absolutely no axe to grind. He proposed that the BBC should be funded through the so-called 'RPI-X' formula, pegging rises to an amount lower than the inflation rate each year. He said 'The BBC should be given certainty of its income for the whole ten years of the charter . . . by giving it an annual increase of inflation minus 1 or 2 per cent.'

Well, if we had followed his inflation minus 2 per cent prescription, the licence fee would now be £87. In fact it is a full third higher. By the end of the current Charter in 2006 the BBC will have 42 per cent more money than he thought it would need to do its job. The person making the suggestion was, of course, the present Director General [i.e. Greg Dyke]. To get back on track with his funding formula, the licence fee would have to be cut by over 5 per cent in each year of the new Charter.

Separate from the argument over the quantity of public-service broadcasting required in the UK is the question of the structures required to deliver it. We need to make sure that the governance and accountability of the Corporation are radically improved, and that the BBC's role and remit are clear to everyone in the industry.

Let me outline three ideas which, I believe, would allow the BBC to flourish, but would set clear limits to its role. In each case, by forcing the Corporation to concentrate its considerable strengths on the things it can do well, we can improve the totality of broadcasting in Britain.

First, every BBC network – analogue as well as digital – should have a specific remit and a set of measurable criteria against which it is judged on a regular basis. Too often the debate about whether the BBC is overstepping the mark is utterly nebulous, because nobody has defined where the mark is.

The government has already decided to impose a clear remit on BBC3. This covers minimum hours per genre per week in peak time, and independent and regional production commitments. There is no logical reason why we shouldn't be equally clear about what we want other channels to do as well. Please note. This wouldn't mean that the government was setting the schedule. Just as with BBC3, the requirements would be broadly drawn. Giving such direction to what a public body is expected actually to deliver in return for our money does not seem to me to be an outrageous threat to editorial independence. Michael Grade famously remarked that the BBC kept the commercial operators honest. I believe that a set of clear enforceable criteria for each service would have the same effect on the BBC.

My second proposal is to set limits on specific types of programming that we licence-fee payers definitely do not want our money spent upon. Some programmes clearly fall outside any reasonable remit for a publicly funded broadcaster. Top of my list would be bought-in American or other foreign programming. Last year the BBC spent over £100 million on such shows, a 29 per cent increase over the figure five years ago. Between them the BBC's two terrestrial networks broadcast nearly seventy hours of acquired programming each week, most of it imported from the US. I really cannot see why public money is being diverted to those poor struggling Hollywood studios in this way. BBC resources should be redeployed to commission more independently produced UK programming.

My third proposal is for a recasting of the relationship between the BBC and the commercial sector, when it comes to UK-produced programming. It aims to resolve two strong arguments made by each side. The BBC argues that, as audiences fragment, only a well-funded public-service organisation will have the resources, the risk-taking attitude and the expertise to make innovative new programming. For their part, commercial broadcasters argue that much of what the BBC shows is not any kind of antidote to market failure, since they themselves would be happy to run the same programmes. I would end this argument by accepting that the BBC does have a role as an innovator and risk-taker. But I would ensure that there is an objective mechanism in place to make sure it's not spending on programmes that crowd out commercial operators. Let's call it Programme Syndication. Here is how it would work.

Under Programme Syndication, every year, a number of established BBC programmes that are a few years old would have to be offered to the commercial sector in a competitive auction. Clearly the process would need to be carefully managed to minimise disruption and guarantee a fair price to the BBC. Not all of the BBC's established franchises could be auctioned at once. But half a dozen or so programmes in the first year would seem a manageable experiment.

Such a scheme would use the mechanics of the market to test market failure. It would help end the arguments about whether the BBC was sufficiently distinctive in its programming. If commercial broadcasters believed a programme could be supported by the market, then they would bid for it. If they did not bid, that programme would clearly pass the 'market failure' test, and continued licence-fee funding of it may be justified.

The proposal would free up time in the BBC1 and BBC2 schedules, and ensure that the licence fee was put to the most creative use possible.

It would encourage the BBC to focus on innovative and risky popular programming. It would give the BBC access to new revenue streams without disrupting the commercial sector. And the latter would come to see the benefits brought by public funding.

For the independent production sector there would be a marked increase in BBC commissions, as the BBC had constantly to reinforce its schedule. In addition, independent production companies would benefit financially if their BBC-commissioned programmes were bought by commercial channels, since they would share in the spoils.

The licence fee would then truly be, in Tessa Jowell's words, a venture capital fund for the nation, stimulating new creativity, to the benefit of the entire industry and the viewing public. But, like venture capital, it would fund risky new projects with a high potential creative return, rather than being used to perpetuate established shows. By concentrating resources on these new ventures, the syndication proposal would, I believe, help to underpin support for the BBC and the licence fee well into the future.

Of course I'm sure there will be objections even to a small-scale experiment. The BBC will no doubt argue that depriving it of some popular shows will cause viewing share to decline, undermining its ability to serve the public. But if all that is underpinning support for the Corporation are old programmes or bought-in US shows that would not be out of place on a commercial channel, then, frankly, in my view, the BBC is already failing in its mission.

The BBC is right to argue that the licence fee can only be justified if it provides something of value to everyone. But it must do more than this – it should provide something of public-service benefit to everyone. As Patricia Hodgson[2] has said, 'beating ITV with *Blue Planet* is a triumph. Beating ITV with *Celebrity Sleepover* is a tragedy.'

Radical surgery at the Corporation is certainly needed, but the aim – I assure you – is to cure not kill the patient. The main driving force for standards will, however, remain the empowerment of the viewer through greater choice. That will lead to a healthier broadcasting industry – one open to change, alive to challenge and eager to serve.

Notes

1. The Davies Committee (named after chair Gavyn Davies) was established in October 1998 to consider the licence fee and the future funding of the BBC. Reporting in 1999, the Committee recommended an additional or 'top-up' licence fee for viewers with televisions capable of receiving digital programming. The Minister for Culture, Media and Sport eventually rejected the idea (20 December 1999), suggesting that

such an additional tax might deter consumers and slow down the 'roll out' of the new digital delivery systems. See *The Future Funding of the BBC* (1999), report of the Independent Review Body (chaired by Gavyn Davies), London: Department of Culture, Media and Sport.

2. At the time of Tony Ball's lecture Patricia Hodgson was Chief Executive of the Independent Television Commission (ITC). She was previously Director of Planning and Policy at the BBC during John Birt's tenure as Director General. She enjoyed a reputation as a strategist and was considered close to Birt. Hodgson was tipped by some to become Director General in 1999 but Greg Dyke was eventually appointed.

The James MacTaggart Lecture 2004

First Do No Harm

John Humphrys*

John Humphrys addresses two connected themes. First, bad television has become 'damaging. Meretricious. Seedy. Cynical' and harms society; second, if journalists engage in self-censorship post-Hutton this will harm democracy. The Hippocratic Oath offers a sound principle for broadcasters and journalists – 'First do no harm'.

Humphrys invited sixteen Channel Controllers to send him ten tapes illustrating the 'case for television'. Having watched them, he concluded that the 'best television' is 'better than ever' but the worst has become preoccupied with sex, confrontation, aggression and violent language, 'even in the soaps'. Reality TV is the real culprit. It turns 'human beings into freaks for us to gawp at' and, significantly, 'erodes the distinction between the public and the private'. Three defences are offered. The '*Blue Planet*' defence emphasises the availability of quality programming, market apologists claim they are simply meeting public demand for certain kinds of programmes, while the 'no brow' argument suggests that programming should no longer be classified into high or low brow, but simply as 'no brow'. But Humphrys argues that good television 'cannot pay the dues of the bad when the bad is indefensible'. Ofcom should intervene to prevent the supply of these 'debit goods' on terrestrial services in much the same way that it attempts to secure the provision of 'merit goods'.

In the second, briefer part of his lecture Humphrys considers how news – 'the most important thing we do' – has fared while other television

---

* John Humphrys is a distinguished television journalist who has presented BBC1's *On the Record*, *Panorama*, *The Nine O'Clock News* and currently *Mastermind*. He has presented BBC Radio 4's *Today* programme since 1987. In 2004 he was named Journalist of the Year in an award organised by *House* magazine and Channel 4. His book *Devil's Advocate* was published in 1999.

output has changed so radically. He details two charges against political journalism. First, Greg Dyke's claim that many viewers find politics boring and that journalists have failed to make it 'less boring'. But politics is not a game show and it is not the job of journalists to 'make it fun'; politics is 'a serious business and it's our job to report it seriously'. A second and related argument, posed by John Lloyd in his book *What the Media are Doing to our Politics*, claims that journalists' cynicism is responsible for voter apathy and poses a threat to democracy, which is greatest 'when the media is at its most fearless'. But Humphrys argues that 'getting it right, abiding by the law' and 'genuine impartiality' are journalists' priorities. Post-Hutton, journalists must not become fearful of politicians and must resist any pressures which prompt self-censorship.

Humphrys concludes by arguing for more, not less, in-depth interviews with politicians, more investigative journalism and more 'straightforward political analysis'.

□

I was not making any great protest by abandoning television five years ago. I moved house, my old telly wouldn't work and I put off getting a new one until the builders had moved out. That took three months and I realised that I simply hadn't missed television so I just never got around to buying another one. Television has changed a lot since I stopped watching.

Let me dispel a myth that pops up as regularly as the weather forecast: there's nothing worth watching on telly these days. It's rubbish. There has been some superb drama, comedy, drama documentaries, art, history, natural history . . . better than ever; children's television ditto. There have been a few (though not enough) great documentaries and investigative reporting is still alive and occasionally kicking hard: The Secret Policeman . . . the BNP . . . Nurseries Undercover. All good stuff. I remember great programmes from my youth and it's tempting to buy into the golden age scenario. But it's wrong. The quality of the best television is not just as good as it ever was. I suspect some of it is even better. Television at its best is very, very good indeed.

But . . . and you can guess what's coming . . . there's the rest of it. A vast amount of the rest is simply mediocre. For me that includes all the stuff that Jimmy Mulville of Hat Trick calls lifestyle porn, which gobbles up so much of the airtime. We all know why there is so much of it. Michael Grade has talked about the 'market-driven drift towards programme-making as a commodity'. We know that process produces increased choice (in theory) but reduced range in practice. Ofcom has complained about a 'narrowing of range' and a 'perceived lack of innovation and originality'. It wouldn't matter too much if all this stuff was cheap to produce, but it costs money and that's money that can't be spent on decent programmes. The fashionable defence of it is to say that it is 'no brow' television: not high brow, not low brow . . . just no brow. It is no brow because it is no content . . . no nourishment . . . no good.

There is, of course, the classic BBC defence against this kind of television: the Blue Planet defence. You know it well: 'Yes, of course there's some pretty lousy television around but what about the *Blue Planet*? What about *Walking with Dinosaurs*?' Well, you might – *just* – get away with that as a defence against mediocre television. But it is not a defence against *bad* television . . . Which takes me to the title of this lecture: 'First do no harm', the first principle of the Hippocratic Oath, which doctors have been swearing for the past two and a half thousand years. It's not a bad principle for broadcasters.

I said that the good television of today is probably better than the best television of the old days. The bad television of today is worse. It is not only bad. It is damaging. Meretricious. Seedy. Cynical.

Let's try to apply the *Blue Planet* defence to it. Go back in time. Imagine you're in London and you take the family to the Globe Theatre for a wonderfully entertaining and stimulating evening of Shakespeare. The next day you cross the river and take them to Tyburn to watch a public hanging. Does the one balance the other? Silly question. Of course it doesn't. Nor does good television balance the bad. Not if it coarsens and brutalises and turns us into voyeurs. The good cannot pay the dues of the bad when the bad is indefensible. And it is my contention tonight that some of our worst television is indeed indefensible. It does harm.

Call me a timid soul, but I was actually quite shocked by some of what I saw when I came out of my Rip van Winkle state. So much of it seemed altogether more confrontational than I'd remembered. I've worked in newsrooms all my life and I've been known to use the odd curse myself . . . but the violence of the language surprised me. It seemed almost impossible to switch on without encountering some sort of aggression . . . even in the soaps. Of course they're meant to deal in the currency of social realism, but is everything really quite as grim and violent as they portray it?

There has been another change that has redefined television. It is, of course, so-called reality television. Why do I say so-called? Because reality implies authenticity and honesty. And whatever some of this stuff may be, it is *not* authentic and it is not honest. It is frankly outrageous even to think of it in the same terms as the sort of reality television pioneered by Roger Graef with his fly-on-the-wall documentaries.

Programmes that are recognisably reality television make up a relatively small proportion of the output, but their influence has been out of all proportion to their number. Elements of them have infected the bloodstream. Like Henry Ford offering to supply any colour car so long as it's black, we have commissioning bosses accepting any idea so long as it has a reality format. Strands that were once available for others to bid for (*Cutting Edge, Equinox*) are now vestigial. And because the schedules have been taken over by reality and its spin-offs there are no new strands emerging. Broadcasters have less of the schedule to play with. Thus they become more risk-averse. They have to be very sure that anything new is going to work and the best way to guarantee *that* is to go along with the current fashion. What suffers is originality.

Then there is the cult of celebrity. It's always been with us, but now television creates and celebrates its own celebrities. It fosters a set of values that are utterly shallow and kills real ambition in the most impressionable. We tell kids what matters is being a celebrity and we wonder why some behave the way they do. But the people who make a fortune out of this sort of thing brush it off with the old line: it's just a bit of fun; stop taking it so seriously. And what does it do to the 'lucky' ones who make it on to the screen? Most survive unscathed – so far as we know. But then, we would *not* know if they were damaged, because we lose interest in them once they are no longer 'famous'. I'm told the young lad who made the headlines for being the first to get laid on *Teen Big Brother* profoundly regrets it. Does anyone know? Does anyone care?

Reality television erodes the distinction between the public and the private, which is a profoundly important aspect of our culture. Even more worrying is its coarsening effect. That's partly because of the sheer vulgarity. But it's even more that it turns human beings into freaks for us to gawp at. *Wife Swap* was a brilliant idea and the early programmes offered some fascinating insights into the dynamics of a marriage. But it had to go further to keep the ratings and it did. Do we watch it now for understanding or for titillation? I leave you to answer that.

And don't tell me it's just entertainment. You can't use people with real lives and real problems and real children as 'just entertainment'. Well, you *can* . . . but it's corrupting.

The first time I watched *Big Brother* live – just after ten on a Sunday night as I recall – there were two men lying on beds and talking about women. Or rather 'fucking women'. And talking about their responses to them. Or, rather, 'my fucking stiffy'. My, how we've pushed back the boundaries of television. How proud we should be. After all, this is *real* people giving us their *real* thoughts. Can we really argue that the mind-numbing, witless vulgarity of so much of this stuff has *no* effect on these perceptions?

Let me give you a quote: 'To apply broadcasting to the dissemination of the shoddy, the vulgar and the sensational would be a blasphemy against human nature.' That was Lord Reith. But what did *he* know? Patronising old toff.

You may ask why I'm spending so much of this lecture attacking something that's already in its death throes. Well . . . because it's not. What happened when *Big Brother* ratings were down last year? The ratchet effect took over. We had to be shocked that bit more. That's what always happens when ratings are the only measure. The *only* measure. And ratchets work only one way. Look around the world to see where reality television is going. Porn idol in Norway? Why not? The fastest sperm in America? Maybe not this time . . . but it'll come.

And even when this reality genre eventually exhausts itself what will it leave behind? It will leave an audience that has been de-sensit-ised because the freak show has been rediscovered. The ratchet has been at work, remember. The next new dispensation will have to build on what has gone before.

But couldn't most of what I've said have come straight from the col-lected works of Mary Whitehouse? They said she was wrong. Was she? They also said she wanted a form of censorship that would be intoler-able in a free society. Now that *is* a powerful argument. There has always been a clash between freedom – especially freedom of expres-sion – and the conservative wish to preserve the old values and mores. Whitehouse was taken apart by the liberal elite, the intelligentsia who defended *Lady Chatterley* and the publishers of *Oz*. They argued – rightly in my view – that it was not just censorious but plain stupid for broadcasters to pretend that sex happened only in the marital bed between people of the opposite sex. What was going on in those days was a genuine debate between two groups of people with radically different views of what was good for society. What's happening now is different.

It is a battle between people who are concerned about society and those whose overwhelming interest is simply to make programmes that make money. Those who fought for the word 'fuck' in *Lady Chatterley* didn't do it to make money. There was no money to be made. There is now. You can hear the cash registers go 'ker … ching' every time there's a fumble beneath the bed sheets. In the bad old days we had paternalists trying to capture the masses for what they believed in their patrician way to be good. Now we have astute businessmen calculating just how far they can push things to titillate or to outrage those same masses to deliver the profits. Which is worse?

Those who admit there *may* be something in what I'm saying have another defence: the free market. 'Sorry,' they say, 'but it's really out of our hands. This is what the market wants and if we don't supply it, we go under.' This brings us to the heart of it. What can people who *are* worried do about it in a television market that is increasingly open and free from regulation? That's the big difference between now and when Whitehouse was going on about it. If we did try to limit the harm it would *not* amount to censorship. People who want the stuff that I find offensive will still be able to get it if they're prepared to pay. Fine. Let them.

The question for us is do we want to keep part of the television world within the boundaries of regulation or not? I think we do – all of us. We believe in something called public-service broadcasting and that *must* form part of the future. Ofcom is examining its regulatory role in relation to public-service broadcasting. It will soon be coming out with the second stage of its conclusions. It is interested in what it calls the 'citizen rationale' for regulation. That is 'to secure wider social benefits'.

Economists talk about 'merit goods' – a useful concept to apply to television. Public-service broadcasters *must* provide goods which individuals and advertisers are not prepared to pay for. I'd like to suggest to Ofcom that there is an obverse of merit goods: debit goods. Just as it intervenes to make sure that merit goods are provided on the terrestrial channels, so it should intervene to *prevent* the supply of debit goods. It may indeed be moving in that direction. It's planning to remove proscriptions on taste and decency and replace them with guidelines on harm and offence. Much better.

By the way, some say Ofcom may not have the power to muck about with its regulatory framework. Well, if it doesn't, then Parliament should give it that power. Remember: if people *want* this stuff there are plenty of other places they can get it.

The question that then arises is: can terrestrial commercial television survive if it is regulated to prevent the sort of harm I've been talking about? In the end it's also for Parliament to decide whether some special help should be given to them in return for a more committed public-service approach. It's either *that*, or it's a free-for-all in which terrestrial television looks and sounds no different from what we get on the digital channels.

The BBC's responsibilities in this brave new world are greater than they have ever been. Like every other broadcaster it produces its share of rubbish and its share of quality programming. It has recently rediscovered the value of genuine public-service broadcasting, or so we are told. Some deeply cynical souls make a connection between that and Charter renewal. Well, I never! If that's true . . . so what? That's what the Charter process is for, isn't it? Maybe it should be renewed more frequently if this is truly the effect it has.

I'm personally profoundly relieved that it has avoided the worst excesses of reality television. Otherwise I'd have spent the last half-hour talking myself out of a job. But maybe I'll manage to do that in the closing minutes of this lecture because I want to talk about that other vital aspect of public-service broadcasting: news. I happen to believe it is the most important thing we do. By a mile. If we get it wrong we forfeit the right to exist.

We are living in what everyone in the BBC seems to call the Post-Hutton Era. I have a problem with this. I don't know what it means. If it means that we should make ever greater efforts to get things right that's fine. Indeed, it's mandatory. But then, we've always tried to do that. But it seems to imply that our journalism needs somehow to be different – specifically political journalism. This is the bit that worries me. It's usually linked to the idea that people have lost interest in politics and that's somehow *our* fault. Well, maybe they have. Certainly fewer people bother to vote these days, but that could be down to any number of things. If we *do* have some responsibility for political apathy, what might it be?

It was Greg Dyke's view that we hadn't properly faced up to the fact that politics is inherently boring and it's our job to make it less boring. I didn't agree with any of that. If it's true, how come so many people were voting when Brian Walden was supposedly boring the pants off us with his relentless political lecture on *Weekend World* in the eighties and there were other political programmes on television that were just as analytical, just as relentless, just as (in the Dyke view) . . . just as boring. As the Americans say: go figure.

But even if it *were* true that politics is boring, it's not our job to make it fun. It's a serious business and it's our job to report it seriously. If people don't want it, that's *their* business, not ours. We shouldn't be trying to lure them into politics by pretending that it's just another game show. Greg got it wrong.

But there's a much more serious charge made against us: we have turned people off politics by our own cynical approach towards politics and politicians. This is the fashionable thesis of John Lloyd's most recent book: *What the Media are Doing to our Politics*. Lloyd claims that the Gilligan affair must be seen in the context of a wider, cynical media narrative that assumes government lies about everything. It's a serious charge. The question is not whether there is cynicism about politics in Britain today. The question is whether journalism is the cause of it. If you believe that then, yes, we need a Post-Hutton Era in which we purge the public realm of this debilitating virus. But I don't believe it.

For one thing, don't politicians themselves have some responsibility for it? What about the so-called Tory sleaze and the way Labour made huge political capital from it? That was the defining event of the closing stages of the last government. The big event of this one has been a war which many believe they were misled into supporting. Lloyd says we are fixated on this 'bigger narrative', that all politicians are lying all the time and that 'celebrity journalists' despise politicians. I don't despise politicians. On the contrary, I respect many of them. I don't know any reputable political journalist – celebrity or otherwise (whatever that cheap phrase is meant to mean) – who is in thrall to Lloyd's bigger narrative. It's just plain silly and lazy.

We should obviously be fearful of many things: getting it right, abiding by the law, genuine impartiality. We should *not* be fearful of standing up to those in power. That is our job: to be fearless in the face of power. It is our job in a pre-Hutton, mid-Hutton . . . a post-Hutton era. In any era. And what it means is that we should approach politicians *not* with an attitude of cynicism, but of scepticism. We should subject them to rigorous and relentless scrutiny. That is what the public wants and that is what the public has a right to expect.

Let me be clear about one thing here. I have *not* personally been leant on by the bosses to go easy in the wake of Hutton. If I had been I would be standing before you tonight as the former presenter of *Today*. But it's not quite that simple. I've read the little paragraphs about the 'knives being out'. Well, there's nothing much new in that. I can't remember when they weren't. And anyway individuals like me don't matter – whatever Mr Lloyd may say about celebrity journalists. What *does* matter is something much more subtle.

It's easy, in the shock waves created by something like the Hutton Report and all that preceded it, for confidence to be replaced by uncertainty – particularly when the phrase 'post-Hutton BBC' is used by the papers to suggest that we have been cowed. It's easy for producers and editors to ask not only 'Is this right?' (as they must) but 'Who might we be upsetting if we pursue this investigation or this line of questioning?' Some things don't have to be put in writing for a particular effect to be created. Let me steal a phrase from the good Lord Hutton himself. It is possible to be 'subconsciously influenced' into thinking that this is what your masters *might* want you to do. I hope the BBC is not subconsciously influenced.

We need more, not less, investigative journalism. We need *much* more straightforward political analysis. Filling a studio with people shouting at each other about the euro is all very well, but it's even more important to explain what the issues are. And let the ratings fall where they may. Easy for me to say, I know, but it is the test of our commitment . . . one proof of our lack of cynicism. Public-service broadcasting can and must make an important contribution to the democratic process. It can do it only if we are not cowed by those in power.

Halfway through my period of abstinence I began to think television actually didn't matter very much. I didn't miss it as entertainment; I have no great interest in sport and I get all the news I need from newspapers, magazines and Radio 4. But you can't live in a television society and escape from it altogether even if you want to. Its influence is everywhere. And I don't want to escape it. Rather to my surprise I've been informed, entertained and deeply moved by some of what I've seen.

I watched *Life of Mammals* with my four-year-old son on my lap. He was quite literally wide-eyed with wonder. It's the oldest television format around – albeit with the latest technology. But it's not cutting edge. It's not pushing back any boundaries. It's not shocking anyone for the sake of it. It's a bit corny. It's old hat. But, like the very best of television, it really does open new windows on to the world. I think my little boy will remember it. It may seem a bit odd after I've spent so much of this lecture attacking television to end on this slightly soppy note. But I've been reminded after my long absence that television can enrich lives. It can lift our spirits. It can give us a deeper understanding of the human condition. It can help maintain the momentum that takes us from barbarity to civilisation. There is good stuff out there. Don't allow it to be dragged down. Rupert Murdoch stood at this lectern fifteen years ago and warned you all that public-service broadcasting would be relegated to a side show. Don't prove him right. First, do no harm.

Appendix A

Edinburgh International Television Festival, 29 August–2 September 1977: Programme

Discussion Programme

The James MacTaggart Memorial Lecture, given by Marcel Ophuls

Drama Documentary

Programme compilation: Jerry Kuehl
Papers: Jerry Kuehl, Gus Macdonald
Chair: Jeremy Isaacs
Panellists: Jenny Barraclough, Brian Gibson, Marcel Ophuls, Leslie Woodhead

Soap Opera and Women

Paper: Richard Dyer, Terry Lovell, Jean McCrindle
Chair: Dipak Nandy
Panellists: Susi Hush, Kevin Laffan, Carol Wilks

Realism and Non-naturalism 1

Paper: Raymond Williams
Chair: Verity Lambert
Panellists: Trevor Griffiths, Barry Hanson, David Rose, Mark Shivas

Realism and Non-naturalism 2

Paper: Dennis Potter
Chair Melvyn Bragg
Panellists: David Hare, James Cellan Jones, John McGrath

Criticism and Television Drama

Paper: Charles Barr
Chair: Chris Dunkley
Panellists: Peter Fiddick, W. Stephen Gilbert, Sean Day Lewis

Censorship and Television Drama

Papers: Clive Goodwin, Anthony Smith
Chair: Phillip Whitehead
Panellists: John Bowen, Penry Jones, Shaun Sutton

Television and Feature Films

Paper: Rod Allen
Chair: Sir Denis Forman
Panellists: Richard Craven, Gavin Miller, Colin Young

Screenings

Monday, 29 August: *A Sense of Loss* (Marcel Ophuls); *Hospital 1922* (BBC 12 October 1972); *Culloden* (BBC 15 December 1964); *Three Days in Szczecin* (Granada Television 21 September 1976); *1844 – The Miners' Strike* (Thames 21 January 1975); *The Missiles of October* (Titus-BBC2 January 1975)

Tuesday, 30 August: *Some Women* (BBC 27 August 1969); *Hard Labour* (BBC 12 March 1973); *Coronation Street* (Granada Television 1962); *Beryl's Lot* (Yorkshire Television 1973); *Bill Brand* (Thames 19 July 1976); *Z Cars* (BBC 1962); *The Glittering Prizes* (BBC 21 January 1976); *Emmerdale Farm* (Yorkshire Television 1972); *Mary Hartman, Mary Hartman* (TAT 1976)

Wednesday, 31 August: *Diary of a Young Man* (BBC 8 August 1964); *Rock Follies* (Thames 4 May 1977); *Brimstone and Treacle* (BBC); *The*

Cheviot, The Stag and the Black, Black Oil (BBC 6 June 1974); *Pend's Fen* (BBC 21 March 1974); *The Paradise Run* (Thames 7 April 1976)

Thursday, 1 September: *Regan* (Euston Films/Thames 4 June 1974); *Clay, Smeddum and Greenden* (BBC Scotland 24 February1977); *Seven Men – Quentin Crisp* (Granada Television 13 March 1971); *The Naked Civil Servant* (Thames 17 December 1975)

EITF Premiere: *The Prime of Miss Jean Brodie* an episode (Scottish Television)

Additional screenings in the library:

After a Lifetime (London Weekend Television); *And Did Those Feet?* (BBC); *Censored Scenes From King Kong* (BBC); *The Enemy Within* (BBC); *I Know What I Meant* (Granada television); *Kisses At 50* (BBC): *The Lump* (BBC); *The Saliva Milkshake* (BBC); *Vote For Nigel Barton* (BBC); *All Good Men* (BBC); *The Bouncing Boy* (BBC); *The Cheaper Mystery Plays* (BBC); *Days of Hope* (BBC); *Follow The Yellow Brick Road* (BBC); *Just Your Luck* (BBC); *Paper Roses* (Granada Television); *Spend, Spend, Spend* (BBC); *Shades, 3 Plays by Beckett* (BBC); *Yesterday's Girl* (Granada Television); *Dixon of Dock Green* (BBC); *Edward VII* (Associated Television); *The Nearly Man* (Granada Television); *Upstairs, Downstairs* (London Weekend Television); *Alternative 3* (Associated Television); *The Billion Dollar Bubble* (BBC); *18 Months To Balcombe Street* (London Weekend Television); *The Issue Must Be Avoided* (BBC); *On Trial: Chicago Conspiracy* (BBC); *The Picardy Affair* (BBC); *The Strange World of Gurney Slade* (Associated Television)

Appendix B

The publishers were unable to secure the authors' permission to reproduce two of the MacTaggart Lectures. The first was given by Ted Turner
(1982), the second by Dr Jonathan Miller (1983). A brief précis of the
key concerns of each lecture is given below.

Ted Turner, James MacTaggart Lecture 1982

Ted Turner, founder and president of Cable News Network (CNN),
delivered the James MacTaggart Memorial Lecture in 1982. It set a prec-
edent by being the first 'ad-libbed' lecture: no lecturer has subsequently followed Turner's lead. Turner's approach was broadly
anecdotal; his modest ambition, to 'tell you a little about my experiences in this business'.

Turner's first business involvement was with what Americans call
the (outdoor) advertising industry. In the UK, this is known as hoard-
ings and billboards which impose a 'blight on the scenery', but they
constitute 'a good profitable business' which funded the purchase of
Turner's television station. He bought the station because he liked old
films and because it was cheap: 'I couldn't afford a real television station
so I bought this Mickey Mouse station' in 1970. Turner knew very little
about television and had no love for the medium. He was not part of a
network and described himself as a 'fringe, fringe player'. But he
argued that success in television rests on skills in programming and
promotion alongside an ability to anticipate future trends in communications. Two technological developments were crucial. First, he placed
his Mickey Mouse station on satellite and 'turned it into a network'.

Second, he moved to a cable delivery system because 'with a UHF station you put out a very fuzzy signal'. Significantly the shift offered Turner 'reception equality with my competitors' and gave him much enhanced audience reach.

Turner wished to separate CNN from the programming of the other major networks, which he described as 'crummy, the lowest common denominator, basically stupid'. Competition between the networks drives standards downmarket, but Turner was committed to high-quality programming since television is 'the average person's main source of information'. His benchmark for quality was the BBC, which delivered the 'highest-quality programming that has been produced anywhere in the world'. This consigned CNN to relatively modest audience figures but 'an all-news channel doesn't get great ratings because we've taken the very highest road that we could. We've haven't become the *National Enquirer*.' Turner started the second news network, which is 'certainly more sensational' as a pre-emptive strike to see off competition from ABC and Westinghouse, which were 'joining forces to put us out of business'. The second CNN channel follows more predictable formats with half-hour forecasts which offer 'thirty minutes of disasters from around the nation . . . if we can show someone being killed we do it and then we go to the biggest murder of the day, the assassination . . . we chase ambulances and police cars in the television journalism business because that's the most exciting thing'.

Turner concludes with a forward glance. Cable technology provided him with the opportunity to create a television network 'to spread my ideas'. It provides similar opportunities for others. New communications technology provides the prospect for greater diversity of programming but no guarantees of quality. 'Whether or not there will be thirty worthwhile channels over here as a result of cable,' Turner concludes, 'only time will tell.'

Dr Jonathan Miller, James MacTaggart Lecture 1983

Jonathan Miller begins his 1983 MacTaggart Lecture by offering a valedictory to his career in television and the theatre, which he later reconsidered. It is 'ironic,' he suggests, 'that I should come back to Edinburgh where I started my career in showbusiness' to end it 'in the same city'.

Miller's thesis is that 'it is the very triviality of what is made on television, the fact that you don't really have to care too much, that you do not have to consult something as painful as choice, that actually renders it so attractive'. Two factors make programmes popular. The first reflects their ready and easy accessibility as part of a scheduled stream of programmes. Miller doubts whether 'any of the quiz shows which fill up television would survive if anyone had to go out and hire them in the form of cassettes . . . or make an explicit decision to fork out cash for them item by item'. But over and above this 'effortless availability' is the second factor which reflects the viewer's shared experience of 'synchronised' watching simultaneously with 'innumerable and anonymous others': the 'Did you see. . . ? phenomenon'.

There are highly beneficial outcomes here. No matter how trivial '*Dallas* or *Coronation Street* might be', their relentless, 'incontinent and synchronised availability' provide 'topics around which people discuss . . . they provide a morality play around which discussion might be convened'. They also provide a medium through which we enter social relationships and, in turn, a sense of community. Miller argues that his thesis applies with equal force to serious as well as trivial programmes, but suggests that those serious programmes that are successful exploit television as a periscope which reaches 'places that no person can normally expect to get to in a lifetime': television provides us with an 'enormous enlargement of our personal experience'.

But Miller also suggests that there are occasions when television 'falters' and these typically involve the 'promulgation and explanation of complex and abstract ideas'. He suggests two areas of television where it not merely falters but 'fails' and 'misses its aim altogether'. The first is the 'transformation of the novel into the dramatised serial', the second is taking 'classic plays intended for another mode and putting them on the box'. Miller confesses to a 'sort of embarrassed impotence about the possibility of doing Shakespeare on television': he believes there are insoluble problems here. The evident benefit of such attempts is that they introduce Shakespeare to a considerably wider audience, but 'televising Shakespeare' also 'introduces people to the regrettable belief that the works fall below par if they are not seen in the visual mode, so that they return to the theatre now disappointed by the fact that the theatre does not live up to the pictorial glamour that television provided'. 'Perhaps this is one of the reasons,' Miller concludes, 'I am finally leaving television altogether along with the theatre.'

Index